VOICES OF AMERICA

Virginia Marmaduke

A Journey in Print From Carbondale to Chicago

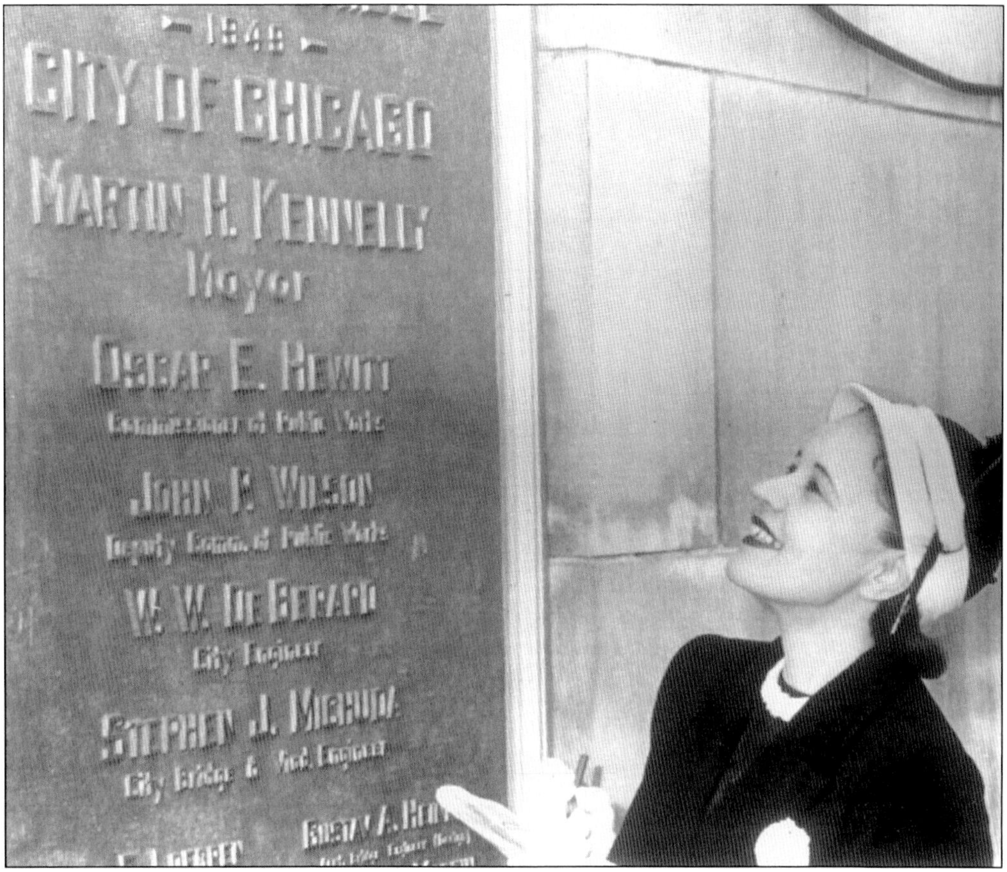

The "Duchess" surveys some of her kingdom.

Dedication

Of course, to the lady herself:

For Virginia Marmaduke,

a great and noble woman.

**Unless otherwise noted, all photographs are copyrighted to the* Chicago Sun-Times, *and were made available to the author by SIU Photocomunications and the Estate of Virginia L. Marmaduke.*

VOICES OF AMERICA

Virginia Marmaduke

A Journey in Print From Carbondale to Chicago

Compiled and Edited by

Cary O'Dell

ARCADIA PUBLISHING

ISBN 978-0-7385-1966-1

Published by Arcadia Publishing
Charleston, South Carolina

Printed in the United States of America

Library of Congress Catalog Card Number: 2002103816

For all general information, please contact Arcadia Publishing:
Telephone 843-853-2070
Fax 843-853-0044
E-Mail sales@arcadiapublishing.com
For customer service and orders:
Toll-Free 1-888-313-2665

Visit us on the Internet at www.arcadiapublishing.com

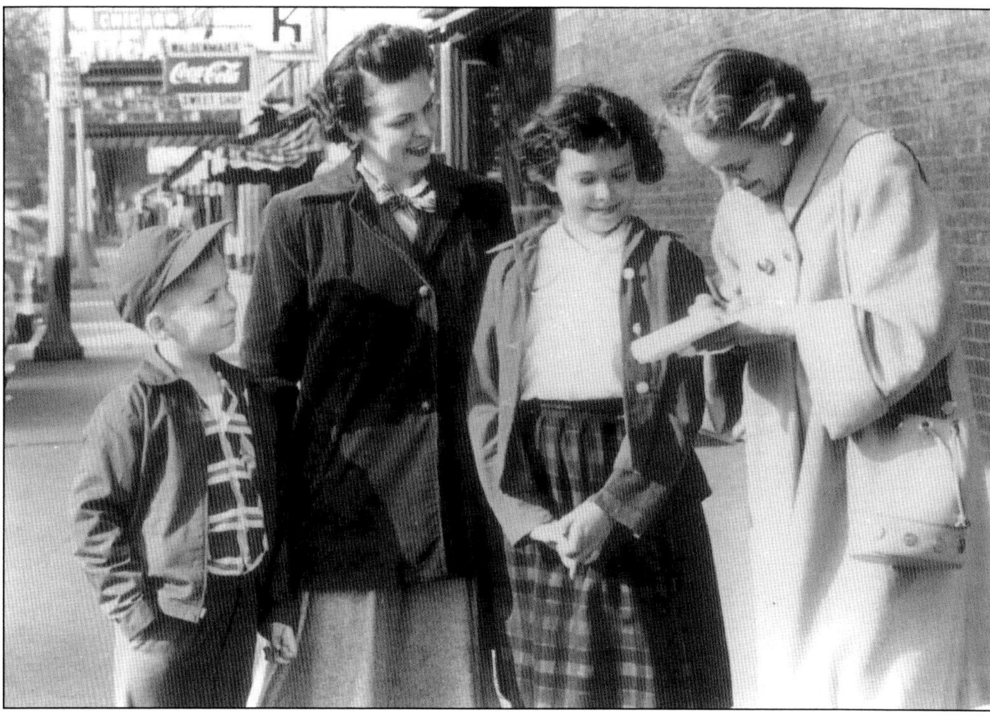

The Duchess conducts an on-the-street interview.

Contents

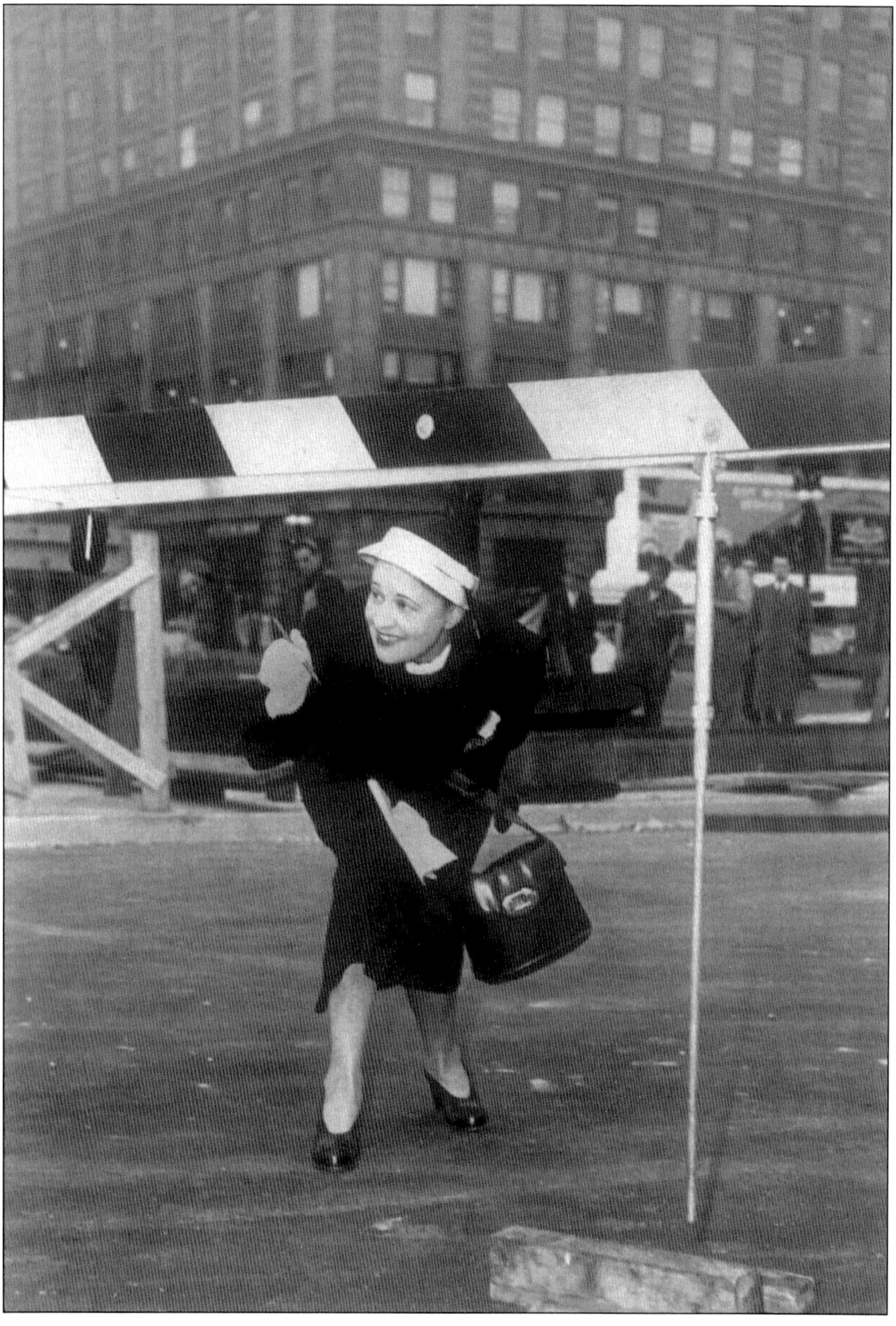

On the job in the late 1940s.

Acknowledgments

In retracing, in print, the life of Virginia "The Duchess" Marmaduke, I had to depend not only upon the vast resources of the Library of Congress in Washington D.C., the Illinois State Archives in Springfield, and other repositories, but also on the dedication and help of various FODs (Friends of the Duchess) whose enthusiasm for and assistance with this endeavor was complete and invaluable. I am forever grateful. They are: Jack Dyer, Jak Tichenor, Genie Wilcox, Don Johnson esq., Sue Davis, Dorothy McCombs, Paula Davenport, and Terri Golembiewski.

Thank you also to a few friends of mine who, unwittingly, got pulled into the process along the way and who then rose, brilliantly, to the task. They are: Mike Heintz, Dolores Ford Mobely, Jody Bales Foote, Frank and Marilyn Black, and Madeline Mancini.

Thank you to Julia Knippen at Arcadia for her early belief in this project.

Thank you to my friend Karmon Runquist.

Thank you to all the newspapers, especially the *Chicago Sun-Times*, for allowing the reproduction of their articles; and thank you to SIUC Photocom, especially Gene Moehring, for assistance with the photographs.

And, finally—obviously—thank you to Virginia Marmaduke, the Duchess, for proving as fascinating and inspiring on the printed page as she always was in person.

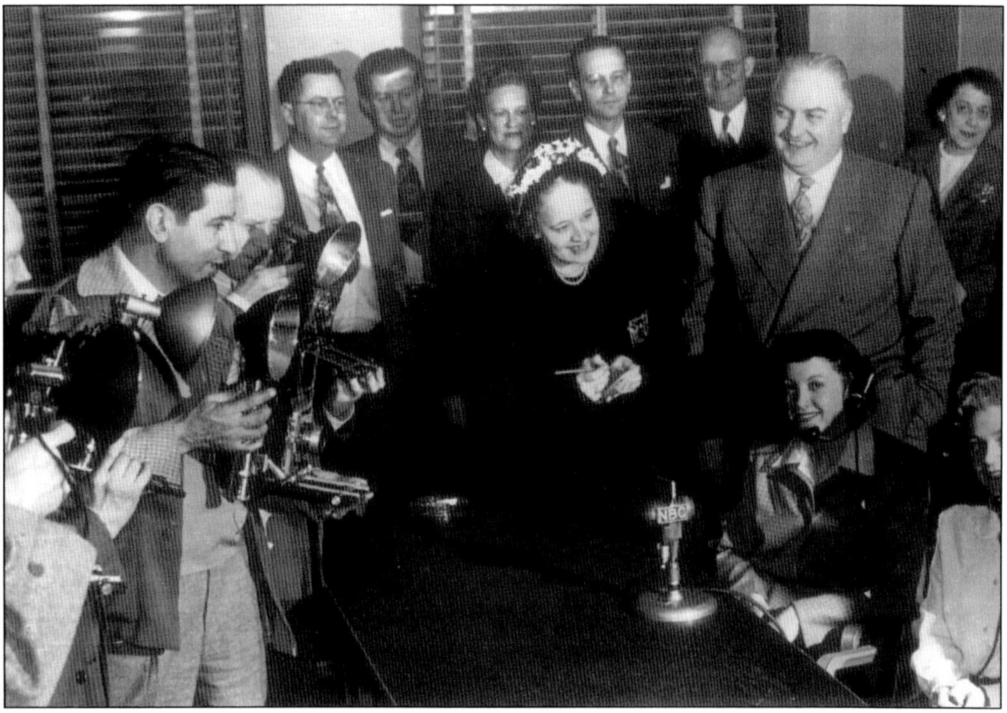

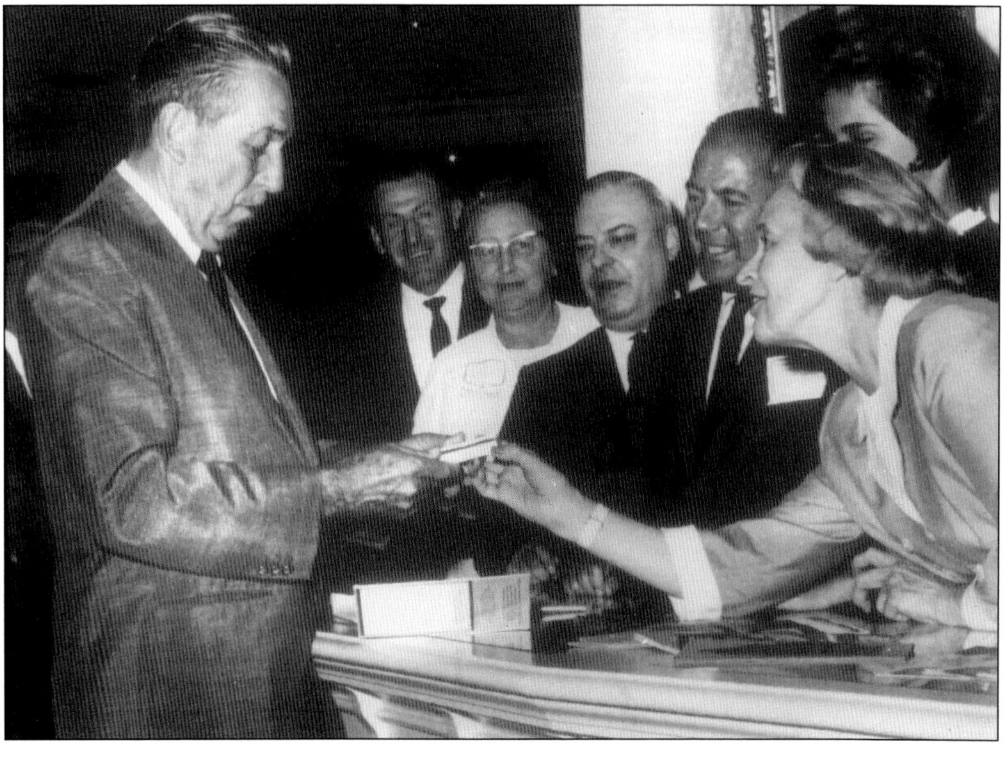

The Duchess at a typical press conference and with the great Walt Disney.

Introduction

What a name. What a dame. What a life!
—Wes Smith on the Duchess, 1992

She is the dambest newspaperman I ever knew.
—Bob Kotalik, Sun-Times photographer, 1992

This is not a biography of Virginia Marmaduke. Rather, what this *is* is a collection of writings by and about Virginia "The Duchess" Marmaduke.

If anything, this book is more akin to a diary as it pools many of the newspaper stories the Duchess wrote during her career, creating a yearly record of what she was doing, the events she was covering, the issues that were affecting her, her city, the country, and the times she was living through.

Of course, as author Annie Dillard has noted, "how we spend our days is...how we spend our lives," and since the majority of the words herein were written by Virginia herself, this book could be considered, in many ways, a memoir—a self-portrait in news clips, an autobiography in articles.

Over the years, Virginia Marmaduke has been widely honored and celebrated. Unfortunately, she has not been widely read. Others have commented on the Duchess's life and achievements through hundreds of articles and speeches, but no one has gone back to quote the primary documents of her career and legacy: the newspaper articles that bore the byline of Virginia Marmaduke.

Mostly this has been because these articles are not easy to find. The Duchess did not employ a clipping service during the heyday of her career at the *Chicago Sun*, *Chicago Sun-Times,* or *Chicago Tribune*; and none of these newspapers have ever been indexed, by story or by journalist, for the time she worked for them.

To compile the articles of Virginia Marmaduke, therefore, it meant a day by day, page by page review of every newspaper during the time she worked for these publications, carefully searching out the Duchess's name.

This done, the reading of these articles in linear order does more than just give a greater understanding of the Duchess's professional life, it also gives the reader a unique sense of the woman behind the byline. What emerges, between the lines of black typeset, is a first-rate journalist and a devoted humanitarian. But there are other insights as well, glimpses of other qualities that made the Duchess uniquely the Duchess: hints of what was important to her, and what was not; her subtly implied opinions; traces of her undefeatable zest for life; and, at times, a little of her salty sense of humor.

Reading the collected journalistic works of Virginia Marmaduke of course begs the question: is there such a thing as a Marmaduke style of reporting and writing? While journalism, per se, does not lend itself to creative flourishes and individualism as easily as prose does, that doesn't mean the Duchess didn't have a certain flair that was all her own. Her work is hallmarked with a certain old-fashionedness (perhaps even old-fashioned for the time), a level of formality which might be accredited to her upbringing or her early, brief career as a school teacher.

Consistently as well, the Duchess's articles frequently show a particular interest in the appearance, clothing, eye color, and demeanor of the people she is covering, be they movie stars, children, or accused felons. Such attention to the visual could be tagged as a "womanly" preoccupation. Or it could be viewed as a more vivid and graphic way of telling a story.

In reading through a career's worth of articles, certain reoccurring themes and topics emerge. Though the Duchess quite famously told her first city desk editor at the *Chicago Sun* that she wanted to be a crime reporter, covering "blood, guts and sex" (and she did!), the majority of articles from her fall instead into the category of advocacy.

Newspapers, those of the past and present day, are too often viewed as presenting "just the facts" in their pages. However, American newspapers, from the days of our founding fathers to today, are often used to shape public opinion, further a cause, or shed a spotlight onto a social concern. This is certainly true of the writings of Virginia Marmaduke. Though she was never an "op-ed" writer, the Duchess nevertheless used her position and the power of her pen to help others.

In her stories the Duchess did not simply recite statistics about post-war housing shortages or children suffering from cerebral palsy, but made a greater impact on her readers by profiling individuals these problems were directly affecting. She also pointed readers in a direction to right this wrong or relieve this suffering—where to send a donation, who to call, what to do—in the process turning a cry for concern into a journalistic call to arms.

These stories, focusing on the poor, ill, or downtrodden, are often labeled, rather dismissively, as "human-interest stories," if not even more harshly condemned as "fluff" or "filler." Though Virginia Marmaduke was not one to play what we would call today the "gender card," in this division between what is considered "hard" news vs. "soft" news, there seems to be an inherent sexism: news that was "hard" (war, politics, crime) was considered the domain of male reporters; news that was "soft," which included everything from health and parenting issues to fashion and social events, was considered the purview of the female reporter. Have certain issues and topics irrevocably been labeled "soft" (i.e. of lesser importance) since women have predominately been the ones to write about them?

In any event, female reporters so frequently covered emotional, tug-at-the-heartstrings stories—and were so adept at getting them—that they were soon referred to, in masse, with the not completely flattering moniker of "sob sisters." (Women reporters were also often called "news hens," so perhaps this was something of an improvement.)

The job of the "sob sister" was not only to write tearjerkers, but also to be the one to take on the task of interviewing the grieving widow or the family just burned out of their home, with the logic that the average person would be more open (i.e. more emotional) with a female reporter than a male one. From time to time the Duchess was called upon to do this sort of on-the-scene interview. Said Virginia about it, "I hated that job."

But however Virginia Marmaduke might have felt about some aspects of her job as a "girl reporter," she didn't seem to take issue with her feminized genre of journalism and the humanitarian issues it publicized. In 1953, when she was feted on TV's *This Is Your Life* as the "typical American newspaper woman," the Duchess went out of her way to tell host Ralph Edwards, "Ralph, all newspaperwomen are the same. We're all cut from the same pattern. By honoring me, you've honored us all."

But this is not to say that all of the Duchess's stories fall into the category of three-hankie weeper or "human interest." In the Duchess's body of work there exists great width and breadth. One will find stories on crime, politics, government, world affairs, education, entertainment, history, fashion, travel, finance, business, medicine, law, ghosts, and grocery shopping. There are also a truly staggering number of articles on the annual Chicago International Horse Show, which Virginia covered each year.

Of course, in collecting and reprinting articles pertaining to Virginia Marmaduke, as with any well-lived life, some things have to be left out. Though the Duchess's actual time spent with big city newspapers was relatively short—less than fifteen years (twelve with the *Chicago Sun-Times*, less than one with the *Tribune*)—she made her time count; hundreds of articles appeared under her byline. Those that are most famous, notable, newsworthy and illustrative of her career are included here.

The Duchess probably wrote and published hundreds of other stories during her career but, as with many reporters, her stories ran anonymously. And since the *Sun-Times* didn't keep track of who wrote what articles—and neither did the Duchess—they are, for all intents and purposes, lost to history. Anonymity of reporters was a common practice for newspapers then (as it is today) especially in regard to stories about criminals still at large. Chicago, though a "big city," was still in some ways a small town, and newspapers had to take into account the personal safety of their reporters (especially unmarried, female ones

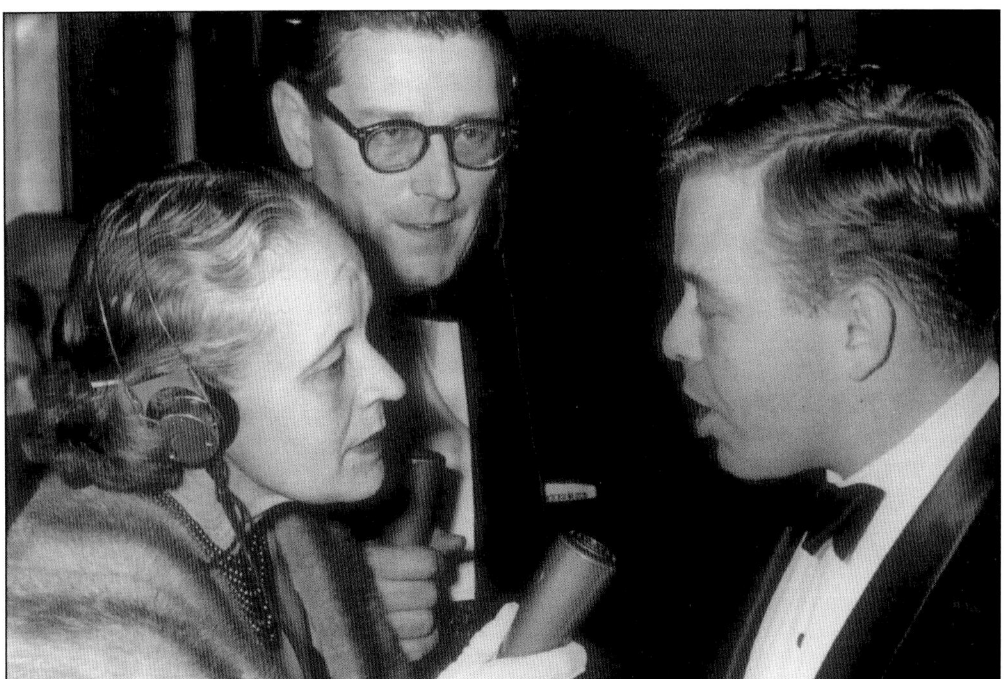

The Duchess interviews singer Mel Torme for one of her radio shows.

like Virginia Marmaduke).

However, thanks to the few scrapbook clippings and personal memories that we do have, we know some of the stories that the Duchess was a writer of or major contributor to that were published with no byline. Most notably these include coverage of the brutal Suzanne Degnan murder of 1946 which were originally printed unaccredited to anyone. To identify these stories in this book an asterisk (*) has been placed at the end of its headline.

Additionally, not every word of every article (for example, information in a story that was redundant to the previous story or a long, non-essential list of names or addresses) needed to be or was reprinted. To note editorial deletions—where part of a story has been omitted—a set of ellipses inside a set of brackets have been placed in the text: [...]. However, it should be noted, that the Duchess sometimes employed ellipses (...) as a punctuation device to indicate a pause in thought or action. These ellipses have been reprinted as they originally appeared.

Sometimes as well, in the rush to get the news out, typesetters omitted a word here or there. Where these missing words could be ascertained, they have been added and also placed inside brackets. Also, many of the original articles contained typos or misspellings; in the interest of readability these have been corrected in the text without notation.

The Duchess lived a rich, diverse, and grand life, which ran parallel with the 20th century, and it reprised in these clippings. Even long-time friends and admirers of Virginia Marmaduke can come away from these stories with renewed fondness for the Duchess and a deeper appreciation for the scope of her achievements.

So if it is true, as legend has it, that Virginia Marmaduke as a little girl in Southern Illinois and then Chicago, said to her father one day that when she grew up she wanted to be a "newspaperman," even she probably didn't foresee where that decision would take her: covering "blood, guts and sex," riding a camel, running an elevator, and helping to bring about social and political change. But she likely did envision and hope for a future that would be adventuresome, out of the ordinary, and far from the status quo. As these articles and recollections attest, by the time the ink dried, she had gotten her wish.

I.

Becoming the Duchess (1908–1943)

Virginia was born the first and only child of Harvey and Blanche Marmaduke and, typical of the time, was born at home in an upstairs bedroom at 500 S. Popular in Carbondale, Illinois, in a house that still stands today. Her birth was newsworthy in its own way in that she was a "preemie," weighing only three and a half pounds at delivery. It was a miracle that she survived at all. In fact, Virginia Lee looked so small and sickly at birth that Virginia later compared her tiny, infant self to "looking like a skinned squirrel." Her father seemed to agree, joking at the time to his wife, "If that's the best we can do, we'll never have another."

Ironically, no newspaper made mention of the birth of Virginia Lee Marmaduke on June 21, 1908. The announcing of births as a regular component of the printed press was a few decades away. Despite having her birth ignored by the local press, it didn't take long for the woman who would become the Duchess to make some news. The first time her name appeared in print was in 1915, when she was seven years old.

CARBONDALE DAILY FREE PRESS

A NARROW ESCAPE

10/21/15

Little Virginia Marmaduke and Margaret Bryden with Miss Katie Vehring had a wonderful escape last night from serious or possibly fatal injuries.

They were sitting in the pony carriage belonging to H.C. Marmaduke just north of the [railroad] division offices. Mrs. Marmaduke left the party in the cart near the curbing and went to the office. In the meantime a man left his team hitched to a farm wagon in front of the First National Bank while he went away to do some trading. During his absence the team became frightened and ran around the square and crashed into the pony outfit and occupants, demolishing the cart and injuring the pony somewhat.

Miss Virginia jumped and was not injured in the least but little Margaret Bryden was injured a trifle. The accident was very dangerous and the occupants of the buggy are very fortunate in their escape.

Virginia Marmaduke spent her early years in Carbondale but often visited her maternal grandparents on their farm in Pinckneyville, Illinois, about 20 miles north. There, despite her earlier horse and buggy mishap (and despite a later horse-riding accident at age ten which left a life-long scar on her forehead), Virginia developed a love affair with the ponies. In her early teens, she owned a Shetland. Her father remembered, "She rode her pony all over that countryside." Later, Virginia would acquire gaited horses and would take them to area showrings. She ultimately fell in love with the showy standardbred trotter that "trotted fast and with an air." Horses would be a life-long passion and hobby and one that would serve her well in her later Chicago journalism career.

Mr. Marmaduke, a descendent of two former Missouri governors (Meredith C. Marmaduke who served from 1844 to 1848; and John S. Marmaduke who served from 1884 to 1892), was employed by the Illinois Central Railroad (I.C.). He began with them in their downstate office in 1901 as a messenger boy, and would eventually work his way up to special assistant to the president of the company. Said Virginia about her father, "He had the same kind of drive I did."

In 1918, after her father was promoted, the Marmadukes relocated to Chicago, Illinois, settling into a house in the then fashionable South Lake Shore area, at 71st and Jeffrey Streets, not far from the South Shore Country Club.

As a student in Chicago, Virginia first attended Walter Scott grammar school, but it was later, at Hyde Park High School, that the name Virginia Marmaduke made its second appearance in print. In the 1923 edition of the school's photoless yearbook, each student's name was listed alphabetically, followed by their grade level and a brief descriptor of their personality. Virginia's entry read:

A-1 Freshmen Virginia Marmaduke—"sweet"

The following year the yearbook repeated the practice, this time positioning their student's personal description as an answer to the question "What makes me think of?" For Virginia:

2-A Sophomore Virginia Marmaduke? "A cure for the blues."

After Hyde Park High, Virginia would spend her last two years of high school at Fontbonne, an all-girl's "finishing school" in St. Louis, Missouri.

Earlier, Virginia's parents sent her southward to her Pinckneyville-based grandparents when each suffered a decline in health. It was also around this time, 1925, that Virginia briefly taught at the Eichholz School, just outside of Pinckneyville.

Her school was the quintessential one-room affair with fifty-some students in her class, grades one through eight, all mixed together. Virginia rode horseback to and from work, explaining later, "I had to. It was too muddy to take a car." While in the saddle, Virginia wore a special "riding skirt," but once she arrived at the school, she would change clothes in the cloak room, re-attiring herself into something more suitable for the young schoolmarm.

During the school week, Virginia stayed with a farm family, the Kellermans, not far from the school house. On the weekends, she returned to her grandparents in town.

After her short teaching stint and her high school graduation from Fontbonne, Virginia did not head directly into marriage or continue in traditional "women's work" but, instead, headed off to college.

Interestingly Marmaduke ended up attending four colleges in almost as many years, traveling widely up and down the state of Illinois and into Iowa and Missouri. According to enrollment records, Virginia attended the all-female Ursaline Academy in Arcadia, Missouri, in 1926. But her stay there was brief. The all-female student body made life boring for Virginia and she was, in her own words, "too fond of the boys" to stick it out at Ursaline.

With her grandparents' health improved, Virginia returned north to Chicago and enrolled at the University of Chicago for the spring semester of 1927. But by the next year she would be enrolled at the University of Iowa in Iowa City, where she would remain for the following two years. (At some point in this time period, Virginia also briefly attended SINU, the precursor to Southern Illinois University.) None of these schools' records make any mention of a declared major for Virginia, in journalism or in anything else.

In later years it was the University of Iowa that Marmaduke would speak of the most. In a 1992 interview, Virginia reminisced, "In grammar school I was always better at essays than anything else. In the eighth grade, a teacher of mine told me I had a knack for writing and should develop it, so I told my father I wanted to be a newspaperman. He supported me and helped me pick a college. At the time, the University of Iowa [...] was the best in the field."

In the *State University of Iowa Directory of Faculty and Students 1928-1929*, it made mention of Virginia, listing her current area of study (A1, general studies for freshmen), her local address and phone number, and her home town:

Marmaduke, Virginia Lee (A1), 8 E. Burlington, 4151, Chicago, Ill.

Though several sources, written many years later, state that Virginia worked, in some capacity, on the college-sanctioned newspaper, *The Daily Iowan*, a thorough review of the newspapers from this era yielded no stories with the byline of Virginia Marmaduke, nor is there any mention of her on the paper's masthead.

Nevertheless, even then Virginia seemed to have a nose for news. In late 1928, she got her name in a front page headline by writing a prize-winning essay on what a new dance hall built by the American Legion should be called.

THE DAILY IOWAN

VIRGINIA MARMADUKE WINS LEGION PRIZE

12/7/28

The $10 prize offered by the American legion for the best name submitted for the ball room in the new American legion building, will be awarded at the dance tonight to Virginia Marmaduke, A1 of Chicago. The winning name was "Shadowland."

"Rags" Wilcox, basketball captain at the university, and Claire Schapp, head cheer leader, from now on have charge of the dancing.

Ever fashionable, Virginia spent her $10 prize money on a new hat to wear to the first dance held at the venue she named.

It was later at one of these dances, sponsored by Virginia's sorority, Kappa Alpha Theta, that the gregarious, outgoing Virginia struck up a conversation with a visiting member of the University of Missouri golf team. His name was Harold E. Grear and he hailed originally from Herrin, Illinois, a town about ten miles north east of Carbondale. Finding they had some geography in common proved enough of an introductory ice-breaker for the two teenagers and, soon after, the couple began courting. (This is how Virginia Marmaduke met Harold Grear, though their later marriage announcement in the Herrin newspaper would, inexplicably, tell it differently.)

For Marmaduke and Grear, it was a lengthy, long-distance courtship but the couple eventually married. Grear's family owned and operated the *Herrin Daily Journal* and when the owner's only son got married, it was front page news.

HERRIN DAILY JOURNAL

WED AT PINCKNEYVILLE TODAY: BEAUTIFUL SERVICE MARKS NUPTIAL TIE

Veteran Southern Illinois Minister Officiates at Wedding of Miss Virginia Marmaduke and Harold E. Grear

By L.B. Sheley, Editor, Pinckneyville Democrat

4/19/30

PINCKNEYVILLE, Ill., April 19, 1930—(Special)—Pinckneyville was the scene today of one of the prettiest society weddings of recent years, when Miss Virginia Lee Marmaduke of Chicago and Harold Eugene Grear of Herrin, were united in the holy bonds of matrimony, in the beautifully decorated First Methodist church, in the presence of a large number of guests from Chicago, Herrin, Pinckneyville, and other surrounding cities.

It was a beautiful ceremony, a striking scene, with the romance of today and a fragrant touch of memories of the past mingled at the Altar, where modern youth plighted its troth in the presence of a venerable minister who had performed the golden wedding ceremony for the bridegroom's great grandparents, John and Cyndonia Grear of Jonesboro, Illinois, thirty-three years before—on April 13, 1897. Rev. H.L. McGill, pastor of the Lutheran Church of Anna, was the officiating clergyman, with Rev. J.E. Devere, pastor of the Pinckneyville Methodist church, assisting. [...]

The bride is the only daughter of Mr. and Mrs. Harvey Creigh Marmaduke, of Chicago. [...] Pinckneyville claims her as its own fair daughter. For many years she has spent her summer vacations here with her grandmother, Mrs. Worth Crain, and has many dear friends among the younger set while having the admiration of all who know her.

She is a girl of charm, and was a picture of beauty in her wedding gown, of egg-shell satin, with slippers and other accessories to match. She wore a tulle veil with orange blossom coronet and carried a shower bouquet of Easter lilies and lilies of the valley. [...]

The marriage today was the culmination of a romance which may be stated to have started in December 1928, when Mr. Grear met Miss Marmaduke at a ball in Pinckneyville, while she was at home from the University of Iowa for her Christmas vacation [sic]. However, the friendship made then really ripened into a love affair last summer while both were attending the summer term of Southern Illinois University at Carbondale [sic].

The newlyweds will be at home at 616 South Fourteenth Street, after June 1st.

After her wedding, Virginia moved with her new husband to Herrin, never finishing her college education. Herrin (population, at the time, about 10,000) was far from being the tranquil small town one might think. It was infamously known in Illinois as the dark heart of "Bloody Williamson County." In the late 1800s and early 1900s, Williamson was a vicious hotbed of bootlegging, mine riots, organized crime, gang warfare, and KKK activity.

Most of the blood-letting and scandal had died out by the time the newly-married Grears settled there but some of the participants and all of the near-folklore-ish stories still circled about the small city.

The *Herrin Daily Journal* was a hybrid of two newspapers, *The Daily Journal* and the *Herrin News* which merged in 1931. By the time Virginia Marmaduke Grear arrived, the *Herrin Daily Journal* had a circulation of about 3,000, and its masthead proudly declared that it was "Serving the Center of the Third Most Densely Populated Area in Illinois."

Though Virginia would often profess later in her life that she had a lifelong dream of going into the newspaper business, the existing records from the time do not seem to

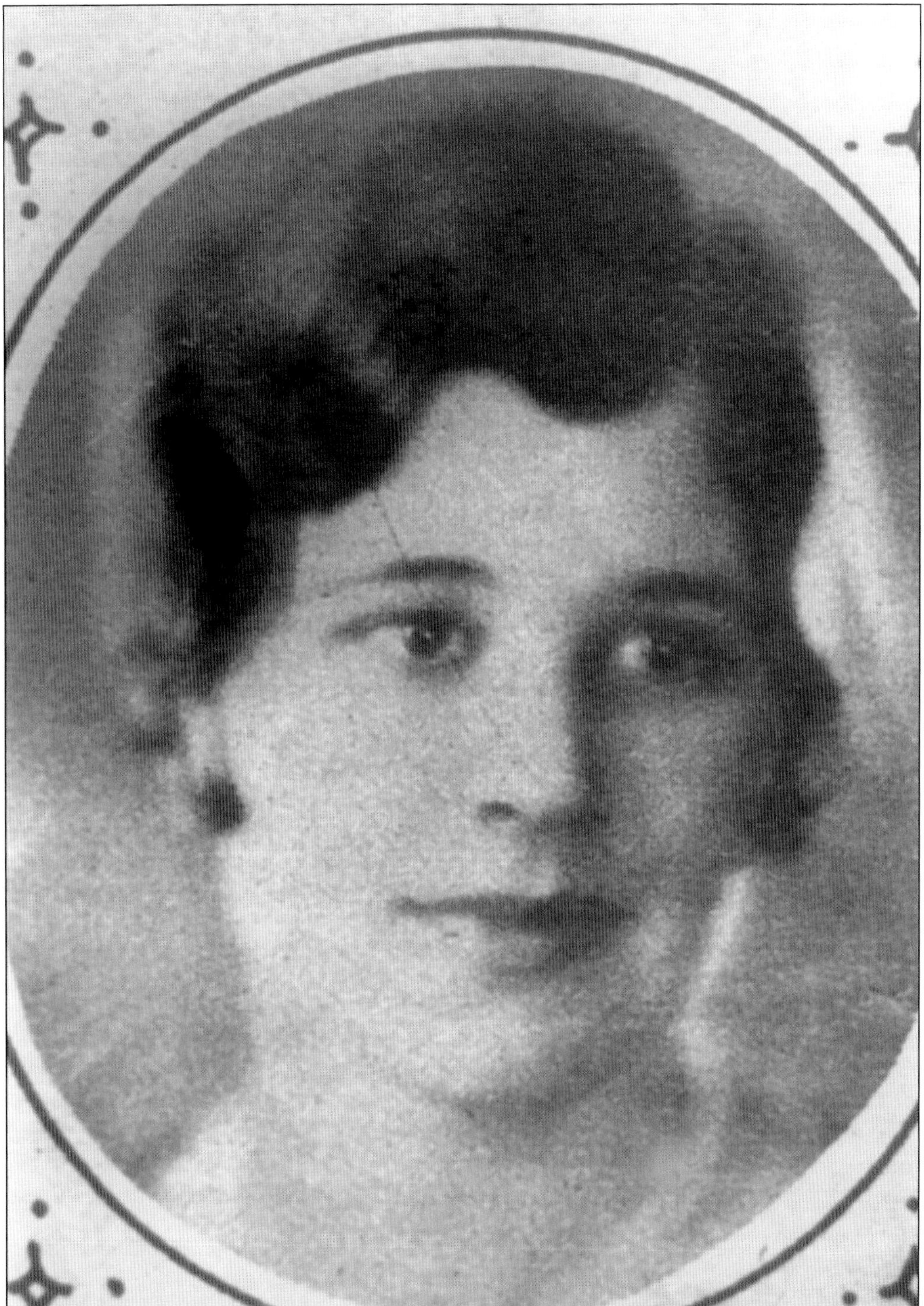

Virginia Lee Marmaduke at the time of her wedding to Harold Grear, 1930. (Author's Collection.)

reflect this interest and she told at least one reporter once, "It didn't matter what my major was, I married the son of the owner." So, whether going to work for a newspaper was the fulfillment of a long-held goal or simply destiny, Virginia Marmaduke was about to embark on a career as a professional journalist.

Her *Daily Journal* work would educate her well, she said years later: "The experience I gained in Southern Illinois prepared me to handle anything in Chicago...in a small town, if you make a mistake every reader knows it. I think it makes you work harder when you work for a small-town [newspaper] where if your name is under it, a lot of people know just who you are."

Virginia's husband served as the paper's advertising manager, leaving Virginia with the task of everything else. During the 13 years she worked for the paper, the size of the newspaper's staff would widely fluctuate, but its chief reporter was always Mrs. Harold Grear.

Years later, Virginia would recall a diverse array of reporting assignments: covering a wedding in the morning, writing a feature story in the afternoon, attending a civic meeting in the evening, and then hurrying to the high school gymnasium to cover the second half of a basketball game.

Sadly, though the *Journal* published a lot of stories in its pages, perhaps out of modesty or out of a need not to look like a small-town, mom-and-pop-type operation, almost none of them carried any bylines. Nevertheless, we know of at least one big story that Virginia Grear certainly did cover: the great Southern Illinois flood which devastated the area in 1937. It would be the biggest story of Virginia's pre-Chicago career.

HERRIN DAILY JOURNAL

JOURNAL REPORTER FINDS SERIOUS CONDITIONS IN AIRPLANE FLIGHT OVER FLOODED DISTRICT

Water Maroons Score of Homes:

Associated Press Asks Help of Journal for Flood Pictures*

1/16/37

A reporter and photographer of The Herrin Journal spent an hour yesterday flying over the flood district of Williamson and Jackson counties, getting pictures and first hand information about the stricken area.

The flight proved successful in revealing information that indicates the flood is much more serious than most people in this section realize. More than a score of homes in the south-western part of Williamson county are marooned by water and there is a question that some of the people might be without food.

It is only possible to get to these houses by boat and only one small skiff was seen in the whole flooded area.

Hundreds of acres in the Crab Orchard Creek district, located in the south-western part of Williamson county and the eastern part of Jackson county, were covered with water. It is estimated that not less than 75 miles of roads in this district are flooded. In many places it is believed some of the roads are under as much as 12 and 15 feet of water.

A great section of State Route No. 13 on the Carbondale-Marion road is flooded. This section is where the highway and Crab Orchard and Creek pass. Water was not only over the road but it was over the fences along the road.

The greater part of the flooded district in the west part of the county is in what will be the basin of the proposed WPA Crab Orchard Lake, now under construction. From the air one got a good conception yesterday of what the lake will look like when completed. The district appears to be a natural basin and from the looks of conditions there yesterday, it appears that most anyone would be glad to sell their land for the lake project.

The road running south from the Carterville cross roads at Highway No. 13 was flooded for several miles through Grassy. All roads leading south from Highway No. 13 were covered with water and the only open roads to the south were out of Marion and Carbondale.

Pictures made by The Journal will reveal many interesting facts about the flood and also give a good idea of what the Crab Orchard lake is going to be like.

The Associated Press of St. Louis solicited The Journal photographer to help get air views of the flooded district. They were made, developed, and sent to St. Louis by bus last night, arriving there at 12:15 this morning. The pictures were then transmitted by wire from coast to coast and appeared in the late editions of the metropolitan newspapers this morning. The Journal also supplied the Associated Press with other flood pictures which are being published today by the string of newspapers they serve.

The news pictures in today's Journal of flood scenes in Williamson county were made Thursday while rain was still falling. They are the first to be published by any newspaper in Southern Illinois.

Fred Valentine of Marion was pilot for the flight over the flood district.

The Journal suggests that the CCC boys, who have been helping flood victims in certain districts, be directed to the Crab Orchard district. No doubt some of the families are in need of food and supplies.

In late 1937, seven years after marrying into her job at the paper, Virginia Marmaduke Grear gained her first regular newspaper byline. "Virginia's Reel," a weekly column running every Thursday, debuted complete with a postage-stamp sized photo of Virginia at the top of the page. Its name was a spin on a square dancing term, a promenade where two sets of couples face each other and, in turn, participate in a series of figures.

Virginia Marmaduke's "Virginia's Reel" column followed a maxim Marmaduke deeply believed: "small town newspapers should offer readers something they can't get anyplace else."

To that effect, "Virginia's Reel" was newsy, charmingly folksy and, in equal measure, editorial and irreverent. And like the do-si-do dance direction it shared its name with, it covered a lot of ground.

VIRGINIA'S REEL
11/10/37

GOOD AFTERNOON FOLKS! Through the generosity of The Journal, I start TODAY on the fulfillment of my life-long ambition for a by-line and a column...and from now on I shall greet you every Thursday afternoon from these columns. Of course, I know that it is only with the aid of you, my readers, that I can make this a success, and in the manner of "Line o' Type or Two," I shall appreciate, heartily, any squib you send to me. Just address it to "Virginia's Reel" and be sure to sign your name, 'cause I sure don't want to go around whispering untrue stories which come to me anonymously. A toast then, to this, the natal day of "Virginia's Reel"! Long may she reel in interesting discussion with you every Thursday afternoon.

VIRGINIA'S REEL
11/18/37

I'M HUMBLY GRATEFUL for the good wishes so many of you have offered me for the future success of "Virginia's Reel." With all you nice people pulling for me I shall try even harder to interest you in some way. As the weeks roll along I'm bound to "run dry" and right then is when I'm really going to need YOUR help. Remember, any little squib will be warmly welcomed. In case you don't like to write letters, stop me on the street...you'll know me...I'm the "nosy" person in the violent green coat who always wants to know if you've been some place or are going some place. It's always the same tune, but I've a new verse to my litany now...It goes like this... "Do you need any business letter-heads or statement blanks? We are fully equipped at The Herrin Daily Journal *office to design and make any type of business stationary you may personally desire."...I am also the walking vitaphone attachment advertisement for our efficient job-work department.*

VIRGINIA'S REEL

12/16/37

I'M PROUD OF THE TOWN IN WHICH I LIVE! I make no claim to its being the most beautiful town in the world...the wealthiest town in the world...nor the most cultured town in the world...but I shout a challenge to any other city, town or hamlet that HERRIN is the friendliest of ALL communities. Just a scanty resume of the past eight weeks' civic movements will prove my arrogation...Our tall Mayor, Fred Henderson, has personally taken the entire responsibility of providing Good Cheer Baskets for Herrin's needy families and has organized the Herrin Good Fellows...Herrin's response to the November Red Cross roll call was the largest enrollment for the past seven years...The Art Department of the Herrin Woman's Club gave a big benefit bridge party and the entire profits go into the Education fund whereby deserving students of Herrin are aided in the continuing of their education[...]The W.P.A. Recreation Workers are painstakingly repairing and re-dolling up old, discarded toys which will be distributed to less fortunate kiddies and thus bring happiness all over again...The Ladies Aids, the Sunday School classes, even the purely social clubs of Herrin are aiding in the collecting of these toys...The Rotary and Lions Clubs lend freely of their membership and aid in ALL these civic promotions—besides which they unostensibly carry on their own individual philanthropy. [...] I could babble on forever—I am permeated with a bumptious glow, and I feel like "The Turk who sat on his throne with no rival near"—I am proud of Herrin! Proud of the good people who make this "The Friendliest City!"

In preparation for the upcoming Christmas holiday, Virginia Marmaduke Grear altered the format of "Virginia's Reel" and turned her talents to prose writing, composing the following little story.

Virginia, at its start, insists that this is a "true story" and perhaps it was, garnered from an experience she had while teaching school in 1925 near Pinckneyville.

VIRGINIA'S REEL

A TRUE CHRISTMAS STORY

12/23/37

It was a recess and the pupils of the little one-room school house played merrily in the deep, flaky snow which had fallen early that morning. They didn't wear smart, woolen, zippered snow suits, but wore plain old-fashioned "long-ones," and stocking-caps. Their cheeks were rosy with good health and their laughter pure and unalloyed.

"Aw," said the school bully, "there ain't no Santa Claus, and if there was, he wouldn't come to your house you ain't even got a Christmas tree and he won't come to a house that ain't decorated up none at all."

The brown-eyed lad, to whom he spoke, hung his head and big, hot tears ran freely down his little chapped-cheeks. He said not a word and slowly walked away from the group of awed children.

Bertha, who had never missed a day of school in her seven years attending the little country school, and who made excellent grades in all her studies, bravely spoke up and said, "James, you shouldn't talk to Danny like that. His Paw is sick, his little brother is blind and his Maw is milking eight cows and you know she hasn't time to get a tree and decorate it up for you. I'm going to tell Teacher that you made him cry."

James, [...], visibly relented and said, "Aw, Berthy, I was only having a little fun. You know there ain't no Santa Claus."

"Whoa there, who says there isn't a Santa Claus?" said the young school marm as she approached the little group.

"I did, and there really ain't," said James. "It's our folks who buy the presents and put them under the tree. I didn't mean to make Danny cry, but his folks ain't got no money to buy him presents with and he ain't got a tree, somebody ought to tell him so he won't expect no Christmas presents and then be disappointed."

"Doesn't Danny have any kind of a Christmas tree at all?" asked the teacher. "Nope, least I don't think so," said James.

The teacher mused aloud, "Umm...I didn't realize...say boys and girls, would you like to play a Santa Claus game this afternoon instead of examinations?"

"Oh Boy! I'll say we would," was the loud chorus answer.

"Then, let's get busy. James, you and Arthur and Eugene go over to Mr. Allerman's across the field and ask him if we may have the young maple I see standing alone there in the fence corner. It hasn't any green leaves or fir-boughs, but we've plenty of green crepe paper and we can wind that around the bare branches. Hurry now, we'll need you to help cut out decorations for the tree soon as you get back." [...]

It was James who said, "But there'll be no presents under his tree; Teacher...Do you think Danny would like this new red pencil of mine? It's only been sharpened once."

"Why he'd love to have it, James, here, let me wrap it up for you."

Furtively the rest of the little kiddies began looking into their desks and dinner-buckets to see what they could offer. "Teacher, I want to give my sling-shot to Danny, it's got three extra rubber bands...Here's a piece of cake my Mamma put in my dinner bucket which I didn't eat...I've got two knives, Danny hasn't any, and he likes to whittle...Teacher, you will give Danny that little whistle you took away from me in school yesterday? HE'LL never blow it during school hours...Here's an orange I was going to eat on the way home."

Teacher smiles, accepted all the proffered gifts and wrapped them in separate packages. She called a holiday for the remainder of the afternoon and laughing merrily they all trooped off together across the fields to Danny's home. When they arrived they found Danny's sick Father and little blind brother there alone. Danny and his mother had gone in the wagon a few miles distant to a neighbor who had kindly offered a bottle of home-made cough syrup for Danny's Father's persistent cough.

It was just as if it might have all been prearranged, for the school-kiddies and Teacher put up the tree, piled the presents underneath and were gone when Danny and his tired mother returned home.

Georgie, Danny's blond brother, greeted him wildly, "Danny! While you were gone, Mrs. Santa Claus and lots of her elf helpers came and left us a real Christmas tree and lots of things...Hurry and unwrap them so I can feel them." Danny hurriedly unwrapped each package and squealed with delight.

"Mother, Father, look Waldo has given me his sling-shot, Arthur has given Georgie his whistle, here's some real cake with chocolate icing, and oh look! James has given me his new red pencil and it's the first real long one I ever had. Mother, don't you think Santa Claus told them to give me these lovely presents?"

Sadly, sweetly and reverently, Danny's Mother answered, "Yes, Danny, a Santa Claus who watches over us all day in and day out, year after year and century after century...A Santa Claus who listens even while little children play on the school ground of a little country school."

—V.M.G.

Despite the heavy workload of the "Reel" and her other newspaper duties, Virginia Marmaduke Grear also found time to work as a Southern Illinois "stringer" for the now defunct *St. Louis Star-Times*. And she even dabbled further in fiction.

Although primarily known for her journalism, a handful of times throughout her life Virginia Marmaduke would turn her pen to the genre of prose. One such endeavor was a short story titled "Fallen Leaves" which Virginia wrote in 1937 and which would go on to win first place in a district short story contest sponsored by the Illinois Federation of Women's Clubs. It would be read at various meetings in and around Southern Illinois and would later be published in brochure form.

One copy, with a personal inscription from Virginia to Mrs. Kent Keller, wife of the Illinois senator, eventually came to reside in the Illinois State Archives in Springfield.

"Leaves" would later be notated in Thomas Kilpatrick's book *Illinois! Illinois!: An Annotated Bibliography of Fiction* where that book's author deduces the location of the story (left unnamed) as Southern Illinois, probably a place similar to Herrin or Pinckneyville.

The story tells the rather progressive tale of young Sylvia Shephard, a city social worker who makes a surprise return visit to her rural family, bringing with her, in her arms, an allegedly abandoned baby. At first, Sylvia (who claims to have found the baby on her doorstep) plans to stay, get a job and raise "her" child alone. But, the lure of the city and pity for her childless brother and sister-in-law, proves too much for her, and Sylvia gives the baby to them and then repairs back to her faraway, big-city career.

The story begins:

It was late October, and the early killing frost of the week before had turned the leaves on the great trees into a riot of fall colors. A gentle but persistent wind fanned the branches softly, and it seemed that the leaves came floating down to the ground almost willingly...

After her foray into fiction, Virginia returned to the real world of reporting for the *Herrin Daily Journal,* and her weekly column, "Virginia's Reel."

VIRGINIA'S REEL
2/3/38

HERRIN'S MOTHERS hugged their little ones just a bit more solemnly last Saturday when they tucked their kiddies into their beds...Many of them thought inwardly, "I'm thankful that that awful fire didn't wait and break out while YOU were there at the matinee this afternoon...During the fire, when vicious tongues of flames were shooting out of the windows and massive brick walls were crumbling, awed onlookers mumbled, "Thank God this didn't happen this afternoon." [...] I stood with hundreds of others, in safety, and watched the fire from the time the first spirals of smoke crept through the ventilators to the time when all that was left of the Hippodrome was a hulk of smoldering, buckled steel beams and a part of two walls...It was the first completely destroying fire I had ever witnessed and while I was frightened and sorrowful, I was at the same time fascinated! I never before realized what a monster uncontrolled fire really is...Onward it rushed, completely destroying everything in its way. [...] There were no causalities...TODAY while we mourn the loss of Herrin's Hippodrome, we look forward to the new, modern, beautiful and glamorous theater which Marlow Enterprises plan to build in the very near future.

VIRGINIA'S REEL
4/14/38

AND SO WE VOTED! Some of us brazenly, some timidly, and I'm sorry to say, some of us furtively... At any rate we VOTED! And as WE walked into the poll we stopped and thought how lucky we are to have the privilege of casting a vote for the man we thought could best aid in the government of our country and the state...We thought of the Russians who have little opportunity of voicing their personal opinions—we thought of the countries where only the Dictator's voice can be heard—and we thought, too, of the days not so long ago when the King's word was law. [...]

VIRGINIA'S REEL
4/21/38

THE OL' PROSPERITY CRY of "There's Gold in Them Thar Hills" has changed to "There's Oil in These Here Prairies" and the song is being echoed over many of the square miles of Southern Illinois. Why, the tune is even being hummed right here in Herrin and if things keep on the way they've started we'll all be yelling it at the top of our voices before very long. Even if we did stick up for "hitch-rack scenery" some time ago, we sure will welcome the oil well background to our Herrin picture and we'll join right in the chant [for] liquid gold.

VIRGINIA'S REEL
6/23/38

YOU'LL EXCUSE US IF WE BRAG A BIT on our recent Herrin Daily Journal Staff Photo of the King and Queen of England, won't you? Maybe you will join in this complacent, self-satisfied feeling the Reel is exuding, for after all, WE are yours—The Herrin Daily Journal is yours and the picture of Queen Elizabeth and her very dressed-up spouse is yours also...In fact, the picture was taken especially for us all... Our very competent Staff Photographer, Harris Jones, is vacationing in England and Europe and he has his Speed Graflex camera right with him for the express purpose of sending us some special tidbits which we might not otherwise have. Somehow I feel especially proud of the newspaper cut which lies so unassumingly on the shelves of our morgue, and which is simply labeled, "King and Queen of England."...To brag even more disgustingly, we lift our noses and say that we are perhaps one of the very few small-town daily newspapers in the entire world to own such a splendid "personal property" picture of England's most important Mr. and Mrs. [...]

VIRGINIA'S REEL
7/7/38
THE GENTLEMAN IN THE CENTER OF THE RING—(he usually carries a cane) doffs his hat, when ladies are riding in the show ring, and calls, "Trot your horses, please!"...And then the riders of the sleek and beautiful show horses which you gaze upon from your seat in the grandstand, usually send their horses around the ring in a spirited, showy trot. In judging this first of the required five gaits of a saddle bred show horse, the judge looks for that certain air of carriage, ears pointed forward at just the right angle, head proudly high, tall straight and motionless and a good speed while doing a square and rhythmic trot. In his mind's eye, the judge selects from the performing horses around him, the one performing best at the trot. Then in a stentorian voice, either he or his assistant ring master, call commandingly for a "Walk!" 'Tis then that the rider must exert gentleness in calming the high spirits of the finely bred saddle horse, and make him do a good flat-footed walk, with no jumping or jiggling around. While the walk is a natural gait of the horse, it sometimes happens that it is extremely difficult to quiet the horse down to the required walk. Then the judge may call for a "canter." In other than the glorified circles of the show ring, it is sometimes called a "short-lope" or when done at more speed it is sometimes a "gallop." [...] From the canter it is usually customary for a judge to call for "Slo-gait, please!" It is then that the showing animal must set himself in a slow rack or a glorified single-foot. The slo-gait is easy to ride and the rider barely moves in his saddle. From the slo-gait the judge usually sends the horses into the "Rack," that very fast, beautiful, smooth and most important of the five gaits. We have heard it said that the gait received its name because of the likeness to the swift but shuttling manner in which the raccoon moves along on its four legs. [...] The competing five gaited saddle horses give their all and when the judge has selected his favorite, he calls "Line up, please" and the horses and their riders form in front of the grandstand. [...] Good size, good height, fineness of neck and head, beauty of back and body manners go a long way in the receiving of the coveted blue ribbon and the prize money...And now, it isn't at all necessary for us to add that herein lies the "Reel's" hobby, for you've already guessed that to just sit and watch these handsome horses perform or better still to be riding and driving one ourselves is our favorite sport and hobby[...]

VIRGINIA'S REEL
10/6/38
IT'S NATIONAL LETTER WRITING WEEK and we intend to swing right into line. We plan to write letters to Mother, Dad, Aunts and Uncles, cousins and friends. [...] Whether we say "Atta-boy," "Thanks," "I Don't Agree With You" or "I Love You"—the ultimatum is that A LETTER NEEDS NO EXCUSE! So along with Lincoln, Franklin and Washington, today we engage in the sweetest, gentlest and most useful of all the arts—LETTER WRITING.

OPEN LETTER TO ADOLF HITLER
Your Excellency:

You have adopted new children, the Sudeten Germans. Remember that as their foster father, you must assume responsibility for their education, their future welfare and their happiness. We personally shall intensely resent any rough treatment which you might give to your new "chickens" and we hope that you will see to it that they have a comfortable and happy life as new members of your flock.

The Reel.

VIRGINIA'S REEL
10/13/38

THIS WEEK THE NATION salutes the "working gal" and joins in the celebration of National Business and Professional Women's Week. 'Tis said that with the possible exception of ditch digging, there just isn't ANY job which a woman can't do as well as a man, but because we really want to be fair with our opposite sex we will admit there are certain professional fields in which we just wouldn't be interested...Once we asked a politician if he thought there was a definite place for women in politics. Because it was close to election time, he said emphatically that some of the ablest politicians in Washington today are members of the fair sex, and he added that he could see no reason whatsoever why women could not, and do not, aid materially in the governing of our nation...You've notice probably, as we did, that he said "AID in the governing," not "DO the governing"...Then again, not so long ago, we asked a city banker why there were not more women bankers than there are. He replied that banking is a highly specialized and technical field and that perhaps women did not care for the study so necessary to being a banker...Be that as it may, there is no open fight between the sexes in this matter of JOBS—it's every brain for itself, and the scramble doesn't eliminate the petticoat wearer. For instance, we know a woman who manages a six-room house, who feeds eight mouths three times daily, who washes, scrubs, cleans, sews, mends, and DARNS. Is there a gentleman in the crowd who would like to beat her out of her JOB?

VIRGINIA'S REEL
1/26/39

BECAUSE WILLIAMSON COUNTY will soon celebrate her one hundredth county birthday, we've become allergic to all old country histories, and in our readings we ran across a beautiful, old copy of the "History of Alexander, Union and Pulaski Counties" published in a big, bulky volume back in 1883... [...] ...As we read, we found a story of the first newspaper in Union County—and if you will forgive a bit of bragging, we are thrilled to tell you that John Grear, our husband's great-grandfather was its owner[...] The country editor of the history berates the early newspaper editor and concludes gruffly saying, "The quality of the writing of the Country Press has definitely deteriorated"[...] So even if you occasionally find us out of accord with your opinions, remember that even back in 1883, editors were "getting the dickens" and weren't pleasing ALL their readers ALL the time.[...]

VIRGINIA'S REEL
2/16/39

THE POPE OF PEACE, Pius XI, is said to have often gazed at the space reserved for his body in the crypt of St. Peter's Basilica at Rome and said, "Here, I, too, will some day find sweet repose." Today he lies at peace, his face covered with a silken veil, his body sealed in a walled niche in the final resting place of Popes of the Catholic Church...We like to feel that the soul of Pius the XI is today in conference with the souls of his predecessors—that he is telling them that the world is growing better, that there is less hardship and suffering and that he left the world a better place in which to live...In yesterday's edition of The Herrin Daily Journal we carried a list of the names of Herrin people who have had personal audiences with the late Pius the Eleventh—but we forgot one name—we forgot to mention that you paragrapher, Virginia of Virginia's Reel, too, once stood and looked on as Pius the Eleventh spread a Papal Blessing over his visitors... In the Latin of his Church, he spoke a blessing over the pilgrims who had come seeking an audience with him and tho' we understood not the meaning of his words or gestures, we sincerely felt that we were in the presence of Holiness and we join with our Catholic friends in mourning the earthly passing of the head of the church, Pope Pius the XI.

In all her years with the *Herrin Daily Journal,* surprisingly, Virginia's name appeared only twice as the author of a non-"Reel" article. The first time was in late 1939.

A MIGHTY ARMY MOVES ON CHICAGO
Legion Convention Gets Under Way: Because of European Tension, 1939 Legion Conventions Has Serious Side
By Virginia Grear
9/29/39

CHICAGO, Sept. 25—Those jaunty little American Legion caps are out in bloom again although this time in their chosen garden they are seriously in danger of a "frost nip." Chicago is again their scene of "blooming" and the temperature is crisply cool.

Although the 21st annual National American Legion Convention doesn't actually start any of its business procedure until Monday morning, the vanguard of their great army has already moved into Chicago.

Friday afternoon a railroad train coming from Southern Illinois into Chicago was turned from the prosaic usual monotonous train trip into a jolly party and the Legionnaires typically "stole the show." Groups of Legionnaires boarded the train at each of its stops. Hearty greetings of "Hi Buddy" were exchanged to each joining contingent and jollier and heartier were the greetings as the train steamed on toward convention city. [...]

They gathered in groups of four or less, and serious were their discussions of the present world situation. Possibly the many resolutions which will be passed and adopted on the floor of the convention meetings at the Coliseum in Chicago this week will reflect the general American Legion sentiment, but it's a good bet that the resolutions will be couched in words less plain, less sincere and less commonplace than the sentiments which were heard voiced in the more informal groups when they spoke in a language familiar to each other.

The tension in the world today will undoubtably make unusual tension in this 21st annual Legion Convention. Legionnaires will discuss the present war and will discuss it from the angle of "experience." Their resolutions will be sent to the law making bodies of the United States and the current opinion seems to be that those who sit in judgment should lend a "hearing ear" to these straightforward words from the men who really know what war means.

More than 30,000 Legionnaires had registered at general headquarters at Chicago's Palmer House hotel by Saturday afternoon. More than a quarter million are expected. Chicago is ready for them. Michigan Avenue is a veritable Avenue of Flags, but in this case they are ALL American Flags for this is an All-American convention. [...]

VIRGINIA'S REEL
1/4/40

WELL, THE HOLIDAYS ARE OVER—some say, "Thank goodness"—others say, "It's been so nice I wish it could last forever."... [...] We lucky Americanites spend our holidays exactly as we choose. We eat, we drink, we make merry or we pull in our ears and toast our toes at a cheerful fireplace. We do EXACTLY AS WE PLEASE and we're proud of our right to do so but we're not selfish in our security. There's probably not a one among us who didn't at some time during the holy week of the Nativity whisper a silent prayer of "Please bring peace on earth."

VIRGINIA'S REEL
10/6/40

ARE YOU A HEADLINE READER?

COMPARABLE TO THE Little Red Hen who felt something fall upon her tail and then ran real fast to her King to tell him that the sky was falling is the person who hastily scans his daily newspaper and reads

ONLY THE HEADLINES. [...] Tedious too is the task of the headline writer! He must be almost a magician to match up words and letters and fit them into a rather small and limited space. He must put the "heart" of the news story into a scanty eight or nine words at the top of a juicy news feature...He tries to make you WANT to read the whole story, so don't skip the "meat around the bone"—it is often the most savory!

These are days of "screaming headlines" and screeching, static-studded news flashes. DON'T TRUST TO QUICK IMPRESSIONS! Don't read JUST the headlines. Read intently and listen closely. Innuendoes of vague meaning are mouthed from out of the air; scrambled words of subtle depth are placed before our eyes. Let's be a careful what we take in through our ears and eyes as we are what we take in through our mouths.

We hear persons who say, "I get so nervous trying to understand all this world chaos that I have decided to read only the comic strips and listen only to 'Amos and Andy.'" They go on to explain that they want to be completely oblivious to the present crises.

Although we are sincerely in sympathy with their wish to "take no sides" we CANNOT AGREE that they should keep themselves WHOLLY UN-INFORMED! We have our two precious freedoms—press and speech—through them we are able to cope with almost any form of "national frenzy." Let's study closely so that we may be mentally equipped to make decisions.

Though a seemingly popular feature of the *Herrin Daily Journal* since 1937, in mid-1940, Virginia Marmaduke Grear's "Virginia's Reel" came, unceremoniously, to an end.

Three years later, Virginia's second non-"Reel" byline appeared in the *Herrin Daily Journal*. It was a near-editorial piece she penned for the paper and which was printed on the front page. (Note the presence of Virginia's maiden name in her byline, it was absent from her earlier story in 1939.)

THERE'S ALWAYS A LITTLE GOOD IN EVERYTHING BAD
By Virginia Marmaduke Grear
3/15/43

Nationally thrown brick-bats can't hurt Herrin and Williamson County. They've dodged 'em for years and always come out on top. That's why they can shrug their shoulders like the ladies they are and "consider the source" of the recent blast from the pages of the Washington Post.

A HASTY reading of Agnes E. Meyer's feature article on Williamson County's Illinois Ordnance Plant has provoked wrath and rebuttal from many citizens of this area.

A COOL and CAREFUL reading of the story reveals some paragraphs worthy of reprint.

"Here is one war project whose social effects on its environment are all positive, all constructive and all invigorating," she writes.

Mrs. Meyer is the wealthy wife of the wealthy owner of the Washington Post. She wrote her feature story after a flying survey made in this area on the afternoon of February 28.

Mrs. Meyer had a special interview with Plant Manager E.E. Ware. "Never have I met such willing people," he told her. "Our women workers are particularly enthusiastic. They get after the laggards themselves and are constantly speeding up the work."

"We expected a wild, restless population," Mrs. Meyer quotes Mr. Ware as saying. "Instead we find them to be the finest people with whom we have ever associated. There are 50 to 60 lay preachers on the line. The scholastic rating of the community is very high and in spite of limited facilities in the neighborhood we have a high percentage of college graduates."

Mrs. Meyer said that her survey revealed that the employment turnover at the Illinois Ordnance Plant is less than any other factory she has visited. She says that absenteeism is negligible. She said that at any plant where people need the money they are only too glad to work.

Mrs. Meyer made a short visit to some of the actual work lines at the Ordnance Plant here. She said that she found there the buzz of machinery accompanied by the singing of gospel hymns and that the management is kept busy attending birthday parties during the lunch period. "In fact, the labor-management relations are probably unique for their intimacy and warm concern for the individual," she writes.

Some of the inaccurate, rumor-based sentences in Mrs. Meyer's feature article were gleaned, she says, from short interviews with "natives." From them she gathered the erroneous impression that Southern Illinoisans are direct descendants from distillin', feudin' Kentucky mountaineers; that plant-installed shower baths were a novelty; that the majority neglect to pay taxes; that only a few have automobile licenses; that marriage is not regarded as a moral institution, and that earned money is enjoyed no more than relief dole.

Maybe it was her haste which caused the resulting job of "poor reporting."

Maybe it was the type of person she chose to interview when talking personally to the "natives."

Maybe she had an honest desire to show that after the war plant has been discounted, Williamson County will NEED and WANT industry to keep from falling back to top place on the nation's relief rolls.

Herrin and Williamson County have only one big job to do today. They're out to WIN THIS WAR.

They have no time for "bickering."

1942 and '43 brought big, abrupt changes for both the country and for Virginia Grear.

For its first 13 years, Virginia Marmaduke would remember her marriage and her work at the family newspaper in Herrin as "hunky-dory." Despite the Depression and the escalating war in Europe, the newspaper made money, and the Grears enjoyed the Herrin high-life: driving a convertible, dancing at the Elk's Club and tripping up to Chicago on the weekends to visit Virginia's parents.

But in late 1942, Harold Grear, a former member of the ROTC, was called into service, made a First Lieutenant and shipped out to work at the Pentagon in Washington. Virginia stayed behind in Southern Illinois to run the newspaper on her own. Virginia would later remember that, with time, her husband's calls home became fewer and farther between.

Virginia eventually traveled out to D.C. and met her husband at his apartment in the city. There he confessed to infidelities and then admitted to having a new steady "girl." Then he asked for a divorce. As Virginia would later recollect, she didn't say anything and she wasn't surprised; other women she had suspected. Virginia agreed to the divorce and returned first to Chicago to tell her parents and then to Herrin to tell his.

Then she and Harold discussed a divorce settlement. The future "Duchess" said she didn't want alimony or property. In ending the marriage, she only wanted one thing. In a gesture quite emancipated for its time, Virginia wanted to reclaim her maiden name. She said years afterward, "I wanted to start afresh—in every way."

Since continuing to work for the *Herrin Daily Journal,* the paper owned by her soon-to-be ex-in-laws, was not an option, Virginia would soon find herself not only single but also jobless. And though she had made her home in Herrin for over a decade, the idea of staying there brought with it the enduring stigma of small-town divorcee. She said once, ruefully, "Everyone there knew me and knew I was going through a divorce..."

Though most records, and Virginia's own memory, say she left Herrin for Chicago sometime in 1943, her divorce from Harold Grear did not become final in the Marion, Illinois courthouse of Williamson County until January of 1944, perhaps with the legal finalization taking place with Virginia *in absentia.* In the court record of the dissolution, Harold Grear was listed as the plaintiff; Virginia as the defendant. For the divorce, they were levied a fee of $33.64.

Decades later Virginia would grow both philosophical and fatalistic about the failure of her one and only marriage, saying, "It could just have easily been me [that found someone else]," adding, "Anyway, I would never have gone to Chicago if things hadn't turned out the way they did."

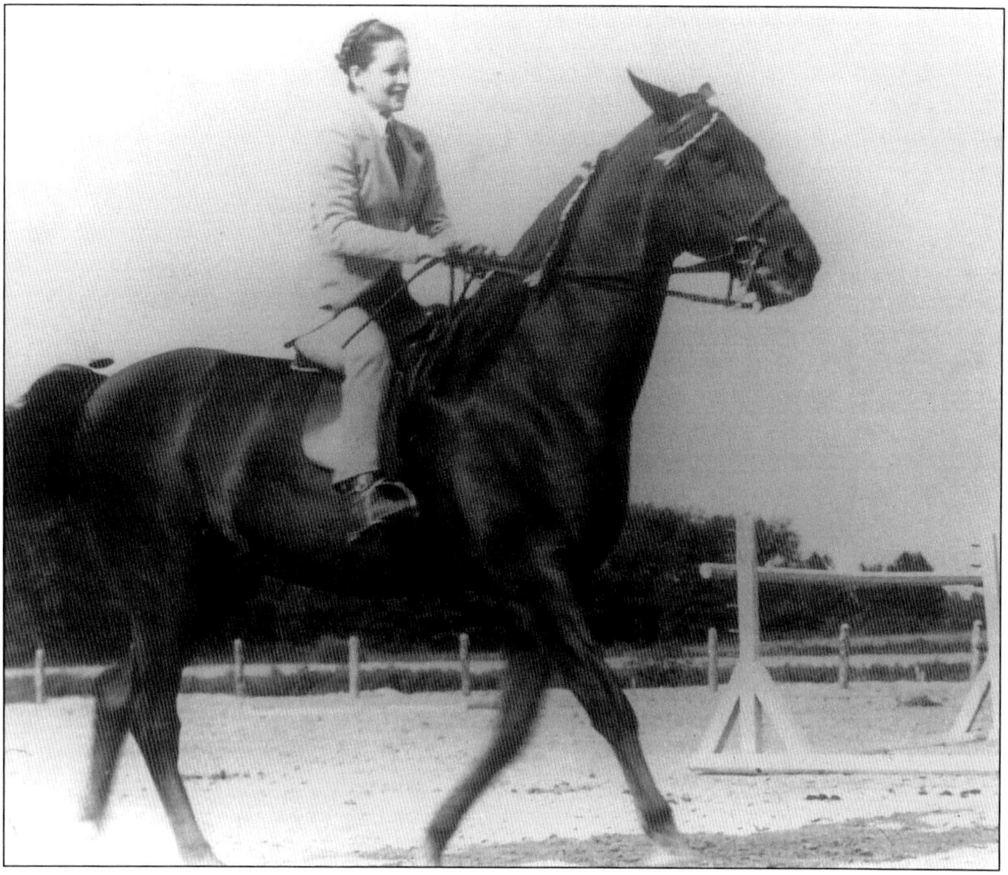

Virginia, a life-long horsewoman, astride a four-legged friend.

II.
The Duchess (1943–1955)

1943–1944

In the early 1940s, with her childless ten-year marriage, and her job, at an end, Virginia Marmaduke had to move on. Her parents were still living in Chicago and Virginia hoped to take her twelve years of newspapering experience, move there, and start over in the Windy City.

Once settled into her parents' home, Virginia spent two weeks knocking on the doors of the local newspapers. She said, "I went to the *Daily News* first. They said, 'Don't call us, we'll call you.'...The *[Chicago] Sun* wanted to know when I could start. I was lucky. All the good men were at war." She later added, "the editor wanted a girl who was not going to be called into service and who had experience and knew the town."

When she applied for the job, Virginia left blank on the application form the types of stories she wanted to cover. "You want to write about nothing?" the editor growled at her at her job interview.

Marmaduke responded, "Well, I didn't like the choices. I don't want to write about society or entertainment or fashion."

"What's left?"

"I want to be a newspaperman. I want the blood and the guts and the sex and the greed. I want to cover it all..."

When the editor asked if she could cover the Chicago city council, Virginia replied, "Why not? The Chicago City Council isn't any different than the Herrin City Council. They just deal with more money." Knowing spunk when he saw it, the editor hired her.

Virginia said of her early days in big city journalism, "I was the new babe in the newsroom. I was standing next to my editor trying not to be nervous because there were 31 men staring at me. I knew what they were thinking. They were thinking, 'Will she or won't she?' You know they were."

Later, Virginia spelled out her reasons for not making, in her own words, "a big deal" of her gender while on the job. "I worked awfully hard at it, and I let my fellow police reporters know I wasn't using my sex to scoop them. I wanted to compete on the same level with them.

"You can't think that just because you're born a little different than a man you have more right to chance because you don't. If you get an exclusive interview with sex, you'll only hurt yourself with your fellow newspaper people and it's not worth it. Not in the long run."

She added, "It didn't really matter then and it doesn't now if you're a man or a woman—the editor doesn't pay any attention to the name. He's just interested in getting the best story. I got those stories."

But, "you know a female smile can open more doors than a $10 bill."

Early on Virginia adopted two rules for getting along in her new work environment: "Don't drink on the job and don't date any man you work with."

But living by her latter rule didn't mean that the Duchess would ever lack for male companionship. Over the years she could be seen around town on the arm of movie tough guy George Raft when he was in Chicago and also out and about with Papa Bear George Hallas.

Along with her new job, Virginia Marmaduke also very quickly acquired a new and lasting nickname. As legend has it, her first editor/boss, Tom Michelmore, on her first day on the job, found "Virginia Marmaduke" or "Miss Marmaduke" too much of a mouthful to yell out across the newsroom when he wanted her. He asked her, "What did they call you in school?"

Virginia replied, "'Ginny.'"

"Well, that's no name for a newspaper reporter," the editor said, thinking, "Well, you've got a 'duke' in your name but you ain't got one in your life...so we'll call you 'The Duchess.'"

Weird logic to be sure, but it wasn't a moniker Virginia objected to and she would carry it, proudly, for the rest of her life.

Her first full day at the *Sun*—working the 2 p.m. to midnight shift—the Duchess later remembered doing nothing much other than helping the obits editor when he got behind at deadline time. But soon, she was out learning the ropes and covering stories.

In keeping with the unwritten newspaperman's code, Virginia was seldom seen on the job without a hat. And in keeping with Chicago press tradition, she adopted the Billy Goat Tavern, at 430 North Michigan Ave., as her favorite after-hours hang-out. Later to be made famous in the "Cheeseborgie! Cheeseborgie!" skit on *Saturday Night Live*, the Billy Goat was *the* place for city reporters at the end of the day. Said the Duchess about the bar, "it was a place of beer, hot dogs, and cheeseburgers and things like that and you'd go and meet a lot of people that you knew. [You'd] exchange items, exchange opinions, all of us together, but we knew we weren't trying to scoop each other, so it was a friendly place." Today, among the newspaper-related memorabilia adorning the Billy Goat's walls, there are three photographs that feature the Duchess.

Though the Duchess's records and most other reports state that she arrived at the *Sun* sometime in 1943, she did not get her first, coveted byline until almost mid-1944. That was just the beginning.

<u>CHICAGO SUN</u>

VOTER GROUP HITS CHANGE

By Virginia Marmaduke

4/26/44

Heavy opposition to a proposed by-law change in the constitution of the National League of Women Voters, which would do away with the medium of State Leagues, is expected when the delegates meet today for the second day of their convention at the Hotel Stevens.

First indication of the strength of the opposition was revealed yesterday when a "request vote" of 198 to 105 brought Miss Ruth Mitchell, St. Cloud, Minn., unopposed candidate for president of the National League, before the body in an official endorsement of the plan.

When questioned as to whether or not she would withdraw her candidacy if the convention rejects the proposed change, Miss Mitchell said she would rather not answer until after today's discussion discloses the "true spirit and sentiment of the delegates."

* * *

Mrs. Walter T. Fisher of Winnetka, treasurer of the National League, and one of the board members who helped frame the proposed change in the structure of the National League, explained that under the new plan "the federated club idea" would be discarded.

"It would give National a more direct contact with local leagues," she declared, "and would eliminate [the] time and expense in transmission of directives first through state and then to actual membership."

State leaders of the opposition contend that State Leagues have done a good job under the present system and that continuation of accomplishing their common purpose necessitates the State League organization. [...]

WAUKEGAN 'CASINOS' DINGY AFFAIRS
Gamblers Crowd Stuffy Back Rooms But Bets Are Small
By Virginia Marmaduke
8/30/44

It cost a Chicago Sun reporter just 18 cents to make a round trip yesterday from the Loop to Waukegan—by the Chicago, North Shore & Milwaukee electric line—a trip of 45 miles.

After rubbing elbows in a stuffy, unventilated, dark room one flight up behind a Washington St. cigar store, watching the town's sports bet 10 cents on dice and 25 cents on horse races, she reported the trip was hardly worth the $1.50 saving.

The bus that was reputed to meet all trains was nowhere in sight when the reporter alighted at the Waukegan station, but a taxicab driver acted as her guide to Waukegan bookmaking. When she asked to be driven to a handbook, he asked:

"Which one?"

Then he volunteered the information that the town has eight or nine gambling places, adding:

"But there's only two you'd like."

He let her out of the cab in the heart of the downtown section and told her to go to a cigar store in the 100 block of W. Washington St.

<u>WOMAN LEADS WAY</u>

As the visitor searched for the place, a neatly dressed woman sidled up and asked:

"Looking for the handbook? Come with me."

She led the way through a cigar store to gloomy stairs leading to a second floor loft. The dingy room was filled with more than 100 persons, about a third of them Negroes, who were gathered in knots before "run down sheets" on the races posted on one wall while a loud speaker blared results.

Most of the horse race bettors wagered quarters and half dollars. Only an occasional bet was as much as $1. The dozen or so seedy looking men around the dice table bet dimes and hung on each roll of the dice as if their fortunes depended upon them.

A quick inspection of the patrons indicted that this was hardly a "gambling palace," so the reporter, acting on information volunteered by one of the bettors, walked directly across the street and into another "casino" every bit as discouraging as the first one.

The reporter showed the cashier her ticket back to Chicago. He marked it with a scrawling "C" in crayon and gave her $1.50.

<u>NO HOODLUMS IN SIGHT</u>

Nowhere was there to be seen [anyone] who remotely resembled a Chicago hoodlum or gangster, although there have been reports that some [...] small fry mobsters had been flocking to Waukegan. Suggestions that Chicago hoodlums might have "muscled in" on the gambling caused guffaws.

Last Nov. 1, Bart Tyrrell, chief of police of Waukegan, admitted that the suburb had received a $36,000 two-year "take"—enough to raise police base pay from $65 to $195 a month by "licensing" handbooks. A *varying scale of court fines, based upon the type of equipment operated by the defendant, was in force, he said, and handbook proprietors were arrested monthly and fined according to the scale.*

BOOKIE ARRESTS THREATENED

Last June 18, after a protest by Ald. Ernest Luke against gambling, Tyrrell announced that handbooks had been closed and that he would arrest the operators "as often as they appeared in Waukegan."

It was noteworthy that in neither of the downtown gambling joints was a slot machine to be seen, although thousands are reputed to be in operation throughout Lake County.

Perhaps surprisingly the topic of stories most likely to bear Virginia's byline is...horses. The races and Chicago's annual International Horse Show were regularly covered by the Duchess. She said, "When I started, I was about the only reporter in town who knew a trotter from a pacer." And so the Duchess was dispatched to the track. Woman or no, she proved her mettle and a later editor would say, "give her a story about anything on four legs."

While the horse-related stories, though voluminous, might not be the articles Virginia is most remembered for, but, even today the presence of a woman's name in a byline on the sports page is a relatively rare occurrence. So to have a female reporter with a regular credit in the sporting section in the mid-1940s was radical indeed. And the Duchess did it.

7,000 JAM COLISEUM AS CHICAGO HORSE SHOW OPENS
225 Exhibitors From 26 States Represented
$80,000 Offered In War Bonds to Prize Winners
By Virginia Lee Marmaduke
12/10/44

Nearly 7,000 persons packed the Coliseum last night for opening sessions of the Chicago Horse Show and saw the cream of America's show horse world begin the nine-day competition for $80,000 in war bonds.

The show will continue through Dec. 17, with competition nightly and matinees today, Thursday, Friday, Saturday and next Sunday.

Saddle breds, standard breds and thoroughbreds and hackney and Shetland ponies, valued, with their equipment, at $3,500,000, have been assembled at the Coliseum and adjourning buildings for the nine-day show.

"WORLD'S GREATEST"

Paul Butler, president of the Chicago Horse Show Association, declared last night that with its 450 horses the 1944 Chicago Horse Show is easily "the world's greatest." Two hundred and twenty-five exhibitors from 26 states will be represented in the show's 126 classes.

Mayor Kelly officially opened the show and welcomed the exhibitors. The Mayor and Mrs. Kelly occupied a box with Mrs. and Mrs. Butler and Mrs. and Mrs. John R. Robinson.

GENE AUTRY MISSING

The appearance of Flight Officer Gene Autry and his horse "Champion," was canceled last night. Autry, en route by plane from California, was grounded in Albuquerque, N.M., it was announced. Because the entire proceeds of the show are to be turned over to the Community and War Fund, Autry was to appear by special permission of the U.S. Army Air Force. [...]

Though her first few bylines listed her name as just "Virginia Marmaduke," for a very short time at the beginning of her career, Virginia added her middle name, Lee, to her byline. Then, just as quickly, it was dropped and she remained Lee-less for the remainder of her working days.

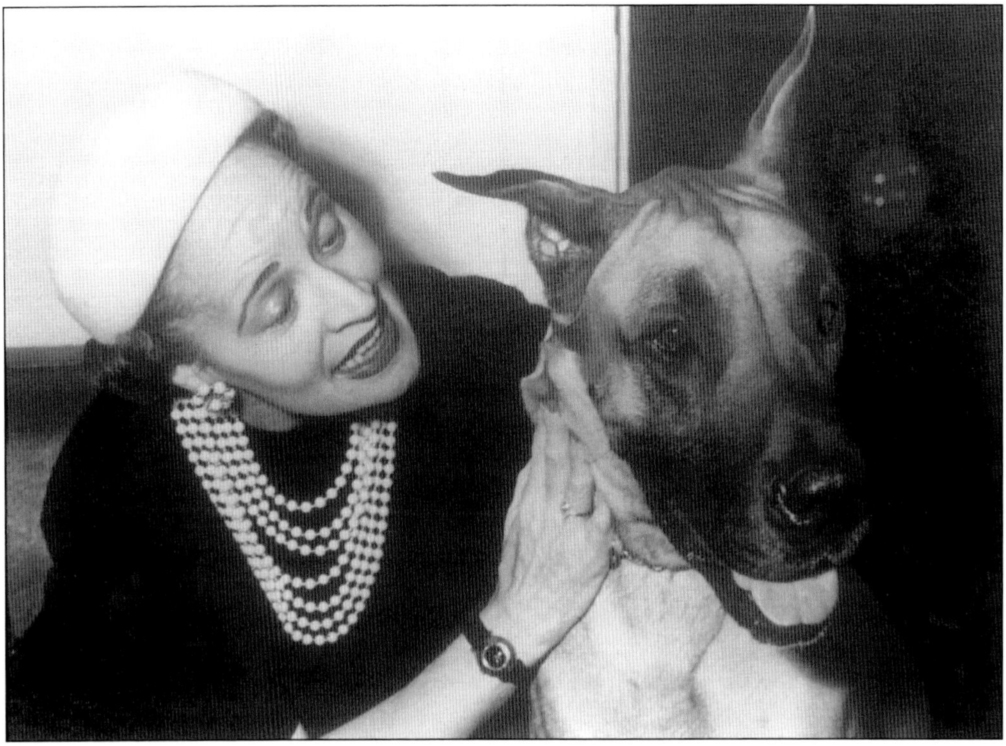

One Marmaduke Meets Another: Virginia with Bruno, the boxer who inspired Brad Anderson's comic strip "Marmaduke" (1954).

1945

For the crime reporters of Chicago, the scene on Kenmore Avenue in June of 1945 was, sadly, nothing too new. One of those reporters was Virginia Marmaduke, who once said, "I enjoyed crime stories somewhat because they led to a rewarding solution." But the "solution" to the killing of Josephine Ross would be over a year away and eventually lead to the arrest and conviction of serial killer William Heirens for, among other crimes, the kidnapping and murder of 6-year-old Suzanne Degnan in 1946.

CHICAGO SUN

MOTHER OF 2 CUT TO DEATH, SUITOR HELD

Brunette's Body Found in Home By Her Daughter*

6/6/45

Slashed to death in her bed, the body of Mrs. Josephine Ross, attractive brunette widow and mother of two daughters, was found yesterday afternoon in her apartment at 4108 Kenmore av. early last evening Town Hall detectives seized Chester Rice, 37, a rejected suitor, who, according to Mrs. Ross' daughters, had threatened her life.

QUESTIONING DELAYED

Rice, an ex-convict and since 1941 a switch engine operator for the Inland Steel Co. plant in Indiana Harbor, was arrested at his home, 916 Cherry st., Hammond. He had been drinking heavily, according to

Detective Peter Harlib and Ellsworth Suckow, who were compelled to postpone detailed questioning.

Rice denied all knowledge of the slaying, which Lt. Thomas J. Murphy described as one of the most bizarre in recent crime annals.

SIGN OF STRUGGLE FOUND

Death was caused by one of four deep slashes which severed the jugular vein. A long, deep cut in the palm of the right hand at the base of the thumb indicated the victim had tried [to] wrest the knife from the hand of her assailant.

At the foot of the bed, whining, and cowering in fright, was the slain woman's bull terrier, Peggy. The body was found on the left side of the bed, but only the right side was saturated with blood, indicating the death struggle had taken place there.

STAINS WASHED FROM BODY

All stains had been washed from the body—apparently after death—and the wounds had been closed neatly with adhesive tape. The corpse was nude except for a red skirt which had been tied about the neck with a stocking and its folds used to cover the features. Mrs. Ross' bloodsoaked pajamas and a dressing gown were found in the bathtub which was half filled with water. The murderer apparently tried to wash them. [...]

YANK MAKES FUTILE SEARCH FOR PARENTS IN NAZI CAMP
Wife Here Gets Letter Describing Heartbreak After Victory in Germany
By Virginia Marmaduke
6/18/45

A story of how victory in Europe brought first joy and then heartbreak to an American soldier was revealed yesterday in a letter from the soldier to his wife, Mrs. Herbert Van Natten of 19015 E. 54th pl.

German-born Pfc. Van Natten, former research tech of the University of Chicago science laboratories, was in France on D-Day as a member of the 11th General Dispensary unit, Army Medical Corps.

PARENTS HELD BY NAZIS

But his heart was near Prague, Czechoslovakia, where his mother and father, Wilhelm and Becky, were interned in a Nazi concentration camp. His every thought was to see the parents he had not seen since he left Berlin in 1938 to come to America.

When Pfc. Van Natten's unit was sent to Heidelberg and billeted in the famous old University buildings, he immediately applied for permission to travel the 400 miles on to the camp at Theresienstadt (Terizn) to see his folks.

Permission came June 2 and an American Red Cross director was assigned to take him there in a jeep. Pfc. Van Natten loaded the jeep with food delicacies. One of his pals loaned him a practically new field jacket to wear and he shined the buttons on his G.I. uniform.

DRIVE ROUGH BUT HAPPY

"Mother and dad will be proud to welcome me in my American uniform," he told all his buddies. It was a rough two-day drive to Prague but a happy one for the soldier. He still had in his pocket the last letter he had received from his parents. It came more than a year ago through the Red Cross in Switzerland.

They finally reached the concentration camp, a few miles out of Prague. The prison director, a Nazi, but under heavy allied guard, was still in charge. It took him one hour to find the registration of Pfc. Van Natten's parents.

RECORD SHOWS TRANSFER

When he did, he handed them silently to the eager soldier. Wilhelm and Becky Nattenheimer (the German family name) had been transferred to another camp, one called a "liquidation" camp in Poland, on Feb. 7.

They were two of 1,400 who had been marked "too old or too sick to work." Their consignment papers had been signed personally by Heinrich Himmler. [...]

NO HOPE OFFERED

The prison director gave the soldier no hope for the lives of his parents. He talked openly and frankly of "gas chambers" that followed torture when prisoners became too weak to work. [...]

"That's all right with me," he declared. "This has made me want even more to help in the extermination of Germany's Japanese partner."

One day, in Chicago's Cook County Hospital on the city's North Clark Street, Virginia Marmaduke, while covering another story, saw a doctor she knew through a doorway. He was busy examining a little boy named Adam. The Duchess said, "It was Dr. Pearlstein, and he told me the child had cerebral palsy."

Affected by the child's plight, the Duchess decided to write a series of stories on these "forgotten children." The Duchess said, "Polio was getting all the attention then in the medical world. Dr. Pearlstein told me that doctors weren't exactly sure what caused [cerebral palsy], they didn't know how to treat it, but something had to be done to help the children who had it."

After the series of articles were published, it prompted the state legislature of Illinois to vote monies, for the first time, to Cook County Hospital for the specific study and treatment of the illness. Illinois politicos were so moved by the Duchess's story, that they were read into the record of the General Assembly in Springfield.

Virginia would say years later, "That was my ego joy; I felt I was responsible for doing something really good."

NEW LIFE FOR THE 'FORGOTTEN'
Science, Patient Training Open Future of Hope for Victims of Cerebral Palsy
By Virginia Marmaduke
7/19/45

In Illinois there are more than 2,000 children suffering from cerebral palsy, an affliction that manifests itself in loss of muscular control—in spastic limbs and spines. This series of articles tells what is being done for these children and what may be done for them under legislation passed at the last session of the General Assembly.

A tot named Andrew sat alone the other day—for 10 full seconds.

This act, simple enough for most 14-month-olds, was almost miraculous for little Andrew, who accomplished it only after being tied in a sitting position half an hour each day for the previous eight weeks.

In his crib, lying flat on his back, Andrew looks like a young prizefighter. He is handsome and sturdy. His well-shaped head is cleanly bald.

But his gentian-blue eyes, fringed heavily with long, black lashes, are sightless and his handsome little body is helpless. He cannot control his spinal muscles or limbs or arms.

He is a cerebral palsied child. His brain is impaired due to an injury at birth.

There were tears in the eyes of Andrew's mother when she saw the baby, youngest of her eight, sit alone. There were tears in the eyes of nine other mothers who witnessed the victory too.

★ ★ ★

But all were tears of joy—and of hope. The other mothers hugged their helpless little ones close to their hearts when they saw the progress Andrew had displayed. Their children, too, were victims of cerebral palsy.

Not so spectacular as Andrew's feat, but as big an event in her life and as much of a thrill to her mother, was six-year-old Patsy's exhibition. She has learned, in two weeks, to make her hitherto uncontrollable left leg do the bidding of her brain. That it took a lot of concentration was plainly visible on her grim, thin, little lips.

But her brown eyes sparkled when for three consecutive times she was able to lift, and then plant, that crippled foot in the very center of a chalked circle which had been drawn on the floor. There was general applause and Patsy's auburn curls bobbed as she bowed her appreciation.

★ ★ ★

[...] These were the characters in a human drama more compelling than fiction and the scene was the cerebral palsy clinic at Cook County Hospital, headed by Dr. Meyer A. Perlstein. The mothers had brought their children to the once-a-week free clinic. They were learning how to manipulate the spastic limbs and spines of their children, to try to strengthen them.

The children? They were only 10 of the more than 2,000 children in Illinois who suffer from cerebral palsy.

They were the children, who, until the last decade, have occupied the farthest and darkest corner of our national conscience. The "forgotten" they have been called because of all crippled and handicapped children they have been the most neglected, the least understood and the most needful of attention.

* * *

For many years a blanket of shame was pulled over the head of the cerebral palsied infant, in many instances his own parents helping to hide him. Pathetically, they feared their child would be considered the result of a blemish on their family strain.

Ignorance even led to mass classing of such helpless children as "imbeciles" or "morons." Nothing could be farther from the truth than both suppositions. Medical research has established that cerebral palsy is caused by injury to the brain at birth, by faulty development of that organ or by injury or disease during the first years of life. [...]

* * *

That's what those mothers at Cook County Hospital clinic [were] thinking about when they saw little Andrew sit alone, Patsy tap the bullseye in the circle and Clorina walk unaided.

They had heard, too, the story of another "graduate" of cerebral palsy. It came from his mother's lips. He is a young man of 20 who is working toward his master's degree in mathematics at the University of Illinois. [...]

* * *

What the mothers probably were remembering more hopefully is that he can work trigonometry problems in his head and already is on his way to becoming a research specialist in mathematics.

That's the lifeline that has been tossed to these once "forgotten" children and it has all come about in the last 10 years. All is not hopeless now, for the cerebral palsied child. The right attention, early enough, can bring him a useful life. Doctors, surgeons, volunteer workers trained in muscle building, legislators, even the man on the street, have joined to help release the palsy victim from a life of captivity and torture.

NEW HOPE FOR THE FORGOTTEN
State Law Now Gives A Better Opportunity to 2,000 Stricken Children
By Virginia Marmaduke
7/21/45 (Last of series.)

For a few of the more than 2,000 cerebral palsied children in Illinois the road to improvement and a fuller life has been opened. But only a few, and their rehabilitation has come about because they lived in cities where clinical care was available or because they were fortunate enough to have parents with adequate means.

Under the guidance of a medical specialist and an expert body builder, a tot named Andrew finally learned to sit alone. But he lived in Chicago, where both were made available to him without cost.

A young man who attended college in a wheel chair is on the way to a self-sustaining status as a mathematician. His parents were able to "buy" a better life for him.

Andrew and the student have found escape from the shadow under which they were born. They are the salvaged among the "forgotten."

But there are not specialists and qualified body builders in every town or village. Local school districts are not financially able to offer special services for the crippled children in their areas. Only a few hospitals in Illinois maintain clinics, and none have space for these little patients who are not actually ill.

* * *

That's where the state of Illinois has recently seen fit to add stronger support to the lifeline the medical world has extended to the cerebral palsied child.

Three new statutes, all designed to help crippled and handicapped children, were passed at the last session of the legislature. All involved the appropriation of funds for financial aid to the handicapped child whose parents cannot give him the opportunity he deserves. Individual application for the benefits should come from the parents to the local school district in which they reside. School officials then will route the request to proper sources.

★ ★ ★

[...] What does all this mean to the crippled child?

It means that anything the crippled child needs that public school can offer him he now can have.

It means, too, that Illinois, for many years a laggard in its responsibility toward its crippled children, has forged to the front. It may mean that other states will follow and new heights of human goodness will have been achieved. Above all, it means humanity is realizing that every human life, however handicapped, has its purpose and can be of use.

1946

The Suzanne Degnan killing in Chicago on January 8, 1946, is widely known as the night that Chicago began to lock its doors. Before that, even in the "big city," a random, brutal kidnapping and killing did not seem feasible in neighborly Chicago. That though came to a permanent end when a little six-year-old girl was taken and murdered one night on the city's north side.

It would become one of the city's biggest news stories ever. And Virginia Marmaduke was on it, finding herself at the gruesome beginning when the decapitated head of the Degnan girl was pulled from a city sewer.

The crime and ensuing investigation dominated the Duchess's worklife for most of 1946. "I must have interviewed 600 to 700 people," she said about covering the "Crime That Shocked Chicago."

In true "sob sister" tradition, Virginia was specially assigned to interview and write about the grieving parents of Suzanne Degnan and, later, to cover the parents of Suzanne's accused killer, William Heirens. The Duchess said years later, "By the end of it, I really knew the mothers and fathers. I worked with them a lot and all I felt was sorrow for them all."

CHICAGO SUN

FIND CHILD SLAIN!

Police Discover Head in Sewer: City Crew Search Basin Near OPA Official's Home*

1/8/46

The head found in a sewer catch basin was identified as that of Suzanne Degnan last night by two friends of the family, Jack Hartnett and Walter Butler. Coroner A.L. Brodie said that the decapitation had been made cleanly with either an ax or a cleaver. The death, he said, was recent.

The head of a golden-haired girl was found at 5:30 p.m. yesterday in a sewer catchbasin half a block south of the home from which Suzanne Degnan, 6, was kidnapped from her bed early in the day. Chief of Detectives Walter G. Storms announced he was satisfied that the head was that of the Degnan girl. He said that he was convinced by the hair and the features.

The head rested four feet down on muck which filled the sewer bottom. In the search for a body, detectives pressed poles into the mire, but were unable to touch bottom. Sewer department crews were called at 7:40 p.m.

PARENTS INFORMED BY PRIEST

A priest from St. Gertrude's Church, 1420 Granville av., broke news of the discovery to the parents, Mr. and Mrs. James E. Degnan, 5943 Kenmore av., who had spent an anxious day at home.

The father, price control board operations officer for the Metropolitan area office of the Office of Price Administration, in repeated radio appeals to the kidnappers, had said that he would raise the $20,000 *ransom asked.*

The catchbasin opening was in a cement areaway between a 35-apartment building at 5900 Kenmore av. A 20-inch manhole cover is over it.

FOUR PERSONS HELD

Detectives Lee O'Rourke and Harry Benoit, among 75 men sent out by the Detective Bureau to search the neighborhood, made the discovery. [...]

NOTE WRITTEN IN LONGHAND

The ransom note was in pencil, part in longhand and part in blocked capital letters. It appeared to have been written by someone accustomed to "printing" rapidly with a pencil. Police Commissioner John C. Prendergast said he believes the note had been prepared ahead of time and not written on the scene. [...]

PARENTS' HOME ACROSS HALL

Suzanne was put to bed at 9 p.m. Sunday in her room. The rest of the Degnan family retired later, with the parents sleeping directly across a hall. Degnan arose at 7:30 a.m., and went to wake the two girls. He found Suzanne's bed empty. The window was wide open. Outside was a short drop to the first steps leading to the back porch. Mr. and Mrs. Degnan spent a long day—of hope and despair.

As if covering ruthless murders in Chicago wasn't dramatic enough for the Duchess in 1946, she was also on the job when one of the most dramatic stories in Chicago history occurred, when the grand downtown La Salle Hotel caught fire near midnight one hot June evening.

Virginia was in the newsroom when the "five-eleven" fire alarm went off. She and all other available reporters and photographers were immediately dispatched to the scene. Virginia ran the four blocks from the *Sun* to the hotel and quickly positioned herself near the ambulance squads to carry out her assignment—keeping track of the casualties as they were pulled from the blaze.

As the Duchess would recall years later, in her haste to leave the office she forgot to grab a note pad. While she had pencils, she had nothing to write on. So she began to look around the street for any piece of paper she could use, finally finding a discarded brown paper sack lodged under the wheel of one of the ambulances. She crawled down onto her hands and knees and pulled out the sack and began to take her notes.

For the next three hours the Duchess stood guard by the trucks and kept the official casualty count, noting how many bodies had been carried out and tagged by rescue workers "unknown male," "unknown female" or "unable to determine sex yet." From time to time the sight of the dead and the smell of their scalded flesh became too much for her to handle, and Virginia would become nauseous, going to throw up in an alley across the street before returning to her post.

By noon the next day, twelve hours after she got to the hotel, Virginia turned her paper sack, now completely covered with her notes, over to her editor, who sent her home for some rest. The Duchess would later reclaim that brown sack from her editor and keep it for the rest of her life.

IT CAN HAPPEN AGAIN: MORE FIRE HAZARDS! CITY ORDERS CLOSINGS
5 Inquiries In Hotel Blaze: 58 Dead; La Salle Warned Last Month on Danger*
6/6/46

Twenty-six days before 58 lives were lost in yesterday's La Salle Hotel holocaust the City Fire Prevention Bureau had given the hotel 15 days to rectify 10 fire hazards. City authorities did not produce official records, but Avery Brundage, chairman of the hotel management, asserted that every precaution had been provided for safety of the building.

Brundage insisted that the hotel had complied with the Fire Prevention Bureau's orders. Reporters, however, found rotten fire hoses in the hotel that could be torn easily with the hands. They also learned that some corridors were obstructed by furniture. The hotel has but two fire escapes, both on the north side.

The state legislature adopted a joint resolution calling for appointment of a 10-man commission to look into the fire and examine fire prevention laws. [...]

All day a steady stream of dazed guests who had escaped death or serious injury returned to the fire-blackened hotel to reclaim what could be found of their belongings.

CAN'T REMEMBER ANY ALARM

Many of these persons, when questioned by reporters, could not recall being given any alarm of the fire, which first was discovered at 12:35 a.m. in the Silver Lounge, a crowded lobby cocktail room.

Those who survived were mainly guests on floors above the fifth story, who had groped blindly down fire escapes or been carried down ladders after being awakened by the smoke and noise. As the patrons ran from the cocktail lounge the flames burst into the lobby and roared up elevator shafts shutting off that means of exit.

SEVEN PLUNGE TO DEATH

Hundreds were trapped, leaning from windows with wet towels wrapped around their faces. They threw lamps and other objects to the ground to attract the attention of rescuers. At least seven of them jumped to [their] death. Many more were suffocated or trampled to death in the confusion of the dark, smoke-filled corridors.

This drama of terror continued for three hours until 75 of the city's fire-fighting units—one seventh of the all available equipment—brought the flames under control at 3:30 a.m. [...]

EXACT CAUSE UNKNOWN

Although the fire was first discovered in the Silver Lounge, the exact place and cause of its outbreak remained undetermined. Fred Wolf, hotel maintenance engineer, told Fire Attorney Earl Downs, that a cigarette butt tossed into an elevator shaft near the cocktail lounge ignited the building.

"I saw the lighted cigarette tossed into the machinery of the pit and when I opened the door leading to the pit, the fire was raging so hotly that it drove me back," Wolf said. [...]

DEGNAN PRINTS FIT

Surgical Kits Found in Room: Student Formerly Lived In Neighborhood of Victim*

6/29/46

A 17-year-old University of Chicago youth whose finger prints matched those on the Suzanne Degnan ransom note "on seven points," was being questioned last night by leading investigators in the kidnap-murder case.

"He looks like the one," said Chief of Detectives William J. Tuohy. The youth is William Heirens, who lives at Gates Hall, 59th st. and Ellis av., on the University of Chicago campus, and whose parents live at 4175 Touhy av., Lincolnwood. Tuohy said police had connected Heirens with 13 burglaries in which his loot included two surgical kits. He was arrested Wednesday when he was felled by a flower pot thrown by a policeman as Heirens fled from a Rogers Park apartment which he had broken into. [...]

Heirens is 5 feet 11 inches tall, weighs 180 pounds and is powerfully built. He has black hair and heavy black eyebrows. He is of German descent. The youth suffered a head injury when he was captured but, despite that fact, it took William G. Milota, superintendent of the Bridewell, and six policemen to hold him in bed at the Bridewell hospital.

YOUTH STRAPPED TO BED

He was shackled to the bed by straps, which held his arms and legs. For two days, physicians at the hospital attempted to take X-rays to determine whether his skull was fractured, but Heirens refused to remain quiet long enough.

His fingerprints were taken, however, and were found to match the partial print of one finger and the print of the heel of one hand found on the ransom note. Tuohy, Storms, Lt. Phil Breitzke, and Capt. Tim O'Connor rushed to the hospital to question the youth.

LOSS OF MEMORY FEIGNED

Heirens feigned unconsciousness, however, and then a lapse of memory. Before yesterday, he would only repeat the questions put to him. Dr. Andrew J. Toman, medical superintendent of the Bridewell, said his temperature, pulse and eye reaction were normal, and that he could not repeat the questions if he were in a coma.

"The fingerprints corresponded with those on the ransom note on seven points," Tuohy said, "I put it to him cold and told him he was suspected in the Degnan case.

"He won't say a word. He is feigning delirium." [...]

FATHER OF VICTIM DOUBTFUL

The slain girl's father, James E. Degnan, [...], was advised of the new development in the case. "This appears to be better than anything they've had so far," he said. "Of course, one day it's one thing, and the next it's another, so I hate to get all excited for a big letdown.

"If he's the one, I hope this thing is settled pretty quick. All parents wish to see the guilty man penalized, and so do we." [...]

NOT THAT, NOT THAT!'

Can't Believe It, Cries Mother Of Suspect*

6/29/46 '

"Not that! Not that! I know he's been in trouble before—I can believe other things about him—but not that!"

Mrs. Margaret Heirens, attractive 40-year-old brunette mother of William Heirens, 17, University of Chicago student and latest suspect in the kidnap-murder of Suzanne Degnan, was near to fainting. [...]

Neatly attired in a yellow house dress and with her dark hair showing only a few touches of gray, she greeted the officers with one question. "Is it true?" she demanded, "about the fingerprints—do they match—do they match his?"

"I'm afraid they do in some respects, ma'am," was the reply. Mrs. Heirens staggered back as though she had received a physical blow. She slumped into a chair.

"No!" she moaned. "God, no—how can I stand that—how can I take it—" In a few moments, however, she had revived and, strong in her mother's instinct that her son could not be guilty of the terrible crime, was able to talk more freely about him.

William, she said, attended the St. Mary's-of-the-Lake Grammar School and later St. Bede's High School. "He was a very bright boy in his studies," said Mrs. Heirens, "but he didn't mix so well with the other boys until the last year or so, I was glad when I saw him beginning to make friends. He had been in trouble before, and—"

"You mean the time he was involved in that burglary on Pratt blvd.?" she was asked.

Mrs. Heirens shook her head. "No," she said. "Before that—it was—well, I don't like to talk about it. He was sent to a private reform school and we paid for his schooling there." [...] Tears came to her eyes as she recalled that he was home last Christmas Eve, on Christmas day and on New Year's Eve.

Where he was on the night of Jan. 6, the night 6-year-old Suzanne Degnan was kidnapped and brutally murdered, she does not know. "I recalled I talked to him about the terrible murder," she said. "I said to him I was glad he wasn't mixed up in anything like that and that he was getting along so much better."

And William, she said, replied: "Why, mother, you know I wouldn't do anything like that."

TWO WORDS MATCH WITH RANSOM NOTE

Heirens Writes 'Waite,' 'Safty'; 2d Lie Test Taken*

7/2/46

At his own request, William Heirens was being given a second lie detector test at the Detective Bureau last night after the 17-year-old University of Chicago youth had been further linked to the Suzanne Degnan ransom note by misspelling two words which were also written incorrectly on the note.

State's Attorney William J. Tuohy and his first assistant, Wilbert F. Crowley, went to the bureau for the test, which was expected to produce the youth's second coherent statement on the accusations against him. [...]

MISSPELLING MATCHES

Heirens, whose fingerprint matches the print of a little finger of a left hand found on the ransom note, also misspelled the words "wait" and "safety" when the note was dictated to him yesterday. He wrote "waite" and "safty," using the same spelling employed by the kidnapper. [...]

Chief Storms and Capt. Ahern, accompanied by three squads of police, brought Heirens to the bureau at 2:30 p.m. Heirens was dressed in brown slacks, brown shoes and a short-sleeved shirt with hospital markings.

CHANGES MIND ON PICTURES

As Heirens walked to the police car, photographers flashed his picture and he made no attempt to cover up. When he was seated in the car between Storms and Capt. Ahern, however, he covered his face from the photographers and mumbled: "Please don't—please don't!"

When he was leaving the Bridewell, he pretended that he couldn't walk. "Cut out the act!" Storms told him. He then walked to the car. [...]

Before Heirens was turned over to police, he was questioned for two hours by Crowley at the Bridewell. Tuohy said later that Crowley reported the youth still held to his story that he was innocent of all crimes except the burglary. Tuohy, recalling the five-hour interview which ended at 2:15 a.m. yesterday, said Heirens said "certain things" which caused the authorities to believe that he should be watched closely to see that he does not harm himself. Tuohy declined to discuss the statements.

Heirens asked to see Tuohy and Capt. Ahern after he had dinner Sunday night. He gave a rambling statement, claiming his own innocence in the Degnan murder and other crimes with which police had sought to connect him, speaking rationally for the first time.

"Once, in a previous interview," Tuohy said, "I purposely addressed him as George. [Heirens had earlier claimed to have a split personality, an alter ego named "George."] 'I'm not George, I'm Bill,' he replied. Then he caught himself right away, and lapsed again into his pretend delirium. It was almost humorous—it was so obvious he was shamming." [...]

ATTORNEY PROTESTS

Attorney Coghlan protested that he had not been permitted to visit the youth. He said that from newspaper accounts he learned that Heirens was kept shackled part of the time, and that a "truth drug" was used to induce him to talk. He referred to sodium penthathol, administered to the youth Saturday night.

"Detention of the youth for six days implied coercion under the law," Coghlan said.

'INNOCENT OR INTELLIGENT'

"For six days," he continued, "this lad of 17 has had to pit his intelligence against the state. He is either innocent or extremely intelligent." Crowley interrupted to declare that Heirens would be charged with a "series of crimes" and that the youth had not been mistreated. "He's been asleep since 2 o'clock this morning," Crowley added, "and that's more sleep than I had—I got only one hour." [...]

"NO MATTER WHAT YOU'VE DONE—": 'YOU ARE STILL OUR SON!'
Parents Whisper to Heirens*

7/4/46

"No matter what you've done, you're still our son!" The boy heard those words yesterday as he lay on the cot in the hospital ward of the County Jail, his hair a shock of unruly black against the white of the pillow slip. He heard them from his mother and father.

It was the first time in eight long, suspense-ridden days that they had a long interview with the boy—William Heirens, 17-year-old University of Chicago student accused of multiple crimes and suspected of the kidnap-murder of little Suzanne Degnan.

There was father—George Heirens, [a] 6-foot, broad-chested, dark complexioned Luxembourger. There was mother, Margaret—brunette, attractive—her face and figure belying the fact that she could be the mother of the husky young man on the cot before her. "No matter what you've done, you're still our son!"

The boy was lying with his left arm against his head as though he was soothing a hurt, when Warden Frank Sain led in Mr. and Mrs. Heirens. [...]

F.B.I. CONFIRMS 'LIPSTICK' CLUE
Degnan Note Reveals New Heirens Print: Federal Experts Back Evidence in Ex-Wave's Death*
7/14/46

Identification of the fingerprint found in the apartment of the murdered Frances Brown, former Wave, as that of William Heirens, was confirmed last night in a telegram from the Federal Bureau of Investigation at Washington.

The message was received by Chief of Detectives Walter G. Storms only hours after he had announced the discovery on the Degnan ransom note of a third discernible print that he said checked with one of those of the University of Chicago student.

NET OF EVIDENCE CLOSING

These two developments coming in rapid succession, seemed to close tighter about the prisoner, the net of evidence implicating him in two of the most brutal murders in Chicago in decades. Miss Brown was shot and stabbed to death in her apartment at 5943 Kenmore av. on the night of Jan. 6,[...]

First identification of the print found on the door jamb in Miss Brown's apartment as that of Heirens was made by Sgt. Thomas Laffey, fingerprint expert of the Bureau of Identification. To provide a double-check, Chief Storms forwarded the prints to the F.B.I. [...]

SUSPECT TURNS TO RELIGION

At the County Jail, Heirens apparently has turned to religion. Warden Frank Sain reported that the young prisoner had spend much of the night in prayer.

His mother, Mrs. George Heirens, who has staunchly maintained her belief in the innocence of her son, sent him a copy of "Novena Notes"—a guiding pamphlet put out monthly in connection with the Perpetual Novena to Our Sorrowful Mother at Our Lady of Sorrows Church, 3121 W. Jackson blvd. And at 8:15 p.m. Friday, Heirens asked and received permission from the warden to hear the regular Friday broadcast of the novena services. [...]

YOUTH QUOTED—BY ATTORNEY

It was then he reported that Heirens was showing the first signs of crumbling under the strain. He quoted his client as saying, half-hysterically: "How long is this going to go on? I understand they are trying to blame me for something that happened in 1943!" [...]

HIS LAWYER PUZZLED

Coghlan shook his head, as if in bewilderment. "I have never met anyone who baffles me as young Heirens does," the lawyer said. "He is either awfully smart or awfully stupid. The manner in which those crimes were committed was not smart.

"I have the utmost confidence in him. He has made full, complete and honest disclosures to me. I believe I am the only one in whom he has confidence." [...]

MOTHER HEARS HEIRENS CONFESS 3 MURDERS
Youth Admits Slaying of Degnan Girl: Tells His Parents Details of Ross, Brown Killings*
7/26/46

William Heirens told his mother and father yesterday how he kidnapped and killed little Suzanne Degnan and how he murdered Frances Brown and Mrs. Josephine Ross. From their son's lips the mother and father heard the full story of the murders for the first time. Heirens told all the shocking details.

PARENTS STUNNED, WEEP

The 17-year-old youth poured out his confession while he sat with his parents and three of his attorneys around a table near the altar in the Country Jail chapel. Heirens spoke freely in the deeply religious atmosphere, and needed little urging. The parents were stunned at their son's words. The mother cried throughout most of the two-hour session and the father also wept.

HE TELLS OF KIDNAPPING

Their son told them how he took the 6-year-old Degnan girl from her bedroom at 5943 Kenmore av., how he strangled her to death, how he cut her body into pieces, and how he hid the parts in sewers in the neighborhood last Jan. 7.

He told them how he went into Frances Brown's room at the Pine Crest hotel, 3941 Pine Grove av., last Dec. 10, and how he stabbed her in the chest and in the neck and shot her in the head and arm. He told how he picked up a lipstick and scrawled on the wall: "Catch me before I kill more. I cannot control myself."

FIRST MURDER DESCRIBED

He told how he climbed a fire escape on June 5, 1945, and entered the fifth-floor apartment of Mrs. Ross at 4108 Kenmore av., found her lying in bed, and slashed her throat four times. It was his first murder.

He admitted to his shocked parents that he had committed countless burglaries. He told them he had been leading a life of crime for years, while they thought he was a quiet, normal boy, engrossed in his religion and his studies. [...]

SATISFIED WITH ATTORNEYS

The mother and father both expressed themselves as "well satisfied" with the manner in which the attorneys had handled their son's case. At the jail, it was learned, they were given an opportunity to veto the agreement for their son's confession in exchange for a life imprisonment recommendation. [...]

'I DON'T REMEMBER!' BALKS HEIRENS QUIZ
Youth Spurns Parents' Plea: Return Him to Cell in Jail After His Refusal to Confess*
7/31/46

William Heirens upset elaborate plans to take his long-awaited confession to the Degnan, Brown and Ross murders yesterday when he balked at answering questions about the slayings before a roomful of the city's top law enforcement officials.

Although the 17-year-old University of Chicago youth had promised his attorneys and his parents that he would give a formal confession in an attempt to escape the electric chair, his only answer to questions was: "I don't remember—I don't know." State's Attorney William J. Tuohy, the boy's five attorneys and his parents pleaded with him, but to no avail. [...]

STATE TO PROCEED WITH CASE

Tuohy said that meanwhile the state would proceed with its case. The boy's admissions to his attorneys are privileged under the law, and may not be used as evidence against him. Under the law, the defense attorneys could not even testify on a witness stand about the admission.

The state's attorney is known still to be receptive to a confession, principally because he believes it to be his responsibility to prove Heirens' guilt beyond a doubt, not only to a jury, but to the people of Chicago. Only a confession will answer the many questions involved. [...]

PRECAUTIONS TAKEN

A short time later he was transferred from Cell 52 to Cell 1, a more secluded spot just across the corridor, and further precautions were taken to prevent a suicide attempt. As in the past, his belt and ties were taken from him. Henceforth, it was announced, his guards will be changed each hour instead of every eight hours.

In the brief questioning, he admitted no crimes, Tuohy said. He gave his name and address and other pertinent facts about his life, then balked when the questioning turned to the kidnap-slaying of little Suzanne Degnan early last Jan. 7. "Where were you on the night of Jan. 6?" Tuohy asked. [...]

REPORTERS CALLED IN

At 2:15 p.m., Tuohy called in the crowd of reporters who had been waiting outside his office and said to them: "We had Heirens in this morning, as I told you we would. We talked with him for a few minutes, and we asked him a number of questions. His reply was, 'I don't know—I don't remember.'

MOTHER PLEADS WITH HIM

The parents and defense attorneys talked with Heirens. The boy's mother said to him: "Bill, tell the truth!—Bill, you've got to tell them!" But the unpredictable youth refused. [...]

LAWYER HAS "BUTTERFLIES"

"I have butterflies in my stomach," the lawyer said. Perhaps involved in the reversal in Heirens' attitude is his personality. Psychologists have reported he is suffering from schizophrenia, a split-personality. He has

at times ascribed his crimes to "George Murman," his alter ego and at no time has he admitted his guilt officially.

He had admitted orally that he killed Mrs. Ross, 43, a twice-divorced widow on June 5, 1945, in her apartment at 4108 Kenmore av. He slashed her throat four times with a knife, stole her purse, and fled down a fire escape.

WAVE SLAYING RECOUNTED

Next, on Dec. 10, 1945, he beat, shot and stabbed Miss Brown, 33, an ex-Wave, in her hotel room at 3941 Pine Grove av. He picked up a lipstick and scrawled the prophetic words on the wall: "For heaven's sake catch me before I kill more. I cannot control myself." The murder of the 6-year-old Degnan girl was the next.

Heirens had told his attorneys all of the details of the slayings, and had said he had not [...] committed the crimes "for thrills." He indicated that he believed that a Commando-type knife, found in a mailbox at Bryn Mawr and Winthrop avs., is the one he used in the Degnan slaying.

125 BURGLARIES ADMITTED

He said further that he committed upwards of 125 burglaries and four assaults, but he denied that he had ever committed rape. One of the attorneys, asked about the admissions, said: "They made me sick to my stomach." [...]

Reporters who had seen [Heirens] before said that for the first time he exhibited fright. He clenched and unclenched his fists and looked around furtively. His face appeared puffed, his eyes were moist and his lips bloodless.

Despite William Heirens's refusal to confess that day, he was later found guilty of the three murders and was sentenced to three consecutive life terms.

For Virginia Marmaduke, having covered the Heirens case from its grisly beginnings (with the murder of Josephine Ross in June of 1945) until its close, she was one of the few who had a unique first person, eyewitness understanding of both the crimes and the criminal.

After Heirens's conviction, the Duchess fashioned her experiences and reporter's notes into a detailed, atmospheric true-crime narrative. At the same time, eccentric fitness guru Benarr MacFadden, already heading a vast publishing empire, decided to branch out by launching his own crime-centered magazine. The Duchess's story was seemingly tailor-made for the new periodical and she sold it to them for $1,500.00.

Under the never before—and never again—used byline of V. Crain Marmaduke (a name designed no doubt to obscure Virginia's gender), the Duchess's story was the lead article in the debut issue of *Bernarr MacFadden's Latest Detective Magazine.*

The magazine did its sensational best by declaring on page one that the story was:

"The Uncensored Diary Of A Twisted Mind—Which Turned A Bright College Student Into America's Most Dangerous And Hunted Killer—Told By A Chicago Newspaper Reporter Who Was Present For Every Development In This Frantic Race Against Time By Police To Find The Man Who Warned Them And The World That He Could Not Control His Lust To Kill..."

BERNARR MACFADDEN'S LATEST DETECTIVE MAGAZINE

"THE LIFE AND CRIMES OF WILLIAM HEIRENS"

By V. Crain Marmaduke

1/47

[William Heirens] was the youth who was to invent an alter-ego named George Murman and pretend he was a Dr. Jekyl-Mr. Hyde personality.

But he was eventually to confess in such detail and re-enact his crimes so thoroughly that police were satisfied no George Murman existed except in the criminal cunning of William George Heirens' mind.

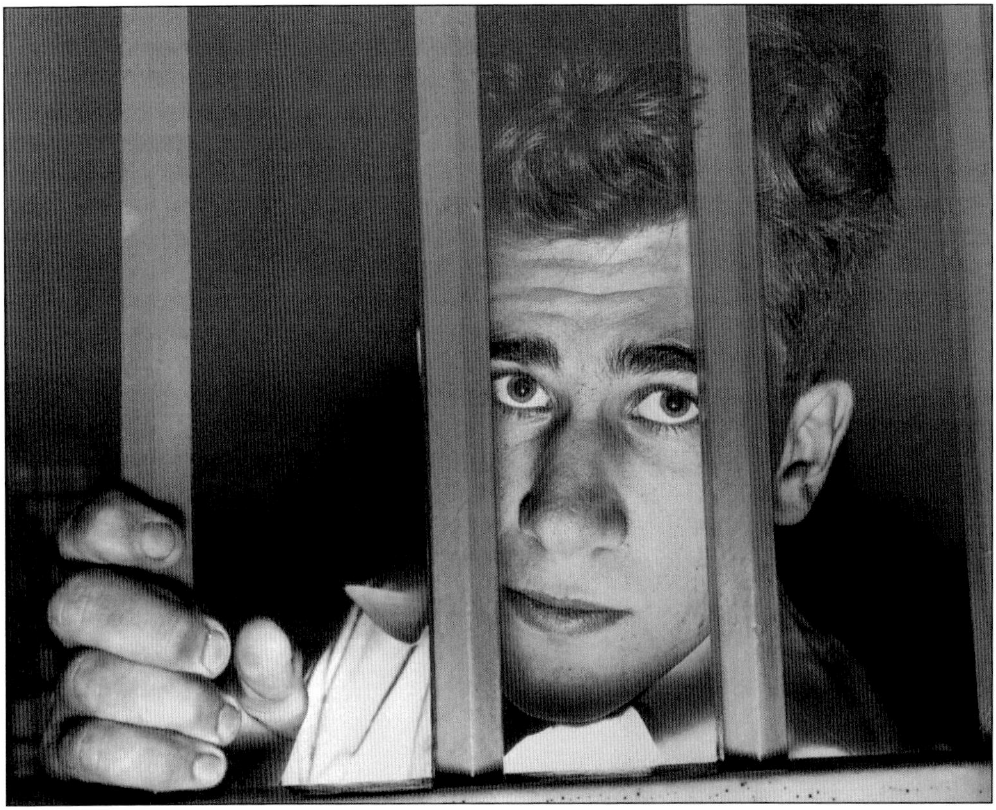

William Heirens behind bars. (Corbis.)

The real manhunt for this killer was to begin in the eerie half-darkness of an early winter night when two Chicago detectives lifted a doll-like human head from a sewer catchbasin in an alley areaway between two buildings.

The manhunt was to end—almost like it began—in a back alley in a Chicago residential section. The curtain was to fall about six o'clock in the evening, the same light of day when the Degnan child's head was discovered. The kidnapper was to re-enact his crime exactly seven months from the day it was committed.

The spark that set a fire of fear in the hearts of parents throughout the nation was ignited last January 7 when James E. Degnan, 36, [...] went to the bedroom of his six-year-old daughter to awaken her for school.

It was the day after Christmas vacation and Suzanne was to return to her studies in the first grade at Sacred Heart convent. She had gone to bed early the night before, shortly after eating a bacon, lettuce and tomato sandwich fixed by her mother, Helen, 35.

Suzanne's room was directly across the hall from her parent's bedroom on the first floor of the 12-room tan brick mansion at 5943 Kenmore Ave. in the rich Edgewater section of Chicago. Her sister, Elizabeth, 10, also had her own room. It was two doors down the hall.

Suzanne had awakened about midnight and was taken to the bathroom by her father. But when he went to wake her the next morning, her bed was empty. The bed clothes were turned back, neatly. The window, which had been left open three inches during the night, was pushed all the way to the top.

Degnan became alarmed. He and his wife looked through the house. They called their friends, attorney and Mrs. Flynn, occupants of the second floor of the large home and owners of the residence. Flynn called the police.

A bit of paper on the bedroom floor, unnoticed before, was picked up by Inspector Ed Daly of the Chicago Detective Bureau when he arrived. Daly was a close friend of the Degnans and Flynns and a resident of the neighborhood. The paper was an oil-smeared, penciled noted with printed letters and two misspelled words. It read: "Get $20,000 ready & waite for word. Do not notify FBI or police. Bills in 5's & 10's." On the reverse side was printed: "Burn this for her safty."

Initial inquiry disclosed that Ethel Hargrove, a maid who lived upstairs with the Flynn's had heard the little girl say drowsily, "I don't want to get up, I'm sleeping now." Mrs. Hargrove fixed the time at 12:50 a.m. She said she had glanced at a clock while reading a prayer book in bed.

Degnan also recalled hearing the child's sleepy remark but said he thought Suzanne was just talking in her sleep. Both he and the maid and several neighbors remembered hearing the Flynn's two Boxer dogs bark at various times during the night.

News of the kidnapping spread to the world. [...]

Chief of Detectives Walter Storms was the first to reason [...] that the kidnapping had not been done solely for ransom. "There are too many richer families in this neighborhood for the kidnapper to deliberately select Suzanne Degnan," he declared.

For that reason he ordered a 75-man detail to search every sewer, every catch basin, every coal bin, every garage can and every basement in the area. The detectives were split into teams, each given specific assignments. One team, Lee O'Rourke and Harry Benoit, had orders to search the area of the building at 5900 Kenmore.

They had already looked into half a dozen sewers when they reached the gangway between buildings at 5860 and 5900 Kenmore. O'Rourke noticed the soil was loose around the circular edge of the lid. "This has been opened recently," he said. O'Rourke used the point of his star to pry up the heavy iron lid so that Benoit could get his fingers under it and lift it. As Benoit swung the cover away, O'Rourke thrust his flashlight into the grimy hole.

He recoiled at what he saw. Benoit looked down. He saw what his partner had seen—a little head, face upward, just four feet from the top. "Maybe it's just a doll," O'Rourke whispered.

"It's no doll," Benoit answered. They both trembled, knowing it was the head of a child. A tall, well-dressed man stepped forward. It was Butler, long-time friend of the Degnan family.

"That was Suzanne," he said in a chocking voice.

The Duchess goes on in her story to recount the frenzied search for the Degnan killer and the eventual apprehension of young William Heirens. She then expanded upon an interesting episode from the incarceration of Chicago's Public Enemy #1:

It was then that the suggestion to use sodium penothal ["truth serum"] was made to State's Attorney Tuohy. A man who had made extensive use of the drug in treating battle shock during his war service was consulted.

He was Dr. Roy Richard Grinker, chairman of the department of psychiatry, Michael Reese Hospital.

The drug, he told police officers, induced a state of inactive consciousness in battle-shocked men. It made the patient answer questions and talked about his horrible experiences as he would not do when wholly conscious.

"It made it possible for us to ferret the hidden causes of the veteran's psychosis," Dr. Grinker said, "and if this youth has a psychiatric disturbance the same treatment might clear up his clogged mind."

The stage was set for administration of the "truth serum" on William Heirens. An emergency operating table was prepared on the third floor of Bridewell hospital. The small operating table was shoved to one side and a cot brought in.

Two screens were set in place at one end of the cot. Behind them sat Tuohy and his first assistant, Crowley. A stenographer sat on one side of the cot. Drs. Grinker and Heirens on the other.

Young Heirens was brought in. He laid down on the cot with his head still bandaged and mops of his unruly black hair sticking out. Black stubble covered his cheeks and chin. He kept his eyes closed, resolutely.

His left arm was bared and sterilized with alcohol. The sharp needle of a hypodermic syringe, expertly manipulated by Dr. Grinker, eased into a vein. Slowly Dr. Grinker pressed the plunger of the syringe.

Thirty seconds later William Heirens had slipped into a state of narcosynthesis. His active consciousness had been blotted out. The questioning began. "Did you kill Suzanne Degnan?"

Heirens whispered his answer. "No, George did it." [...]

After recapping the trial and conviction of Heirens, Virginia Marmaduke ended her sad story:

To insure that William Heirens will never again be free, Criminal Court Justice Harold Ward sentenced him to consecutive twenty year terms for each of the three murders; to one to fourteen years for assault; to one year to life for burglary; to one to fourteen for robbery; and to one year to life on twenty-five other burglary and assault charges. Heirens has already made three attempts at suicide. He may be successful in some future try, but it will be the only way he will ever be able to escape spending the rest of his life behind bars.

After writing this narrative of the murders and the trial, the Duchess closed the book on the subject and actively moved onto other stories and pursuits.

Years later, in 1996, when asked about the "Crime That Shocked Chicago," the Duchess still seemed somewhat haunted by the memory of Heirens and his victims. She said, "I don't talk about it much. . . . Heirens took [responsibility for] it all. He did it. And he has served out his life." Today, William Heirens remains incarcerated in Dixon Correctional Center.

1947

CHICAGO SUN

FINE PORTABLE HOME ENDS FAMILY'S CRACKERBOX DAYS

By Virginia Marmaduke

4/23/47

It was the same old sun that rose yesterday morning over Chicago's southern suburbs, but the new day it brought to the trailer camp home of Lee W. Williams' family of eight was one they will remember so long as they live.

It even looked like a different day to Lee's wife, Minerva, as she stirred herself and roused the others. It wasn't that the sun was any brighter or warmer than usual or that its light fell any differently upon the huddle of weathered trailers in the camp at 13367 S. Western av.

It just looked different because, she explained, a little tremulously, it was THE day; the day she and Lee and their six youngsters ranging in age from 8 months to 8 years, were to move forever from the eight-foot-square crackerbox trailer which for nearly nine months has been their home. [...]

They thought for a while it would be only a temporary thing, but as the weeks went by and scores of landlords continued to refuse the father a home ("Six kids? Nothing doing!") they came gradually to abandon hope of ever having anything else.

It wasn't as though they couldn't pay for something better. Lee Williams was earning $50 a week as a freight handler for the Illinois Central System, Minerva was a good budgeter, and no one was sick. It was just that there were so few apartments and landlords balked at taking six children.

INVESTIGATION MADE

There's no telling how long it would have gone on that way except that a social worker wrote to The Chicago Sun about the Williamses and said they deserved a home. The Sun investigated independently and found that all good things said about the family were true. Then it made public their case.

Among those who read it was H.L. Spencer, president of the Liberty Coach Co., Inc. At that moment he was exhibiting in Chicago a deluxe 2-story six-room portable home his company had built for Ginger Rogers, the screen star. One like this, Spencer thought, would be a fine thing for the Williamses. [...]

HOME ADDS HEIGHT

[A]fter Spencer pressed a button inside, the big trailer began mushrooming upward and continued expanding until it was almost double in height. Upstairs there now were three private bedrooms, each with a Hollywood-type bed and separated by metal Venetian blinds reaching from ceiling to floor.

A metal stairway, covered by deep maroon carpeting connected up stairs and down. Below there were a little living room, a dinette, a kitchen, and a tiny bathroom with shower, lavatory and toilet. [...]

HOME IS ANCHORED

While the Williamses and the trailerville folk examined all this, Spencer and his men worked on. Cables were anchored into the ground to steady the tall structure in the event of a storm; a septic tank for the toilet was buried nearby, gas, lights, and water were connected, and concrete foundation blocks were placed under the sturdy axles. Then the tires on the heavy truck wheels were deflated and the job was done—almost. [...]

SPECIFICATION MADE

"I want these youngsters to have it for five years until they grow a little older," the elder Spencer had specified. "By that time maybe there will be no housing shortage." There was one last surprise which the Williamses will find out about when they read this. As Allen Spencer was leaving, he slipped a folded $100 bill into the hand of this reporter.

SHOPPING PLANNED

"When you can," he whispered, "go shopping with Mrs. Williams and let her pick out new utensils for her kitchen and the other new things she'll be needing." I'll be seeing you tomorrow morning, Mrs. Williams.

BOGART TAKES SHOTS AT FILM WITCH HUNT

12/4/47

Alternately suave and disgruntled, Humphrey Bogart lounged in a hotel penthouse yesterday and commented saltily upon his recent trip to Washington to protest the inquisition of film stars in the congressional Hollywood-Communism witch hunt.

The screen gangster-bad man, more sleek and more smooth than the genuine Chicago article, was accompanied by Lauren "Baby" Bacall, who is as sultry off screen as she is on. [...] A throng of reporters and cameramen listened as Bogart discoursed.

'WE WENT IN GREEN'

He read a prepared statement in which he said he is an American and detests Communism. He appeared to be still smarting from the rough ride given him by certain segments of the press. The formal statement finished, Bogart slipped into character and rasped his words: "We went in green. They beat our brains out. The idea of the trip was to defend the 1st Amendment. But they kicked that around and lost [it] in the shuffle." (The Hollywood delegation didn't get to protest before the House Committee on Un-American Activities.)

"And get a load of this: When it was all over I had been adopted by the Communist press. My mug was on Page 12. They said I was a great guy. How do you like THAT!" [...]

CHICAGO ERASES HORROR FROM PRETTY GIRL'S EYES

By Virginia Marmaduke

12/10/47

The pretty, blue-eyed 17-year-old girl who climbs aboard the 7:30 a.m. Montrose Ave. bus each morning with her arms full of books looks like any other teenager on her way to school. But she isn't.

She is Lilian Milewski, a Polish war orphan whose memories include nearly five years in concentration camps in Poland and Siberia and the loss of every member of her immediate family through the horrors of war.

<u>HORROR FADES</u>

But those are things Lillian is rapidly forgetting these days. For six months she has known a new world, new tenderness and a new mother. Last July she came to Chicago to make her home with Mrs. Magelena Milewski at 4119 Montrose Ave. Mrs. Milewski, 72, a childless widow, adopted her through the Polish National Alliance, [for] which she once served as vice-president. Today the two are giving each other new happiness through the miracle of companionship. [...]

BEARDED GIRL SANTA GETS COLD SHOULDER
By Virginia Marmaduke
12/11/47

The bell-ringing Santa Claus standing at a paper chimney on the corner of State and Madison Sts. didn't get much attention. More than 6,000 persons walked [by] within a one-hour period Tuesday, but only the children gave the whiskered character much more than a glance.

Maybe they were in too much of a hurry. It could be, too, that the adults—along with one 14-year-old boy—sensed that the bell ringer was no real Santa Claus and was, instead, this girl reporter, properly padded and bewhiskered for the one-hour impersonation.

<u>ONLY 7 STOPPED</u>

At any rate, only seven of the 6,000 passerby stopped to drop a coin down the contribution chimney to help along the year round social service work of the Volunteers of America. The total collection was $1.82. Not members of the Community Fund, the sidewalk collection is the Volunteers' only annual drive for funds.

Largest single contributions during the hour of impersonation was a 50-cent piece, dropped by an elderly Negro woman. Only one other adult, also a woman, stopped to feed the chimney. The others were eager-eyed children [who] dragged their parents over to Santa Claus and the chimney.

[...] Probably the most surprised person on all State St. was a 14-year-old lad who sneaked up from behind and gave a healthy yank to this Santa Claus' flowing beard. "Aw, you're a fake," he sneered.

"Sure, son," he was told in a high, feminine voice. "Even more of a fake than you imagine."

For the Duchess's article on being a "girl Santa," the paper ran several photos of a red-suited and white-bearded Virginia Marmaduke—it was the first, though not the last, time that she would be pictured and portrayed as an integral part of the story she covered. Beginning here, the name (and face) of Virginia Marmaduke would became more recognizable to the newspaper-reading public, beginning her elevation to full-blown Chicago celebrity.

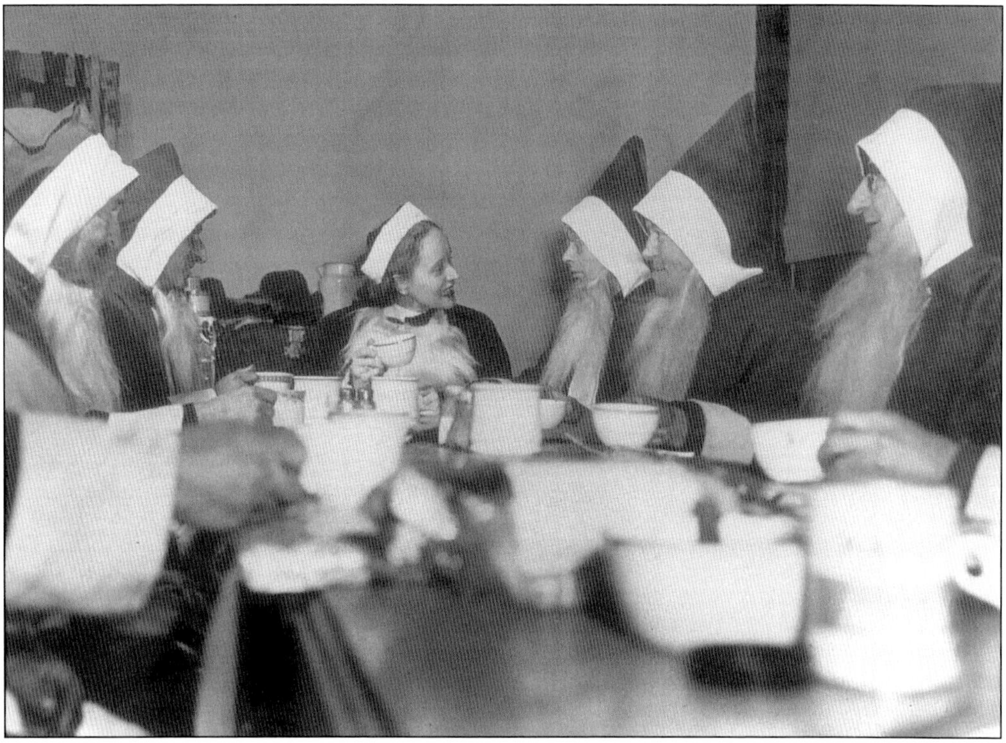

A Most Unusual Santa:
Chicago's only "girl-Santa" meets with some of her fellow Kris Kringles.

1948

One of Virginia's most famous features for the *Sun-Times* was her 1946 series "The Other Guy's Job," where our Duchess, for one day each, took on the occupations of waitress, elevator operator, taxicab driver, zoo keeper, and radio sound effects artist, among others. Each day's story brought with it another tale of the working man or working woman's life. And each brought a photo of Virginia in uniform and at work.

This series of stories is also the only time that Virginia's famous moniker—"Duchess"—was made part of her Chicago byline.

CHICAGO SUN
THE OTHER GUY'S JOB
Riding an Elephant is Scary but Fun
By Virginia "Duchess" Marmaduke
1/5/48

How does it feel to ride an elephant? That's something I always wondered, too—till now. Today I can tell you it's scary but fun. The pachyderm I rode in the curtain-raiser spectacle of a matinee performance of the International Circus at the Coliseum was named Babe. She's 65 years old, weighs nearly six tons and is nine feet tall.

Pretty Helen Scott, veteran circus elephant girl, introduced me to Babe. But first she took me to her dressing room and from a trunkful of spangled costumes selected a little satin number trimmed in rhinestone brilliants. It had an alarmingly abbreviated skirt. "No, you can't wear an oriental costume with balloon trousers when you ride Babe," she explained. "They remind her of clowns and she doesn't like 'em. We think some clown must have pulled her tail or teased her early in her circus career."

CLINGS TO NECK

I must have passed muster with Babe. When it came time for me to climb aboard, she obligingly lowered the business end of her nose. It wasn't easy, but I managed to scramble atop and cling to her neck with the desperation of a drowning gal hanging on to a handsome life guard.

Then began the ride around the circus arena at the head of the parade. Sure I was scared. But by the time we neared the exit I was able to give a weak smile and wave at the audience. I was even able to try a stunt or two, later, and with the aide of the trainer, do a "stand act" on Babe's upraised trunk. [...]

THE OTHER GUY'S JOB

Policeman for a Day Puts in Plug for Horse

By Virginia "Duchess" Marmaduke

1/6/48

If you were a traffic policeman which would you rather have—four legs or three wheels? I tried both. I played mounted policeman first astride a horse and then aboard one of the new three-wheeled motorcycles that are scheduled to supplant the faithful four-legged animals by early spring.

Despite the way I walk today, the horse is my choice for the job. When I climbed up on a tall, handsome bay named Tom at the Chicago Mounted Police barn at 262 E. Illinois St., I already had instructions on how to direct traffic and check parked cars. I didn't need them. Tom, veteran of 14 years on the force, knew exactly what to do. After he got used to his lighter rider (his regular customer weighs 215 lbs.) he settled right down and went to work.

PAUSES AT EACH CAR

First he took me slowly down the street beside a row of parked cars, pausing at each as I jotted down license numbers and the minute of the hour. Then we took up a sort of a guard position at a street intersection. Automobiles honked and backfired. I jumped at every sound. But not Tom. He didn't even flinch. Big trucks didn't faze him either. When they threatened to tie up traffic Tom moved out to them, bravely, and practically stared them to a stop. From my perch on his back we had the traffic situation well in hand.

TRICYCLE DIFFERENT

I can't say as much for my performance with one of the new motor-tricycles. It didn't stop on a "whoa" or start on a "cluck." It took both hands, fast footwork and a lot of concentrating to even pull it into a curb.

But traffic experts say the gas-driven vehicle can cover more ground, operate on a 24-hour basis, offer the advantage of a two-way communication system and don't eat when they are standing still. I might add that they also have nice, soft seats. But those who advocate replacing police horses are overlooking one thing. Motorcycles can't think.

THE OTHER GUY'S JOB

Life of a Waitress: Trifles by Trayful

By Virginia "Duchess" Marmaduke

1/7/48

If you got more coffee in the saucer than in your cup yesterday at the Triangle Restaurant at 225 S. Wabash Ave., it's a good bet I was your waitress. All dressed up in one of D.L. Toffenetti's maroon and white uniforms I tried my hand at waiting tables. One thing is sure. From now on I'll never again get angry at the person who serves me the food.

Juggling those plates while trotting from kitchen to table is an art. So is keeping the customers happy. My first patron was short, fat and bald. After studying the menu for what seemed ages he ordered ham and sweet potatoes and coffee. "And make it snappy," he added.

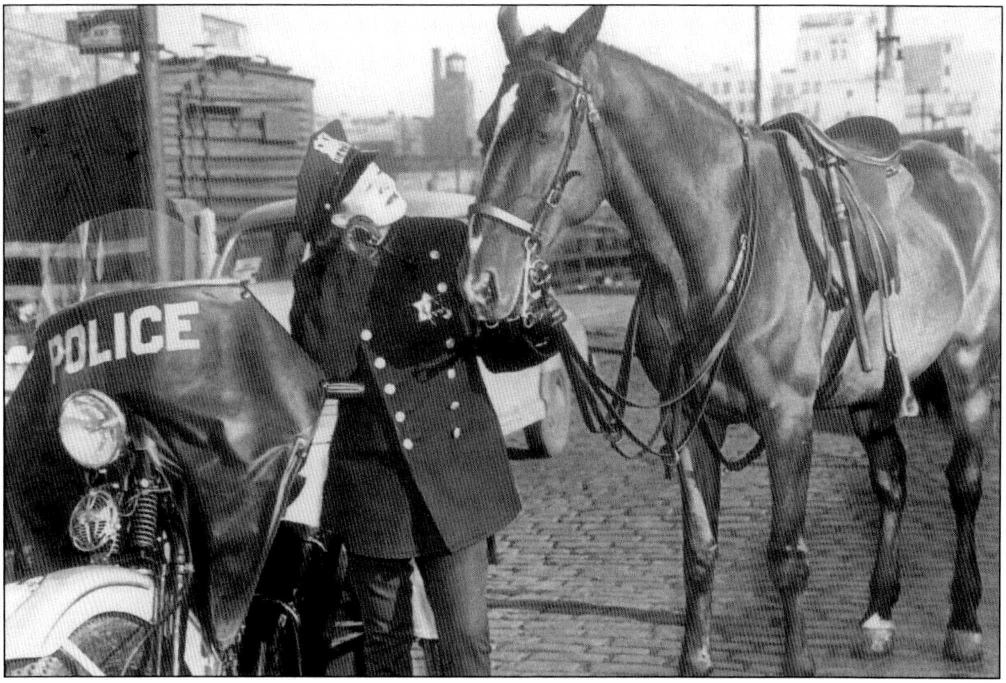

Acting as a cop, Virginia tries to choose between horse and horsepower.

He got his order, pronto. But when I brought his steaming java he barked: "I ordered milk!" Now I know that gentleman changed his mind on me but he got his milk on me and I got a tip—a dime. [...]

One of my customers must have had a hard night. I nearly ran my legs off keeping his water glass filled. He gulped five glasses during one half-hour association and tipped me at the rate of two cents per glass. I'm afraid I'll have to report that we (the customers) aren't pretty as we sit and stow away the food, folks. And as a general rule we aren't very polite to those who serve us.

But most waitresses like their work and make a game of seeing how many regular customers they can get. Regulars are always better tippers. Mrs. Helen Morrow, mother of a 16-year-old daughter, has been a Triangle waitress for 10 years. She is neat and trim. "Serving food to the American public takes the patience of Job," she said, "But it's interesting and often fun."

TOMORROW: What it's like to be a fireman.

THE OTHER GUY'S JOB
Stubborn Drivers Irk City Firemen
By Virginia "Duchess" Marmaduke
1/8/48

The boys were playing cribbage and beefing about the cooking when I walked into 209 N. Dearborn St.

These are favorite pastimes of the members of Chicago Fire Department Squad No. 1 and Engine Co. No. 13 when they aren't out battling fires. But when the alarm ticker beats out a call for their services they hop to duty like streaks of greased lighting. Every man, of course, has a definite station to leap to. My station—for a day—was in the cab of the fire truck on a jump seat behind the driver and Capt. William McDonald. I made it fast enough to go with them when an alarm came in. We roared out of the station with sirens screaming and headed west on Wacker Dr., swerving and weaving our way through the traffic.

GREATEST OPPONENT

It was then I learned that the motorist who won't pull up to the side and stop when he hears a fire engine siren is the fireman's greatest opponent. The driver was muttering under his breath. So was Capt. McDonald. So was I.

We reached 443 W. Elm St. intact but found it was only a rubbish fire in an alley, already under control by Engine Co. 27 which we had been ordered to follow to the scene. We reported to the battalion chief but were waved on to return to quarters. Then I learned more things about firemen.

DO OWN COOKING

The boys at 209 N. Dearborn do their own cooking, their own laundry and their own housekeeping. They take turns at being chef and grouse good-naturedly about every meal. Paper fortunes are won and lost in their card games. And according to the report of each on the other, they all snore.

They keep their boots with pants already drawn up around them on the floor beside their dormitory beds and waken immediately at the sound of a bell. They have tiffin—strong cups of black coffee—at tea time and each washes his own cup.

CAT IS MASCOT

Instead of a fire dog, Squad 1 has a cat [as a] mascot, a midnight black slinker which they obstinately call Brownie. But they do not wear red suspenders. Neither do they slide down the brass pole for recreation. I guess they don't believe all those jokes about firemen.

TOMORROW: The life of a theater ticket seller.

THE OTHER GUY'S JOB
Life a Quiz Game To Movie Cashier
By Virginia "Duchess" Marmaduke
1/9/48

"Two adults and two children, and how long does a full show run?" the man asked.

"Exactly two hours and forty minutes, sir, and that will be $2.50 even." Then, just as if I'd been selling tickets at the Chicago Theater all my life, I pushed $7.50 back at him as change from his 10-dollar bill.

This was just the beginning of my day as a movie theater cashier. Change-making got harder and questions became more difficult as the line grew in front of the ticket window. "Will I be able to see a complete show and still catch my regular train to Wheaton?"

That was one I didn't attempt to answer. [. . .] Children's faces were eager as they offered their money—usually the exact change—and reached for their tickets. One of them, a handsome lad, suffered an embarrassing squeak in his voice when he asked for a half-fare ticket. "My voice is changing," he explained hurriedly. "But I'm really only 11 years old." [. . .]

THE OTHER GUY'S JOB
Ups and Downs Of Elevator Life
By Virginia "Duchess" Marmaduke
1/10/48

They stepped out on the 18th floor and left me hanging. "I'm going to have to talk with him right now," one of the women had said to the other. "And our marriage is over if. . . ."

If what? I never did learn. Such unfinished dramas are everyday frustrations in the lives of elevator girls since they can't help but hear conversations begun right under their noses.

This was one of the things I learned yesterday as a guest jockey at the Palmer House learning about other people's jobs. A few trips later, just as pretty Gerry Walter, the starter, gave me the signal "ride," a radiant young girl was beginning the story of her romance. "It all began years ago when he first sent me flowers," she was telling an older companion.

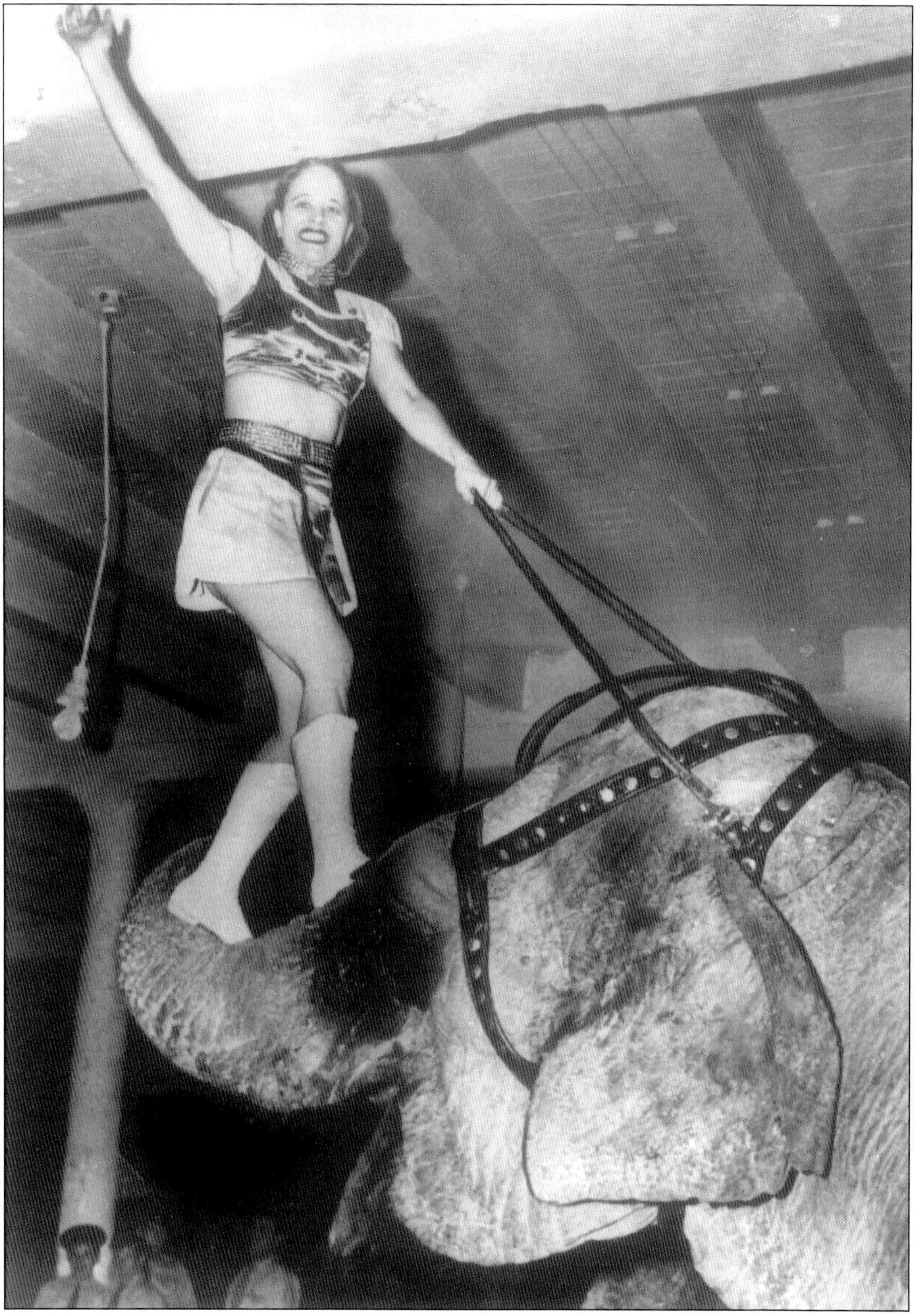

A circus performer for a day trying "The Other Guy's Job."

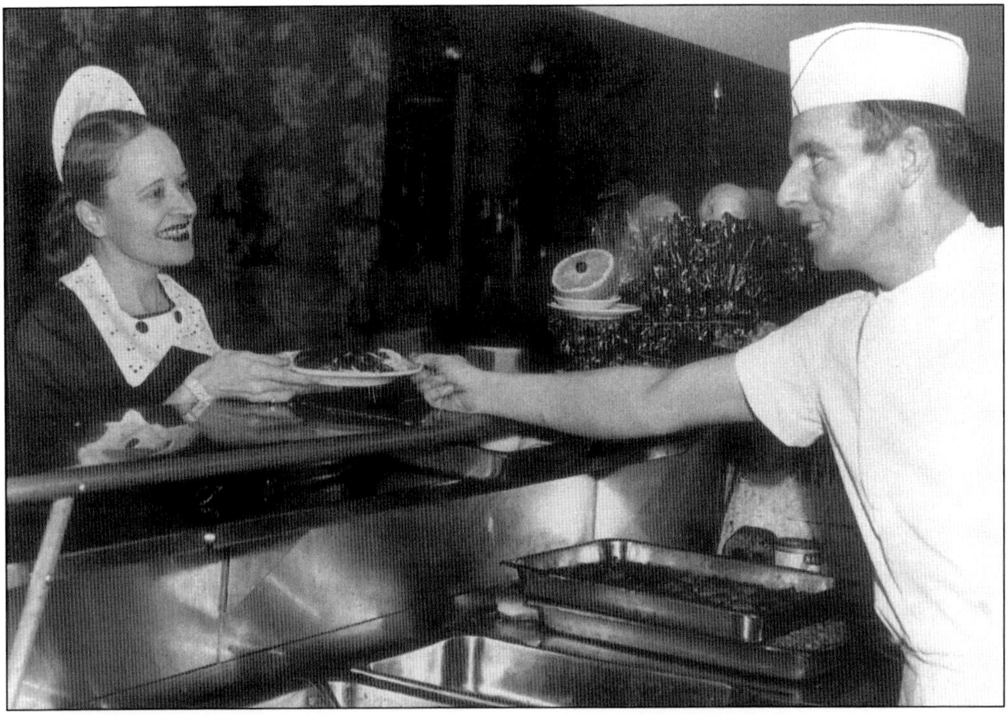

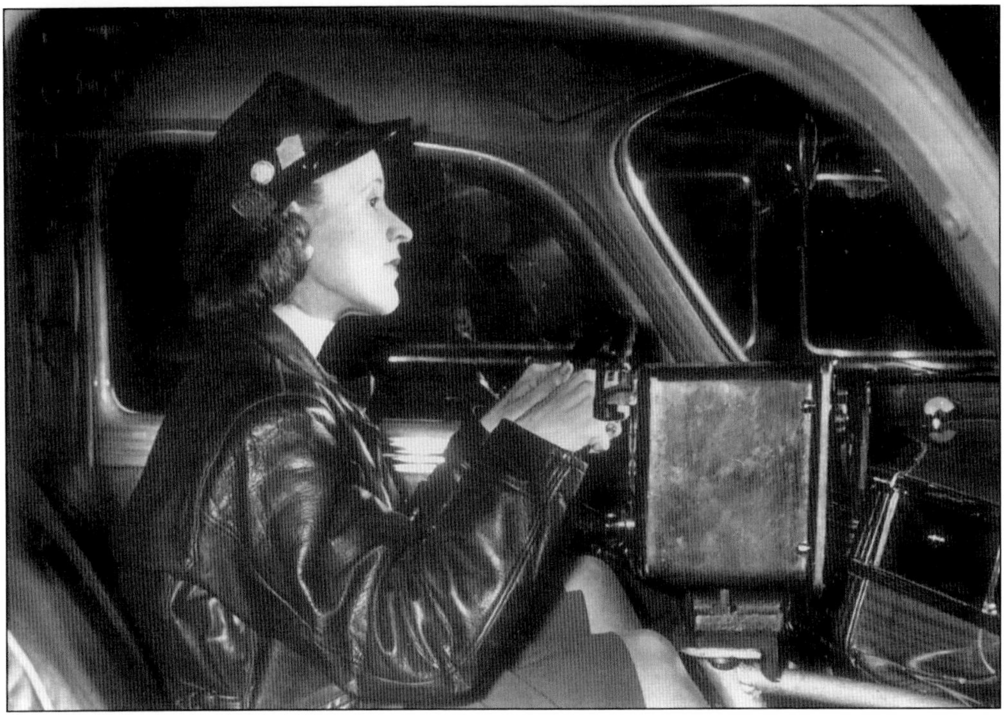

In the top photo, Virginia tries her hand at being a waitress.
Below, for a story, Virginia Marmaduke becomes Chicago's only female taxi cab driver for one day.

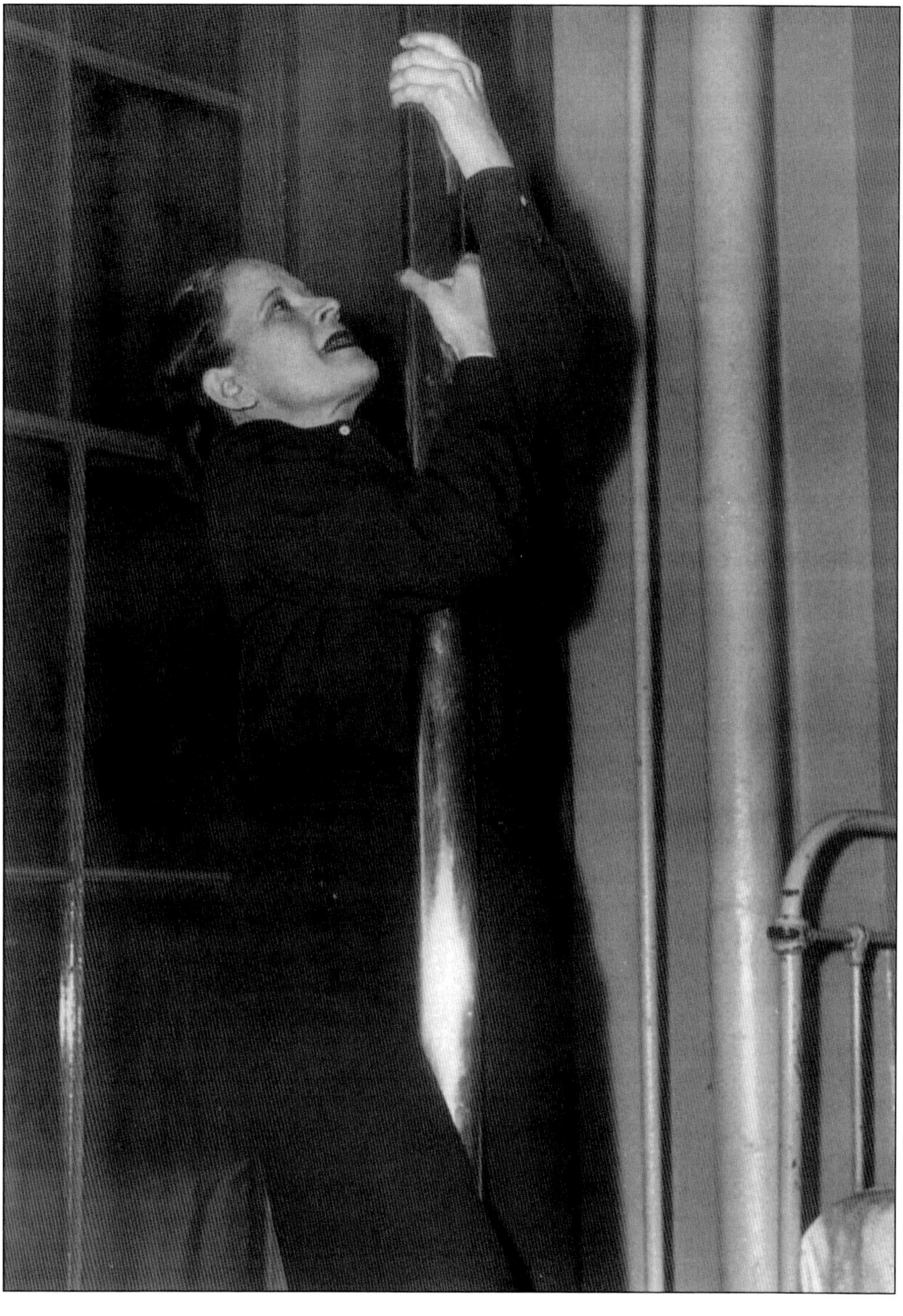

Virginia tries out as a Windy City fireman.

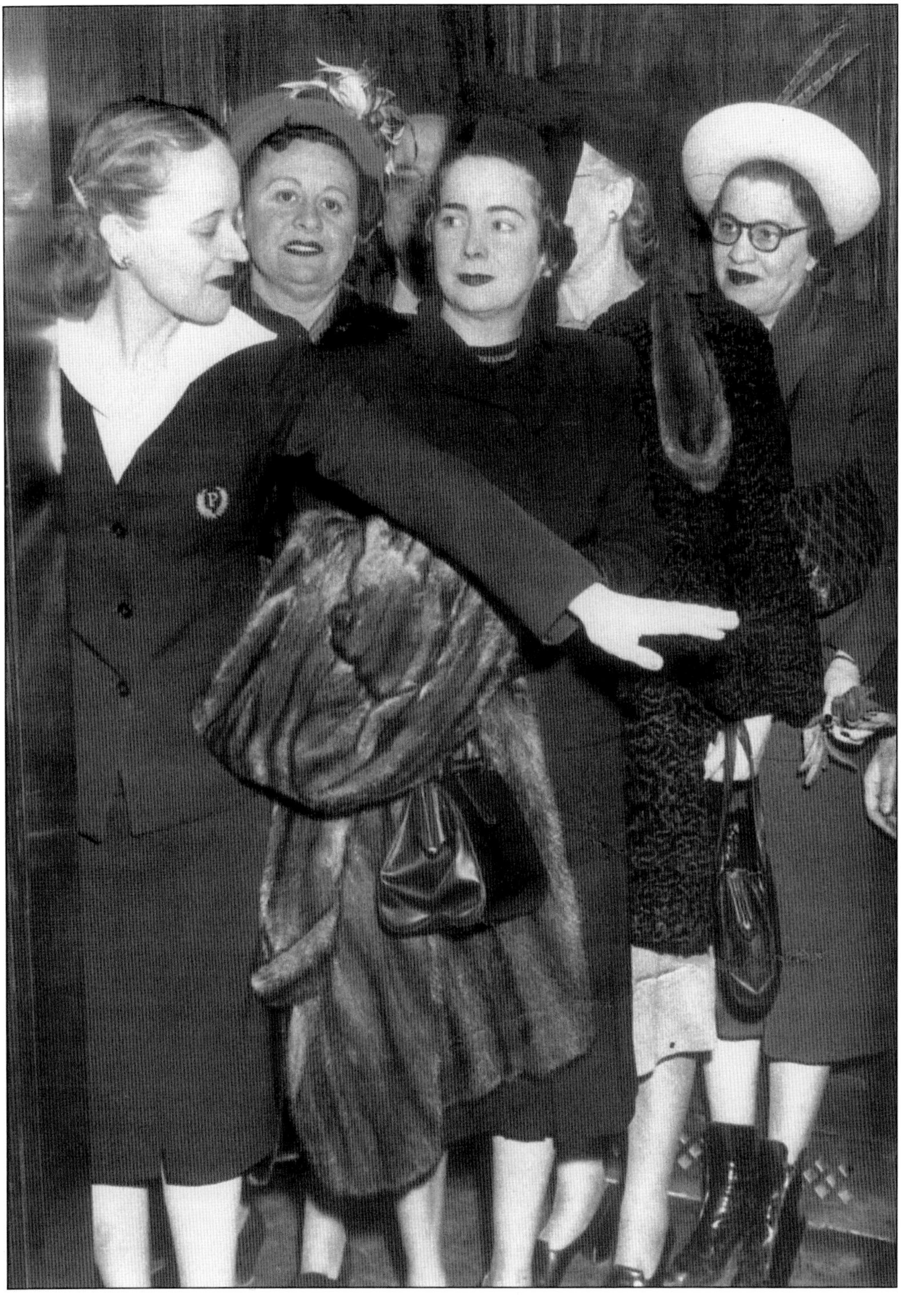

Going Up!: Virginia's next "job" was as an elevator operator.

SHINY, NEW RING

But it was easy to guess that ending. When she stepped out of the 5th floor I noticed a shiny, new sparkle to her wedding ring and she was wearing an orchid corsage. Operating an elevator is not all hearts and flowers, however. Sometimes it's hard to keep the required decorum.

There are "late callers" who announce they want off at the 7th floor when the cage is already at 6 1/2. And passengers with aromatic unlighted cigars butts in their mouths. Feather-spiked hats can also give trouble. I thought the carload was snickering at me until the lady with the extended ostrich plume left us at the 14th floor.

Passengers who board an up car in the middle of the trip just to be sure of space on the down voyage don't help either. Every time it happened I kept waiting for them to call their floor on the way up.

NO CONVERSATIONS

The first rule for hotel elevator operators is not to carry on conversations with passengers. The exchanges are usually confined to "Floor please," and "Thank you." But there's one exception that ought to be made. When somebody remarks (and somebody does on nearly every trip) that her life must be full of ups and downs she ought to be permitted to answer: "I've heard that one before."

TOMORROW: What is a taxi driver's job like?

ADVICE FILLS CABBIE'S DAY

By Virginia "Duchess" Marmaduke

1/11/48

If a Chicago taxicab driver should try to absorb all the gratuitous information tossed at him in a day, he'd be addle-headed before the end of the shift. And four of every five riders seemingly feel compelled to start regaling the helpless cabbie the instant they settle back against the cushions. It's not so much the chatter that grows tiresome, but the unctuous manner in which it's delivered; sort of like a very wise person instructing a half wit.

I suppose it's the feeling of superiority some people get from riding in a cab. Though it could be that relaxation loosens the vocal chords. I found out about these things yesterday when I wheeled a taxi around the town to see what the cabbie's job is like. And here are some of the things I was told:

TRIPS TO HOTELS

Martin Kennelly is making Chicago a fine mayor; Notre Dame is going to be the football team to beat in 1948; it's going to be a tough year for the Democrats. I hauled passengers on trips that covered several loop hotels, the Wrigley Building, 1500 Lake Shore Dr., 4200 W. Washington Blvd., and several other destinations. Most of the passengers sank back with a tired grunt after they'd announced where they wanted to go. Then the talk would start.

The bartender I took home from work told me to put my money on Notre Dame next year. The Homburg-hatted gentleman I dropped at the Lake Shore Dr. address complimented our mayor's regime. Two passengers were responsible for the ill-wind prophecy about the Democrats.

I drove cab No. 2356, a shiny new one owned by the Public Taxi Service Inc., usually handled by Charlie DeLorme, veteran of 20 years in Chicago taxicabs.

MART IS TRIED

"If you get stuck for a haul, try the Merchandise Mart," he had advised. "The big furniture show is on and the place ought to be lousy with live ones." It was and I drew opulent, well-dressed gentlemen who wanted to go to the Morrison Hotel. When he heard my feminine "Yes, sir," he broke out in smiles.

"I thought the war was over," he said. When we got to the Morrison, the bill, according to the meter, was 50 cents. He gave me a half-dollar and three dimes.

"Thank YOU," I said. It was well over the usual 10 per cent tips I had been receiving.

"Aw, it isn't often a guy gets chauffeured around by a cab driver in earrings," he answered. "Besides I'm a furniture buyer and I'm on an expense account."

TOMORROW'S article in THE CHICAGO SUN will describe the trials of a radio sound effects man.

THE OTHER GUY'S JOB
Stealthy Killer's Steps Slither in Sound Box
By Virginia "Duchess" Marmaduke
1/12/48

I killed a man yesterday and got shot for it. The gory business happened while I sat in on a radio show as a sound effects man. I hardly had to move out of my tracks to do it.

To start me off on the right foot, Edward Wojtal, WBBM's chief of sound effects, gave me a pair of his "sound shoes."

"The whole plot of this one moves on footsteps," he explained. It began with the villain's approach over a gravel driveway so I shuffled around in a 2 by 2 foot box of small stones with a microphone at my feet. By rolling a bunch of reeds around in my hand, the listeners learned that I was slithering through some bushes on my way through a window. The next steps were over a small strip of carpet, since I was supposed to be in a house making my way toward a kitchen. Then I poured some water into a glass and waited for a suspenseful second. […]

'DUCHESS' GIVES TIPS TO CHARITY
1/24/48

This is a message to the persons who contributed tips to THE CHICAGO SUN's girl reporter, Virginia (Duchess) Marmaduke, while she was working as a waitress and a cab driver assembling material for stories on other people's jobs. Her tips were donated to the Community Fund of Children "to help other Chicagoans" and yesterday she received a letter of appreciation from Fred K. Hoehler, executive director.

Officially, on February 1, 1948, the media landscape of the city of Chicago changed forever. As was already happening across the country—and which would become the norm evermore—in order to survive, two area newspapers merged. In this case, the *Chicago Sun* merged with the *Chicago Times*, forming a new newspaper, pooling their mutual resources and, hopefully, their readership. Said the Duchess about the uniting of the two dailies, "The *Sun* regarded itself as more aristocratic so the joining of the two was a little difficult, especially when they started cutting costs."

The combining of the two businesses resulted in having a few too many employees—and too little workspace. Said the Duchess, "The place was grimy, it was a dirty crowded place[…] It was a like a hot sheet operation, we had a hot desk. You had to wait for someone to get up to get to a typewriter. The firings took care of that. They'd fire a hundred of the *Sun* men then it was time to fire a hundred of the *Times* men and so on."

Fortunately for Virginia Marmaduke she would not be one of the individuals let go in the transition of the *Sun* into the *Sun-Times*. In fact, her place (and the place of other women) in the newsroom became even more solidified around this time when the newspaper installed the first women's restroom in the city news room, saving female reporters a two-flight hike upstairs. Virginia was given the honor by her bosses of cutting the pink sash in the bathroom's light-hearted ribbon-cutting ceremony.

CHICAGO SUN-TIMES

THE 'HUMAN WAY' FOR LANG—IS WHAT?
By Virginia Marmaduke
2/23/48

Is there a "human way" to deal with a 13-year-old self-confessed killer? Nearly everybody is agreed there should be and that Howard Lang should be given the chance that society has thus far denied him. But there were various ideas as to how it should be administered.

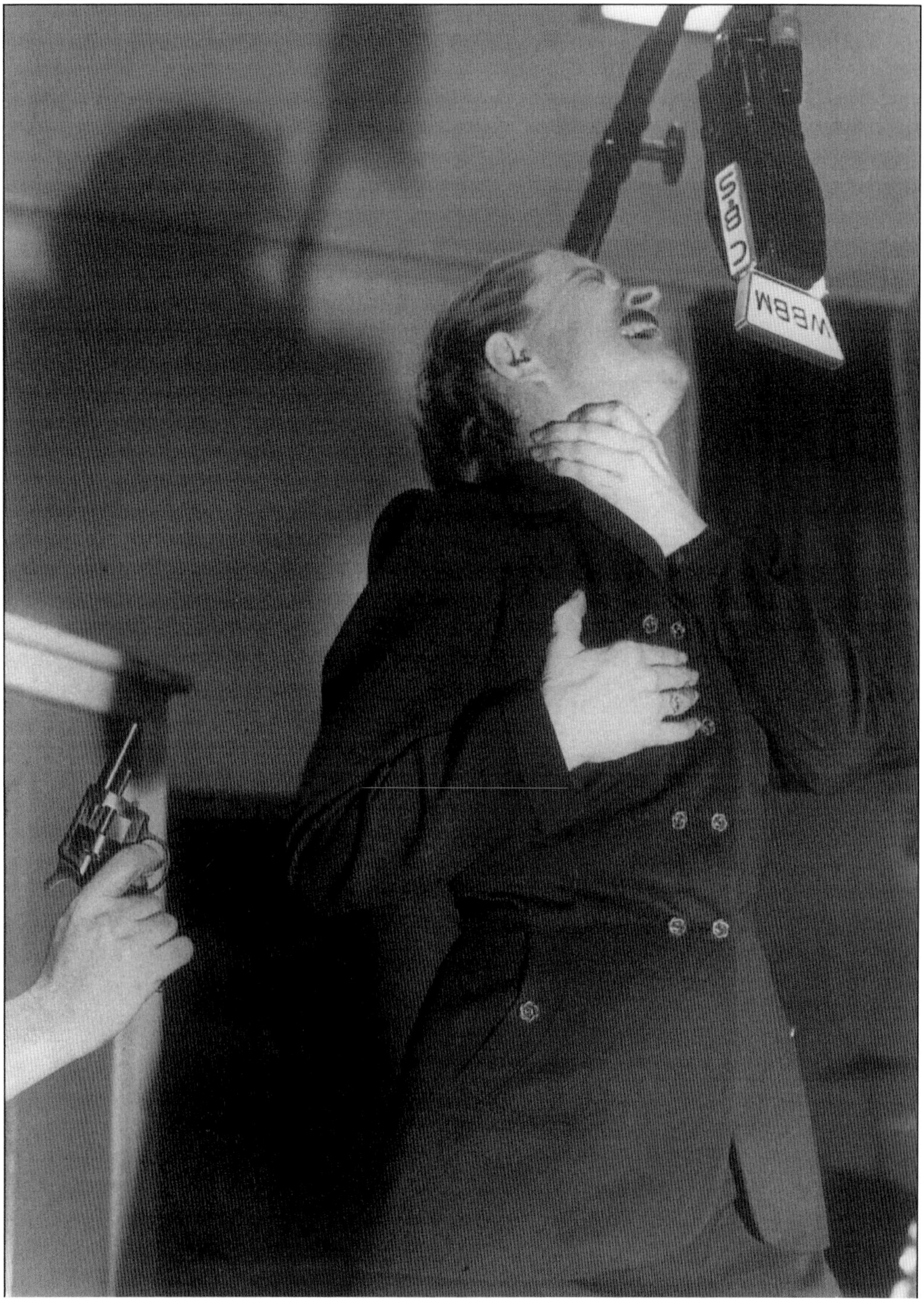

For radio sound effects, Virginia fakes a scream into the microphone with the help of a phony (?) pistol.

UNDER DISCUSSION

With the death penalty eliminated by his plea of guilt, the ultimate fate of the spindly, blond youth was discussed in many places. Everybody was remembering that he had coldly killed his 7-year-old playmate, Lonnie Fellick, and left him to die alone under a pile of leaves. But with few exceptions they were also wondering what Howie Lang might have been if he had enjoyed a normal childhood.

Churchmen, law enforcement officers and educators talked of "the Lang case" in private conferences. Many parents looked at each other and made new resolves about home life for their children. Dr. Clinton Cox, pastor of the Drexel Park Presbyterian church, said the 14-year minimum sentence which Lang faces is all right [...]

The Rev. Ralph Gallagher, S.J., regent of Loyola University's School of Sociology, says the basic problem in the Lang case is how to protect the child and protect society too.

SOCIETY BLAMED

"It's the fault of society that this boy is where he is now," Rev. Gallagher declared. "We must make it up to him somehow." In homes and on the streets there were a few who would like to see Howard Lang "put away for the rest of his life," but none wanted to be quoted. One man, who said he was the father of an 11-year-old girl, hoped that Lang would never again be loosed on society.

WOMAN TO CONDUCT SYMPHONY? OH, NO

By Virginia Marmaduke

2/24/48

Ann Kullmer, 29, of New York, thought she was going to conduct the Chicago Symphony Orchestra next fall. But she is not. Chicago officials of the symphony said her announcement in New York was "purely the result of her manager's wishful thinking."

NO CONTRACT

Edward L. Ryerson, president of the symphony group, said he certainly was unaware of any contract with Miss Kullmer. George A. Kuyper, business manger of the association, went even further. He said the dark-eyed, vivacious young conductress, first woman to lead the Paris Conservatory Orchestra, definitely was not booked for next fall's season and would not be.

DRAMATIC WORDS END GIRL'S SECRET

By Virginia Marmaduke

4/5/48

Hour after hour, a brown-eyed, brown-haired wisp of a girl made a secret of who killed her father and why. Then, with dramatic suddenness, Frances Korbelik, 17, gave the answer.

"I killed him," she told Sheriff Elmer Hoffman and State's Attorney's Chief Investigator Allan Mayers.

As she told the details of how she shot her father and dragged his body to the basement of their home where she piled lumber on it, she appeared almost relieved.

EVASIVE EARLIER

Earlier, as she took lie tests which showed she was lying and giving contradictory accounts of the circumstances of her father's death, she had been more evasive. "Yes, I know who killed him," she had said. Her answers, in an earlier eight-hour grilling, were identical and determined. "I have nothing more to say."

ADMITS LIES

Curious, she asked to see the chart of the lie tests. Myers showed them to her and indicated the spots in which she was not telling the truth. "Yes, that's right," she added in agreement with Myers on points where the chart showed she was untruthful.

Hoping to shake her, Hoffman's men suddenly handed her the gruesome folder showing the police pictures of her father's body. Not once did she wince as each picture was pushed at her. She saw them all. Then, without losing her poise, she stood erect and strode through the door.

REMAINS UNMOVED

Four burly policemen raced after her but put on the foot brakes quickly when she dashed through another door into the woman's washroom. I followed her in there. She was dry-eyed and serene though. Then she walked back for more questioning.

It wasn't long afterward that a jail door closed on her for the first time in her life. "Don't you have something to tell people who are interested in your case?" I asked.

"I have nothing to say," she replied grimly.

"But you are in a spot. If you are as innocent as you say you are, you need help," I suggested.

AS LAST, TEARS

She wept, showing the first emotion since her questioning had started. "Whoever she is protecting, she loves very much," Sheriff Elmer Hoffman remarked. A junior in Hinsdale High School until her father disappeared, the 5-foot 3-inch, 112-pound youngster went to work for the first time in her life last Monday in a hamburger stand at Ogden Ave. and Austin Blvd. in Berwyn. For months she had wanted to work. While her father lived, he forbade it. He wanted her to get the education she didn't want.

EDWARDS VISITS AT LARABIDA
By Virginia Marmaduke
4/16/48

It was a modified game of Truth or Consequences which Ralph Edwards played with the little rheumatic fever patients as La Rabida Jackson Park Sanitarium. It didn't have any of the running around or hilarious antics of his famous Saturday night NBC radio program but everybody had lots of fun.

VISITS CHILDREN

Armed with more than 100 American Beauty Roses, Edwards made a lake shore haven for children with crippled hearts. He stopped at every bed.

"Tell me the truth or take the consequences," he began. "Now what is your full name?" The correct answer—and nobody failed—earned a beautiful, long-stemmed rose.

RESEARCH AIDED

Through the "Walking Man" contest, originating on his program, listeners contributed $1,575,000 for the heart cause. A portion of it will be allocated for research on rheumatic fever. [...]

The Duchess had a long relationship with La Rabida Hospital, adopting it as one of her favorite charities, even for a time editing its newsletter, *The Little Heart of La Rabida*. She said once, "When you don't have anyone yourself, that's when you need to look around and find other people to help...." She would add later, "Working with children has been the greatest happiness of my life."

A $20,000 PARTY TRIPPED UP RICCA
By Virginia Marmaduke
6/17/48

In an extravaganza of champagne, potted palms and hundred dollar bills, Paul Ricca, a parolee and former Capone associate, saw to it that his daughter's wedding reception was done in style.

But the $20,000 super-production, staged last Jan. 24 at the Crystal Room of the Blackstone Hotel, was one of the things that tripped up Ricca's parole record and got him back into federal custody Wednesday.

Among his parole violation charges was that Ricca, who prefers the name of De Lucia, failed to make a truthful report to the parole supervisor on his income and expenditures.

The $20,000 party wasn't recorded on his report. [...]

HOTELS HAVE SUITES READY FOR TRUMANS
By Virginia Marmaduke
7/14/48
PHILADELPHIA—The suite they have been holding at the Warwick hotel for Mrs. Harry Truman and daughter Margaret is going to get its famous visitors after all. National Committee Chairman J. Howard McGarth said it looks "probable" that President Truman will come to Philadelphia to accept his nomination and if he does, Mrs. Truman and Margaret will accompany him.

The President's family had left Independence, Mo., Sunday, with the Philadelphia jaunt, apparently, in mind. It had been no secret—to at least three hotels—that Philadelphia might have distinguished guests from Washington before the week was ended.

The President's housing problem has been well taken care of in advance. There was the rumor that the presidential family would be given use of a palatial private residence while here. But the Bellevue-Stratford, the Ritz-Carlton and the Warwick hotels were holding deluxe suites on direct orders from authoritative sources from the White House itself—pretty sure they would draw Mrs. Truman and Margaret as guests.

The covering of Truman during the 1948 campaign gave the Duchess one of her favorite stories. Posted outside of Truman's suite before his acceptance speech, Virginia took note of several trays of liquor arriving before the candidate headed down to the convention floor.

Later, during Truman's unusually lively, spirited acceptance speech, *Sun-Times* owner and department store tycoon Marshall Field turned to the Duchess and asked, "Is this the new Truman?"

The Duchess replied, "No, it's the Old Grand Dad." She added later, "To this day, I consider that the best repartee of my entire life."

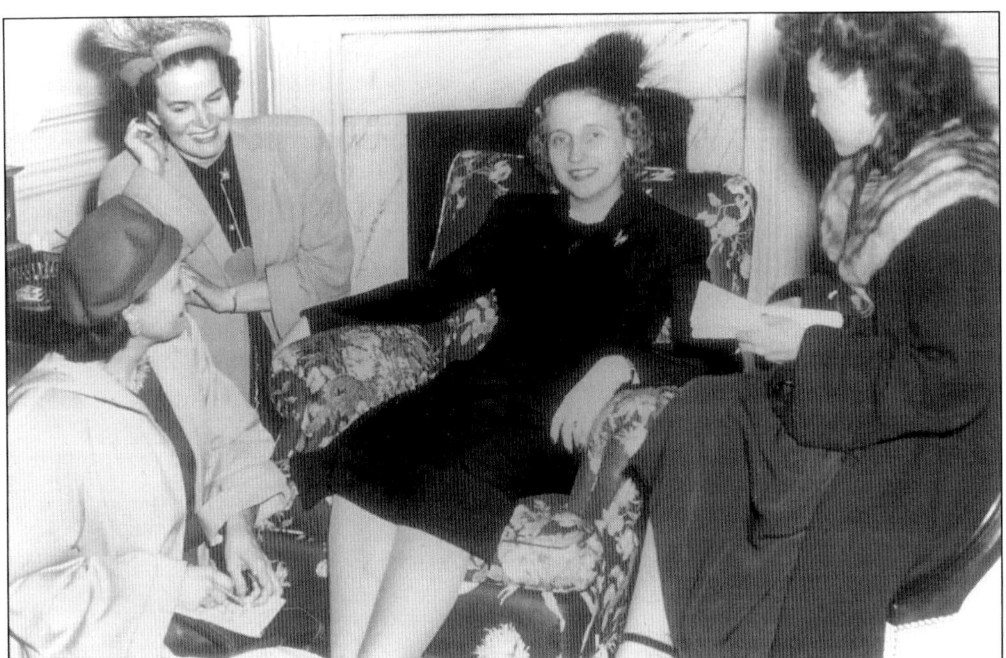

Virginia (lower left) and fellow "news hens" interview Margaret Truman.

LADIES TAKE OVER, SLASH HARD AT GOP

By Virginia Marmaduke

7/14/48

PHILADELPHIA—It was ladies' night when the spotlights centered on the speakers' platform at the Democratic National Convention Tuesday night. California's glamorous Helen Gahagan Douglas and New Jersey's silver-haired Mary Norton formed two-thirds of the scheduled speakers of the program. Texas' Sam Rayburn, a bachelor, found himself smack in the middle when he assumed permanent convention chairmanship.

When attractive Mrs. Douglas, former actress and wife of movie star Melvyn Douglas, took the rostrum. the television cameras had a field day. Her vivid brunette coloring and her vibrant personality proved perfect foil for the lensmen. But Congresswoman Douglas was not acting when she struck out at the 80th Congress and the Republican Party in general for their failure to aid the American housewife.

HITS INFLATION

"Success or failure in economic politics can be measured simply by what a dollar bill will buy at the corner grocery store," she continued, "And that's the way American voters will evaluate the Republican Party."

"There's actually fright today when the housewife sits down to plan her weekly budget."

The Republicans have made no plan to meet the problem of inflation, she said. "All they did for five sweltering days of their convention was dance on the grave of a dead President. They shivered in the fear that the philosophy of Franklin Delano Roosevelt still lives in the hearts of the American people." That drew shouts of assenstion from the delegates and Mrs. Douglas picked up their enthusiasm.

'FEAR WELL GROUNDED'

"Their fear is well grounded," she said. "The spirit of F.D.R. does live and the Democratic Party intends to preserve it." [...]

WILL JIMMY LIVE? BROTHER SEEKS HELP

By Virginia Marmaduke

8/12/48

Th[ere] is [an] advertisement a 13-year-old boy sought to buy in THE SUN-TIMES *on behalf of his 5-year-old brother who needs blood donors. Along with his neatly-penciled plea, Robert Jacobsen of 2435 W. Marquette Rd., enclosed two $1 bills from his sparse savings. News space in this newspaper is not for sale. But this is not the reason Robert's $2 was returned to him by special messenger.*

WHAT IT SAID

This is what the letter said: "Dear Mister Editor: Dad and mother are all broken up because my little brother has leukemia, the blood disease.

"We are trying to find blood donors to help him get better. I am inclosing (sic) two dollars if you will please put a little ad in your paper. I was going to buy a bike fender with the money but as long as my brother lives there is hope. Jimmy is at Billings Memorial Hospital for Children so if you get any donors please send them there and tell them that they should say it's for Jimmy Jacobsen.

"Please try to do something for him so he won't die, please. If anything ever happened to Jim I don't know what would happen to my mother. This is my own money. I don't want my mother or dad to know.

"Yours sincerely, Bob Jacobsen."

A PROUD MOTHER

But Bob's mother and father, Mr. and Mrs. John Jacobsen, know now of their son's letter. They were there when his $2 was returned. "Bob earned that money selling ice cream bars from a streetside stand," his mother said. "I'm proud he wanted to spend it that way."

At Billings Hospital, doctors said young Jimmy may need lots of blood. They said they would be glad to make appointments for "Jimmy Jacobsen donors." Simply call Midway 0800 and ask for the blood bank to help Robert get results from his "ad."

One story the Duchess covered for much of 1948, was the tale of little Pamela Lamphere, whose birth defect complicated her parents' divorce proceeding and became a medical and legal cause celebre.

WOMAN WHO SURVIVED ORDEAL ENDS FEARS OF PAM'S MOTHER
By Virginia Marmaduke
8/15/48

A toddling, blue-eyed child has won for 22-month-old Pamela Lamphere what judges, lawyers and a pleading father had failed to get. She is Christine Ulrich, there months younger than Pamela, and living proof that the dangerous, abdominal operation Pam needs, need not be fatal.

Completely recovered, little Christine visited Pamela's mother at the request of the SUN-TIMES *and won her consent for a similar operation for Pam, if the jury of doctors says she can stand it.*

BROUGHT TOGETHER

Christine's mother, Mrs. Helen Ulrich, 38, of 11430 S. St. Louis Ave., read in the SUN-TIMES *of Irene Lamphere's refusal to let her daughter undergo the needed operation. "Why it sounds exactly like Christy's trouble," she exclaimed. "I liked to talk to that mother and show her my child."*

Through the SUN-TIMES, *the mothers were brought together. So were the little girls, Pamela with her dark eyes and light brown hair and Christine with her big blue eyes and blond locks.*

The meeting took place Saturday evening in the Lamphere home at 2398 Blue Island Ave. The little girls became friends at once, almost as if they knew the thing they shared. So did the mothers, the one young and distraught, the other graying and calm. The little girls played with toys. The mothers talked.

'FELT LIKE YOU DO'

"I felt just like you do, at first," Mrs. Ulrich began. "Then I decide it was Christy's right to happiness and not mine to decide."

The young mother still was fearful. "But I've always been told it was so dangerous and that I might lose Pamela on the operation table," she sobbed.

"There's a chance in every operation," the older woman soothed. "But you'll never be sorry you gave your little girl a chance at a full, normal life."

The young mother unburdened her heart. "I had a hard time when Pamela was born," she said. "Even the homecoming wasn't what a mother wants and expects. They kept Pamela in the hospital and didn't tell me about her deformity until they sent her home to me."

'NOTHING TO LIVE FOR'

But the special care, the daily surgical dressing and the plight of her baby only made me love her more.

"If she should be taken from me now, I'd have nothing more to live for," she added.

Mrs. Ulrich nodded her understanding. "It was exactly the same with Christine for the first nine months of her life," she said. "But when the doctors said she had reached the stage where she had to have an operation or maybe die, I made up my mind to give her the chance at life," she said.

The young mother still was hesitant. "Come into the bedroom with Christy and me," Mrs. Ulrich invited. "We want to show you something."

Little Christine's wholesome young body—free of the ugly deformity with which she had been born—was bared to the doubting mother. Only a small, dainty scar remained. Then little Pamela joined them. The surgical dressing[,] which she has always worn, was removed. "Was Christy like this?" Mrs. Lamphere demanded.

"Exactly," Mrs. Ulrich answered. Irene Lamphere gathered her child to her breast.

"Then Pamela shall have the same chance," she said. "I have seen with my own eyes."

STEER RUNS WILD AT SHOW

By Virginia Marmaduke

11/30/48

Fiddle, a little bay mare, put a little nip into the western quarter horse exhibition and scattered the customers all over the place Monday night at the International Livestock Exhibition and Horse Show. The mare, ridden by Jack Hart, of Marshall, Tex., was doing a fine job of showing how a cow pony "cuts" a herd until it ran into a reluctant steer. The steer was determined not to be kept away from its brother steers. Fiddle was equally determined it should.

STEER JUMPS RAIL

Finally, in exasperation, Fiddle reached over and bit the steer on its hindquarters. The steer let out a bellow and jumped over the four-foot guard rail, landing in the middle of a crowd of 50 persons. The steer was as frightened as the people but none of them, including several policemen detailed to keep the crowd back from the rail, stayed around long enough to look into the matter.

COWBOY TO RESCUE

Cowboy Lloyd Jinkens, of Fort Worth, Tex., saved the day. He leaped off his horse, vaulted the rail and threw a hammerlock on the steer. It went meekly back to the arena. Only one person—Kasper Jerome, 15, of 2022 N. Whipple St.—was injured and he suffered only minor bruises.

NEWLY-BORN TWINS FIND THERE'S A SANTA

By Virginia Marmaduke

12/27/48

Out of work, his savings nearly all used up, James Gutillo, 34, had told his five children that Santa Claus wouldn't be able to bring any toys or goodies to their house at 256 W. 23rd St., this year.

"We'll have to play like the twins are our Christmas presents," he had said. The twins—a boy and a girl—had been born to Mrs. Gutillo Christmas morning in the home of her mother-in-law at 2451 Archer Ave. Rosemary, 9, oldest of the little Gutillos, had told him it was all right with them. "We'll make believe the new babies are our dolls," she said.

NEIGHBORS TAKE HAND

But Papa Gutillo hadn't counted on the good hearts of Chicagoans or the miracle of Christmas. The SUN-TIMES' *story telling of the plight of Gutillos had hardly been published when neighbor-readers began knocking on doors at both addresses. They brought toys, candy, oranges and even layette items for the twins.*

But the gifts from Mrs. Doris Petersen and her three children were the ones they exclaimed about most. Mrs. Petersen, 31, a widow, and her three little ones had shared their Christmas with the Gutillos despite their own strained circumstances. [...]

KILLED IN CAR CRASH

Her husband was killed last summer in an auto accident, Mrs. Petersen and her brood live in the rear of 988 Linden Ave., in Hubbard Woods. Hampers of goodies and toys from wealthy neighbors had been arriving all week for the lonely little family.

Among the two large sacks Mrs. Petersen sent the Gutillos were a large toy taxicab that winds up, a story book doll and a tea set. The taxi was contributed by Buster, 4; the doll by Leilani, 5, and the tea set by Patricia Lynn, 2. Mrs. Petersen sent along a $10 bill in an envelope. "Use this to buy some warm sleepers for the twins," she wrote. "Somebody gave it to me but I can manage without it."

1949

CHICAGO SUN-TIMES

STUDENTS PROTEST SKIMPING ON S.I.U.
By Virginia Marmaduke
1/10/49

CARBONDALE, ILL.—The old, pre-Civil War main classroom building of Southern Illinois University is echoing with its 1949 version of rebel yells. Students had jitterbugged up and down its musty old corridors in a dance of derision because they had no other place to hold a week-end social party.

"Maybe the old thing will fall in on us," one of the young rebels predicted as he danced. "Then the State of Illinois and the budgetary commission would realize how much we need some new buildings." The protest dance had the full approval of the downstate university's youthful president, Dr. D.W. Morris, 41. He even attended.

"It's false pride for us to try to gloss over the true story of our plight any longer," he said. "Our academic facilities are as disgraceful as the recreation facilities. The students have the right to rebel."

LIBRARY CONDEMNED

He was thinking of the library situation under which the school's 3,100 students work. Built in 1903—to meet the needs of an enrollment of 250—the library building has just been condemned as unsafe. They've had to remove nearly 100,000 pounds of reference books in order to even use it as a study room. The new library annex is now in a basement section of the women's dormitory, which also serves as laundry [room] for the girl students—the only available place for it. Now, while some girls study, others hang up their washing on the clothesline.

With enrollment at an all-time peak, the Southern Illinois education institution is asking for an $8,000,000 operation budget for 1948-51. [...]

Dr. Leo Brown, of Carbondale, president of the university alumni association, had declared it was a case of "either-or" for the university, [...] "Either the state and the new governor will have to recognize us or just definitely discard us as unwanted stepchildren," he said.

In an October 1998 article from *The Daily Egyptian*, Southern Illinois University's campus newspaper, this early 1949 Marmaduke visit to SIU, and her meeting with Delyte Morris, was looked back on as nothing less than a watershed event in the history of the university.

Harry Reinert, who was interviewed for *The Daily Egyptian* story, was a student at SIU from 1948 to 1951. He states that Marmaduke's Carbondale visit beget a windfall of financial support to the school from the state legislature. He says, "She took pictures of where foundations had cracks and such. When the *Sun-Times* came out, the whole back page was devoted to our dance and the problems at SIU in terms of funding.

"This is what got it started. The reason you have the campus you have now is because of that stupid little dance we had at Old Main."

The Carbondale visit had been engineered by Virginia. She said, "Well, a very nice Southern Illinoisan, a young man then, became President of SIU and I soon found out that he was very well liked by everybody but that he wanted to do things differently. So I called him from Chicago and I said, 'I'm a native of Carbondale but I've been in Chicago since I was ten years old and I know radio, television and newspapering, if you need me in any way let me know.'"

Of course, this 1949 visit was also a milestone moment for Virginia Marmaduke. Years later, having retired from Chicago-area journalism, the Duchess would relocate to Southern Illinois and adopt SIUC as the number one recipient of her largess, granting it thousands of dollars for scholarships and programs and devoting to it much of her vast, measureless energies.

N.Y. TO DOMINATE VIDEO PICTURE HERE
By Virginia Marmaduke
1/16/49

Unless the picture changes, television's new coaxial cable is going to be a one-way street to New York and Midwesterners will have to face east, figuratively, when they sit down before the television screen. Only a small portion of network time now available will feature Chicago-originated shows. New York-produced shows will dominate nearly 20 to 1.

Local shows—featuring Chicago talent and produced on our own State St.—will still be available from station WBKB, however, WBKB is the only station here not affiliated with national networks. Two network officials, unwilling to be quoted by name, said it was ridiculous for Chicago to hope to be the television center of the nation. [...]

USE ATOM IN HEART RESEARCH
By Virginia Marmaduke
2/18/49

University of Chicago scientists are preparing a new chapter on the use of digitalis which, when completed, may serve as a guide for the cure and prevention of heart disease. The work, being carried on by Dr. Eugene M.K. Geiling and six of his department of pharmacology associates, involves tracing radioactive digitalis in an organism.

Explaining the work of his group, in connection with the Chicago Heart Assn.'s current drive for $1,000,000 for research, Geiling said: "If we are to conquer heart disease, we must know more about the why and wherefore of it. Since it is known that digitalis helps some heart sufferers, we want to know how it helps them."

USED FOR 200 YRS.

Digitalis, a derivative of the leaves of the foxglove plant, has been used to treat certain heart diseases for 200 years. Though its effect and dosages are known, the mechanism by which it acts is a mystery. [...]

The University of Chicago, along with all other university, hospital and sanitarium centers working on heart research, will share in funds raised by the Chicago Heart Association.

TWISTER SURVIVORS TELL OF CLOSE CALLS
By Virginia Marmaduke
5/23/49

WOOD RIVER, ILL.—Bit by bit and very carefully, pretty Mrs. Mary Jane Richter, 22, sifted through the jagged chunks of wood and twisted metal of what used to be her home. She was looking for her wedding ring. [...]

At least five persons were killed at Wood River, across the Mississippi River 20 miles from St. Louis. About 250 homes were knocked flat and 69 persons were taken to hospitals in Alton and Edwardsville.

GLOOMY SUNDAY

The Illinois Militia took charge Sunday, a gloomy, miserable, wet Sunday, and the Red Cross and Salvation Army passed out coffee. Worst hit was a six-block-square area in the northeast section of the town, which has 11,700 residents. It was there that pretty Mrs. Richter searched through the scrappage of a house trailer for her wedding ring, but didn't find it. [...]

SUN-TIMES AND TV JOIN TO MAKE HISTORY
By Virginia Marmaduke
6/14/49

It was a record-setting, award-winning night Nov. 2, when the television station WBKB and The SUN-TIMES *combined skills to tell the on-the-spot story of the 1948 national elections. It was the first time a metropolitan newspaper had ever permitted a public look-see into the inner sanctum of its newsroom and the first time television cameras had ever tried to pick up the drama and excitement of a big city daily newspaper going to press.*

But the event, hailed by more than 50,000 Chicago area televiewers as the most interesting program ever brought to their own living rooms, went off as if it had been a carefully rehearsed and edited movieland production.

ACCLAIMED AS BEST

Television Forecast, foremost video magazine in the Midwest, awarded plaques to WBKB and The SUN-TIMES, *acclaiming the show the "best remote type coverage of election results." Originally planned as a 2 to 3 hour show to keep pace with the election night picture throughout the nation, the telecast ran continuously from 8 p.m. to 3 a.m.*

The unusual and costly spontaneous extension of the telecast came on direct orders from WBKB officials and was in answer to thousands of telephone calls to the studio pleading that the show stay on the airwaves until the election returns indicated which way the nation was voting.

LONGEST IN HISTORY

The 7-hour telecast set a new record as the longest remote show in television history. [...]

A 20-man crew from station WBKB, three cameras and hundreds of yards of cable sent the picture-story out from the SUN-TIMES *Building at 211 W. Wacker Dr. [...]*

FLOOD OF THANKS

At 3 a.m., when the national returns showed a pretty definite trend toward election of Harry S. Truman as president of the United States and Adlai Stevenson as governor of Illinois, the final vote tabulation was given and the telecasters said a tired good night.

Letters of congratulations flooded The SUN-TIMES *and WBKB for the next several days praising the historic presentation, many of the writers saying they never left their television screens during the 7-hour program.*

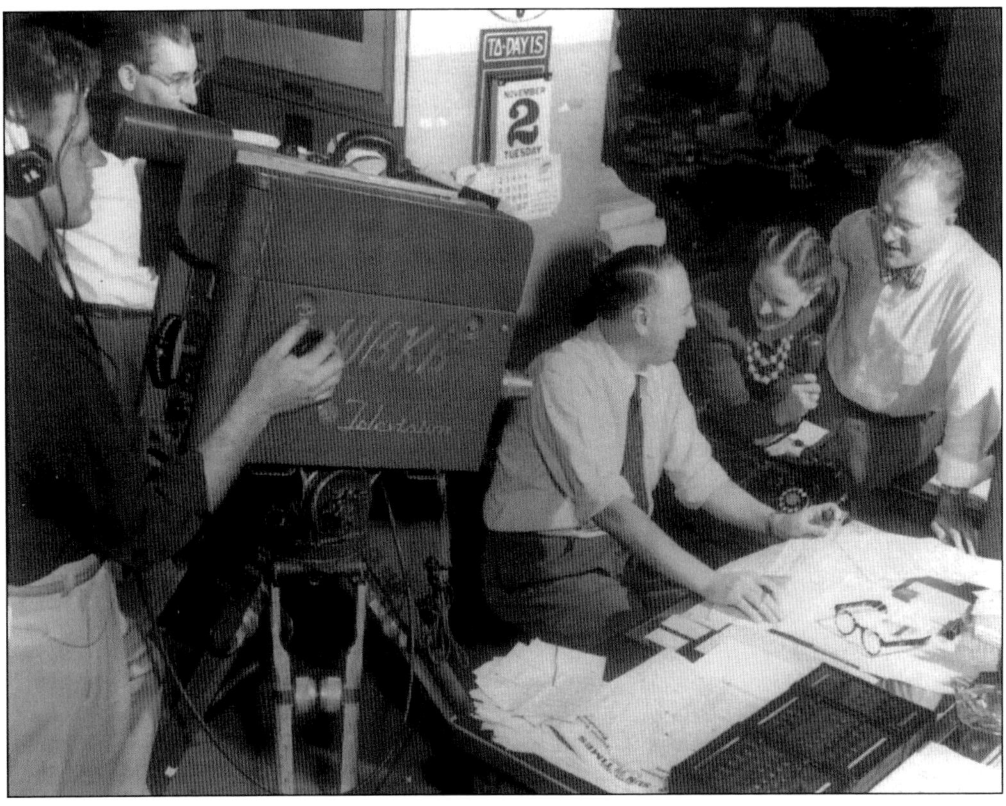

The Duchess takes to the air over WBKB-Chicago (Now WLS).

One of the Duchess's personal favorites among all the stories of her career came in 1949. Dancing legend turned animal rights activist Irene Castle began canvassing the hallways of the Illinois State Legislature in Springfield promoting a bill that would prohibit medical testing on animals. Along with her show biz glamour, Miss Castle was also, daily, parading though the legislature two beautiful white wolf hounds on a dual leash in order to promote her cause.

The Duchess and her *Sun-Times* editor, though both animal lovers, made no secret of having more concern with the welfare of children with weak hearts than animals on leashes, decided to launch a counter attack to Castle's Springfield campaign. With the assistance of the Chicago Medical Society, Virginia located four children who had been born "blue babies" and whose lives had been saved thanks to information gathered from prior animal-based research. She took the kids and their eager parents with her to Springfield.

SMILING, WAVING 'CUTEST KIDS' LOOK IN ON LEGISLATORS' GAME
By Virginia Marmaduke
6/15/49

SPRINGFIELD—Five of Chicago's cutest kids showed they were stalwart, too, infusing their stamina into legislators who advanced the Humane Pound Law Bill to passage stage.

For five grueling hours the kids were in there pitching while the battle raged in the House.

They pitched with a deadly aim, these kids who had been saved from lingering death by medical research that opponents of the bill termed aimless experiments.

<u>MORAL INSPIRATION</u>

Now radiant and healthy, they were the moral inspiration for the lawyers who voted an initial victory for the bill that would make available to medical science unclaimed dogs and cats from city pounds. The young veterans of heart surgery sat in the first row of the spectator's gallery, engrossed in the debate on the measure that can pave the way for full, normal lives for other afflicted youngsters. Here with their mothers to show the legislators how vivisection has advanced cardiac treatment, the juvenile Chicagoans arrived at the State capitol at 8:30 a.m., long before the session opened.

<u>CURED BY SURGERY</u>

Three of them—Ann Kempf, 6, Mitchell Simen, 10, and Robert Reicher, 13—were blue babies before surgery cured them. Heart malformations of the other two—Carol Lavelel, 7, and Barbara Condon, 15—had been corrected—by the miraculous patent dictus operation, also recently perfected through animal research.

Their new-found health was reflected in the faces of their beaming mothers[...]

Wide-eyed at the spectacle of lawmakers in action, the youngsters chattered among themselves, exchanging excited impressions until the speaker's gavel thumped for the crucial bill. "Now they're talking about little children like you," whispered Mrs. Kempf. The young visitors became silent, peering intently over the rail. [...]

"You were right," Rep. Arthur M. Kaindl (D-Chicago) told them when they met the legislators in the corridor after the session. "These children were our sparkplugs." [...]

FAMILY STANDING BY TOKYO ROSE IN TRIAL
By Virginia Marmaduke
7/5/49

When Tokyo Rose, American-born Iva Toguri D'Aquino, goes on trial for treason Tuesday, her father, June, 65, of 1012 N. Clark St., will be by her side. Fred Toguri, 39, a brother, said his father had gone to San Francisco two months ago to be with his daughter during the trial. The father and son are co-owners of a fish and grocery market at the Clark St. address and live in an upstairs apartment. From behind the counter, Fred voiced what he called "the family stand on the matter."

<u>'STILL OUR IVA'</u>

"We say nothing," he said, "until the trial is over. If she is vindicated we [will] be very happy. If not she [is] still our Iva and we love her." He said they had exchanged "several" letters with Iva and her husband, a

Portuguese-born printer, since their arrival in San Francisco last September. "She [is] very unhappy," he added. "She lost a baby just before she came back to the United States and she'll be very glad when this trouble is over."

The Justice Department has charged the 33-year-old former University of California student with being one of at least six English-speaking Japanese women who played temptress disc jokey to GIs in the Pacific.

SUBTLE PROPAGANDA

Using the name "Tokyo Rose," the woman played jive records interspersed with subtle and sinister enemy propaganda. Born in Los Angeles, Iva Toguri went to Japan in 1941. She has declared herself "anxious to clear herself" of the treason charges.

Virginia Marmaduke seemed to have an affinity for Shriners. And vice versa. She wrote about them and their works back in her Herrin days and wrote again about her fez-wearing friends in a couple of stories in mid-1949. The latter of the two articles was one of the Duchess's most remembered and unusual assignments: riding camel-back. Yes, Virginia really did do it.

SHRINER'S RIDE HIGH, AND IT'S GREAT FUN
By Virginia Marmaduke
7/20/49

The secret why there are so many Shriners is out. To become one you get to ride a camel. Initiation into the ancient, Arabic order is [a] deep and mystic secret. But Rufus Wells, potentate of Zor Temple of Madison, Wi., said this much could be told: "Traditionally, we ride the camel across the hot sands to reach the City of Mecca." That's why his Zor Temple carries along a real live camel patrol as part of its trappings for convention parades.

SLEEPY-LOOKING

Through the courtesy of Potentate Wells and Camel Captain, this girl reporter took a guest-ride on one of their camels, coming about as close to being a Shriner as any female has ever come, they added. They gave me Dana, an 8-foot, 6-inch camel claimed by them to be the biggest in this country. The sleepy-looking animal got down on all fours and knelt like a gentleman for me to climb aboard. The rising to his feet procedure was a couple of mighty big jerks, since he gets up first in the aft and lastly in the fore. But from then on it was a swing and sway that explains why so many people want to be Shriners and why Sheiks are such fascinating gents.

IT'S NO WONDER

The hot pavement of Ontario St. changed into burning hot sand and the tower of Wesley Memorial Hospital in the distance took on a Sphinx-like contour. I was an Oriental princess, swathed in mysterious veils, instead of a SUN-TIMES *reporter in a riding habit, and a palm-dotted oasis lay just ahead of me. But someone woke me by yelling "Your editor is on the phone and wants to know what it's like to ride a camel."*

No wonder more than 300,000 Madison, Wis., children have taken advantage of Zor Temple's free Sunday morning camel rides. No wonder the Madison Shriners paid the $1,500 each for their six camels and another $5,000 for genuine Damascus trappings they imported from Syria. No wonder there are 600,000 Shriners on the North American continent. Riding camel-back is fun.

CHICAGO'S WAYWARD GIRLS: POLICEWOMEN'S ANGER AROUSED
By Virginia Marmaduke
11/12/49

These were children. Very little ones, and in need.

"Their mother leaves them alone whole days and nights," a neighborhood resident telephoned Policewomen C and Z. "I want to make an official complaint about it." Child neglect, like anything that promotes the delinquency of minors, is a particular hate of women who carry the badge of the Chicago Police Department. So, pushing aside the endless paper work and report sheets that flood their desks, Policewomen C and Z went to investigate.

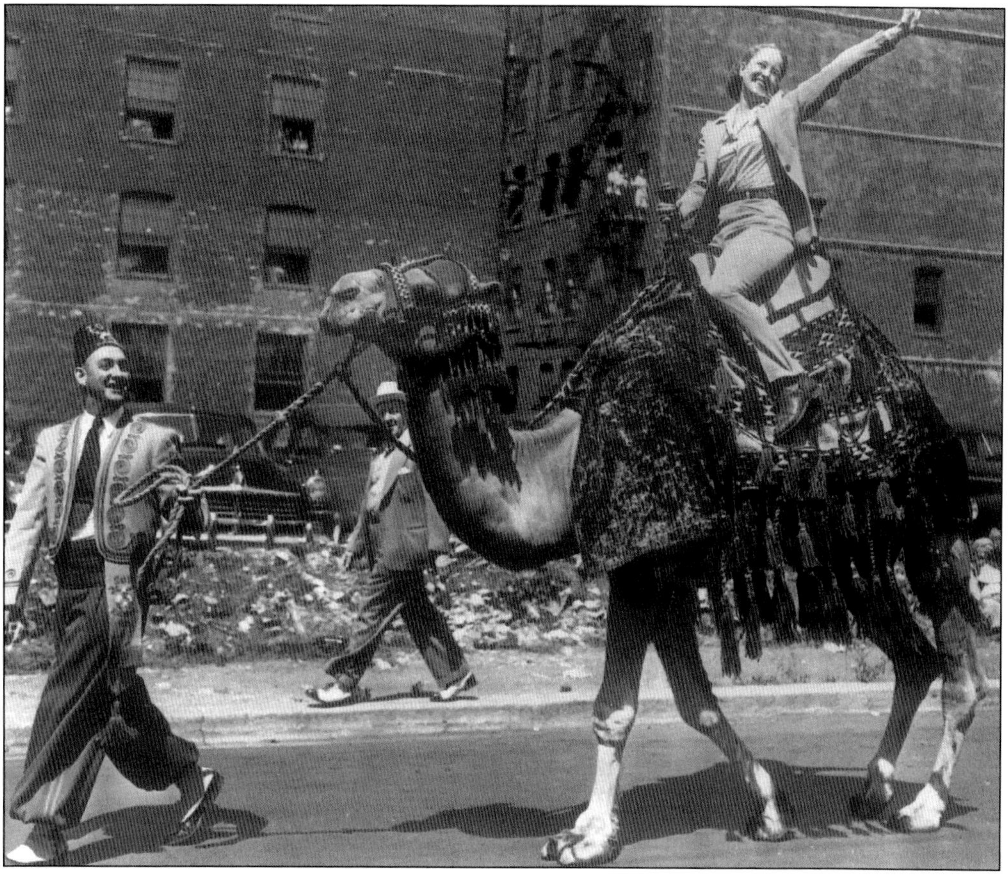

All in a Day's Work: The Duchess rides camel-back in an annual Shriner's parade.

<u>REPORTER TAGS ALONG</u>

This reporter tagged along to gather the data for this series on the little-known activities of Chicago's women of the law. It took the help of three neighbors to lead investigators through the labyrinth of refuse to the loosely-boarded basement coal bin where the five neglected children lived.

Before they reached the dingy hovel, the policewomen had heard a story with a tragic impact that years of repetition never dims. "Their mother spends every cent on liquor," said the neighbors. "All her time is spent chasing men. We want these children taken away from this hole—and from their mother—forever."

<u>'WHAT DOES HONEY MEAN?'</u>

From a concrete pit with a shaky orange crate for a step, a 5-year-old girl crawled out of a pile of ragged bed clothing. Three other children followed her. An infant slept among the rags. "Where's your mother, honey?" asked the Policewomen C, who has six children of her own.

"I don't know," said the little girl. "And what does 'honey' mean?" There was no electricity, and the policewomen lit a candle to examine the filthy bin that was furnished only with packing boxes. Old newspapers and garbage littered the floor. [...]

<u>MOTHER SPRAWLED OUT</u>

Within an hour the policewomen found the mother. She was sprawled drunkenly in a booth at a saloon. Her name was Ruby, but she couldn't answer intelligently. "She's been here all day and all the night before," said the bartender, "Cadging drinks and trying drinks and trying to get men to go home with her." [...]

'APPEARS FEEBLE MINDED'

Judge John R. McSweeney asked her more questions in Municipal Court [the] next day. But she didn't know where she was born, how old she was or whether she had any relatives. "This woman appears to be feeble minded," said the court. "I'm sending her to [a] psychopathic hospital for an examination." The hospital found her sane. Judge McSweeney ordered the children placed in a foster home, and sentenced Ruby to the House of Corrections for contributing to their dependency.

SHE'LL BE OUT SOON

"But she'll be out again soon," Policewomen C remarked bitterly, "free to return to society and foist more fatherless children on the community." Chicago's policewomen will wait for their arrival—and then try to watch over them. [...]

SANTA: MAKE THIS A SPECIAL STOP

By Virginia Marmaduke

12/12/49

Memo to Santa Claus:

If this reaches you before you pack your sleigh, please toss on a few extra presents for a little girl I visited today. She is 3 years old, Santa, and lives on the second floor at 905 W. Concord Pl. Her name is Marguerite Rydlewski, but everybody call her Margie. If ever there was a brave, sweet little girl, Mr. Claus, this is one.

MUST LIE FLAT ON BACK

For seven months she has had to lie flat on her back in bed with her feet tied up in the air. It's a mighty uncomfortable position and you couldn't blame her if she cried and fussed about it. But Margie's mother and dad, Marie and John, say she hasn't caused them a bit of trouble. The neighbors say they've never heard her cry. The milkman and the meter reader say they've never knocked on the apartment door that little Margie hasn't invited them in for a chat. [...]

MAKE IT A LONG STOP

That's why everybody hopes you can make an extra long stop at the Rydlewski home this year, Santa, and drop off any toys you might have left over. She is asking for color books, a doll, some juvenile phonograph records and any game that can be played in bed. She also likes cards with pretty pictures. Maybe some of your helpers can send her Christmas cards. [...]

1950

CHICAGO SUN-TIMES

YUGOSLAV EX-KING PETER HOLDS COURT IN CHICAGO

By Virginia Marmaduke

1/9/50

Ex-King Peter, youthful onetime monarch of Yugoslavia, held court in the Morrison Hotel Sunday, shortly after his arrival from New York. He talked of Tito and the Communists, of his beloved grandmother, the late Queen Marie of Romania, and of the brilliant green necktie he was wearing. He said the cravat was a Christmas gift from his wife, the former Princess Alexander of Greece.

In the Midwest on a speaking tour and to confer with Serbian-American leaders on the disposition of Yugoslav DPs, the exiled monarch will go to St. Sava monastery in Libertyville Monday. He will attend final Christmas mass of the Serbian Eastern Orthodox Church now celebrating its three-day holy season. Tuesday he will address the Kohler (Wis.) Women's Club with what he called a "general, historical lecture on my country." [...]

MARRIAGE CHEATER SOBS AT DEATH TRIAL
By Virginia Marmaduke
1/17/50

Handsome Harvey McDonald, 34, broke down and sobbed loudly at his murder trial Tuesday while testifying how his "weekend sweetheart," Miss Joan Vestal, was shot and killed. On a spectator's bench, McDonald's petite brown-eyed wife, Grace, and two of their six children also were weeping. So overwhelmed did McDonald seem that Judge Leonard C. Reid called a short recess in the trial, before 12 Criminal Court jurors who could send the defendant to the electric chair.

Mrs. McDonald, true to her husband through seven years of philandering, had proceeded him on the witness stand. "I love him and I always will," she testified. "He was good to me and the children. He loves us, too."

GIVES HIS VERSION

McDonald, often told by the girls that he looked like Robert Taylor, the movie actor, then told his version of how Joan died in the apartment they shared weekends. [...]

A—Putting her earrings in a drawer, she then took a revolver out of the drawer. She said: "I'd like to play a little Russian roulette." [...]

Q—What did you do or say?

A—I said: "Don't be silly." She came toward me. We struggled. I don't know whose finger was on the trigger. I heard an explosion and there was blood all over her face. I called for help.

McDonald admitted he first told police that Joan was his wife, and explained that he "was trying to protect her." [...]

One of the most memorable and moving stories of Virginia Marmaduke's reporting career came in 1950.

The State of Illinois had just imposed some drastic cuts in its public aid. The Duchess and her *Sun-Times* editors wanted to know what this really meant to a relief-receiving family. To find out, Virginia moved in for one week with a "relief family," Anna Jacobs, a young widow, and her children. Once again, as is often true in the Duchess's career, here Virginia did not just cover a story but became a part of the story, personalizing it for her readers.

Years later, when Virginia was featured on *This Is Your Life* as the "typical American newspaper woman," the Jacobs Family surprised the Duchess and reminisced with her, and with the nation, about what happened when "Miss Marmaduke" moved in.

Not long after this string of stories were published, the radical cuts by the state were greatly lessened, restoring benefits to thousands of citizens. Most Illinois historians credit that change to Virgina Marmaduke and the *Sun-Times's* newspaper series, "Reporter on Relief."

REPORTER ON RELIEF
Widow's Problem: Child's Heart Must Be Fed
By Virginia Marmaduke
2/20/50

(Reporter Virginia Marmaduke has lived with the Jacobs family on relief. She has shared their stove-heated flat, eaten their food and observed their struggle to survive. This is the first of a series of three eyewitness stories on what the state's cutback in relief funds will mean to 52,000 Chicagoans with no other income.)

It was a major decision for Anna Jacobs, 35. She had to choose between a new hair ribbon for one of her children or another meat ball for the evening meal. Which way should she spend the nickel? Walking through the door of the second floor rear flat at 839 W. 33d was a headlong step into the Jacobs family's struggle to live on relief funds. The mother's dark eyes were mirrored with anguish. A daughter, 7, wiped away tears. Two younger children stood by, quietly. The tearful child had been begging for a new hairbow. It would cost a nickel.

PROBLEM FACED

But to the widow Jacobs, five cents also meant a meatball for the spaghetti supper she could serve her family. She explained the situation, apologetically. Someone had poked fun at the Christmas wrapping ribbon Anna Marie wore as a hairbow. The little girl wanted a real bow, the kind you can buy for a nickel.

"What should I do?" the mother asked. "Feed the child's heart—or stomach?" It was not the only problem I watched Anna Jacobs battle as I lived in her home the next four days. But back at my desk, the plaintive battle of a hair ribbon versus a meatball seems to sum up the basic struggle to make ends meet as a reliefer.

ALLOTMENT CUT

Along with 52,000 other Chicago relief recipients, Anna Jacobs has received a cut in her monthly allotment. The state's February slash in public funds has snatched $14.35 a month from Anna and her children, John Jr., 3; Joan, 5; and Anna Marie, 7.

When I moved in [with] the Jacobs family—to live with them on relief—the Chicago Welfare Department computed my share of the board. The mother must feed me on 41 cents per day. This is what relief allows for an adult female. In addition I got one pint of milk per day through dole tickets.

SAVINGS WIPED OUT

Because Mrs. Jacobs, an American-Lithuanian, is a careful, food-saving cook, I didn't lose any weight. But like her youngsters I soon wished there was enough money for the meals to include some fresh fruits and sweets.

During my first day with the little family on 33d St., the mother revealed some vital statistics. When the father died last May all their saving had been eaten up with his illness. They had never been on relief. It left the widow starting from scratch. Because eligibility for funds from Aid to Dependent Children requires thorough checking and investigating and because birth certificates were not immediately available, the little family's recourse was direct to the Chicago Welfare Department.

TOTAL INCOME, $89.33

Subsequent transferal to ADC rolls may mean a slight increase in Anna Jacobs' allotment, but the state supplemental funds to ADC have also suffered cutbacks. Beginning last May, the widow realized: $72.16 per month from the Federal Old Age Survivor Benefit Insurance, because her husband had made social security payments from his salary during his early years; and $17.17 from state and local funds administered as relief through the Chicago Welfare Department.

But the state's recent slash has snatched $14.35 from Anna Jacobs and her three children. They now get only $2.82 cash from the taxpayers of Illinois and Chicago. Anna pays $20 per month for her humble but comfortable flat. She keeps her light bill to its lowest ebb, around $3.50 a month. By heating only the kitchen she holds coal purchases to 12 sacks (about a bushel each) for a cost of $7.50 a month. A gas stove, for cooking, eats up $1.50 a month.

This leaves Anna Jacobs with approximately $32. It must feed and clothe the four of them for 30 days.

This is why the question of a nickel hairbow has posed a serious problem—and brought tears. What was a struggle before, now looms as an impossibility.

(Tomorrow: Stale bread and hand-me downs.)

REPORTER ON RELIEF

Stale Bread Stretches Food Quota for 4

By Virginia Marmaduke

2/21/50

Some day John, Joan and Marie Jacobs may be able to smile when they tell about how they were raised on stale bread. But right now neither their mother, Anna, 35, nor the youngsters can find anything funny about it.

Stale bread played an important role on the table at 839 W. 33d while I lived on relief with the widow Jacobs. It costs less. Some store managers give it away. We had it for breakfast, dinner and supper in various guises. Dressing up old bread and making hand-me-downs is typical of Mrs. Jacobs' fight for survival. She is trying to raise her little family on relief funds.

'COME AND SEE'

Knowing the state's recent slash in public aid had taken $14.35 from her monthly allotment—leaving only $32 to feed an adult and three children for a month—I knocked on the door of her second floor flat to ask what it was going to mean to her. Nearly 52,000 other Chicagoans are similarly affected.

"Come and live with us a few days," the mother invited. "Then you can see for yourself."

Anna Jacobs is a strong, sensitive, handsome woman of Lithuanian descent. When her husband died last May she thanked God for the few happy years she had known and for the three beautiful children who had blessed their home. Then the struggle began. For the next few years—until the children are old enough for her to leave them to work—she must live on relief.

This is the pattern of life that welfare agencies have set for such a case as hers. Their experience has shown that if a mother in her situation goes to work her expenses for sitters eat up her earnings. The state policy is dictated further by the knowledge that the best interests of the community and the children's welfare are served if the youngsters have association with and supervision of their mother, rather than strangers.

HER BIGGEST PROBLEM

Anna Marie, 7, is in the second grade at St. George's school. Joan, 5, attends kindergarten there. John Jr., 8, is the man of the house.

"I don't have to worry—yet—about clothes for Johnny," the mother explained. "But keeping Anna Marie and Joan presentable so they won't feel the stigma of 'relief' is my biggest problem."

She raised her eyes heavenward when she added that thus far they had all been able to keep healthy. "This new cut has also eliminated medicine money," she reminded. Nothing is ever thrown away by Anna Jacobs. Anna converts bread into French toast, a pie-plate of "fake dressing" made with meat fryings, or bread pudding.

When a friendly clerk gives her a sack of "vegetable shavings" she spends hours paring out the spoiled spots and converts the rest into neck-bone stew or vegetable-barely soup.

'BEST BUY' MEALS

I watched her do her weekend shopping and trudged along as she made preliminary surveys to find the stores with the best prices. After careful figuring, she decided stewing chickens were Saturday's best buy. The store we were in offered old hens at 29 cents per pound.

But Anna thought there was another store—four blocks away—that might do better on chickens, so we walked to it. Sure enough, their hens were 28 cents a pound and Anna selected one that cost $1.05. "This will make three meals for us," she explained. "First I boil the pieces and save the broth for soup. We have the better pieces with dressing, then chicken and dumplings the next day." This is the way Anna Jacobs stretches a $1.05 meat purchase to three meals for her family.

GIRLS SHARE COAT

She works the same miracles on clothing with old items, contributed by good neighbors and friends. One friend brings unwanted scraps from a factory where she works. The cotton pieces are turned into pinafores, pajamas and petticoats for her little girls. Woolen scraps are patched together for comforters, badly needed in the unheated bedroom.

There's one doll in the household. It is nameless so that the one playing with it can call it whatever she wants. There's also one presentable winter coat between the two little girls. They take turns wearing it on special occasions. "This is the difference between living and living-on-relief," the mother said. "I don't think anybody in the world would choose it, if there were a choice."

(Tomorrow: Even a 'Reliefer' can dream.)

REPORTER ON RELIEF
Family's One Luxury—Daydreaming
2/22/50

(Reporter Virginia Marmaduke lived with the Jacobs family on relief to observe their struggle to survive. This concludes her eyewitness series.)

The only extravagance Anna Jacobs permits in her household-on-relief is daydreaming. Huddled around the coal stove in their kitchen, second floor rear at 839 W. 33d, I heard the mother and the three children tell their dreams to each other. I felt privileged to listen.

"It won't always be like this," the mother began. "When you children get old enough I can get a job. I am strong. I can earn enough so that we won't have to be on relief."

A RIBBON, A COAT

Anna Marie, 7, had her dreams: "Then I can have a new hair-ribbon every month, maybe."

Joan, brown-eyed, 5-year-old pixie, had an equally feminine objective: "I'll have a coat all my own—a new one."

Johnny Jr. jabbered about kitties and the zoo. "He means there'll be carfare so that we can go to Lincoln Park every Sunday afternoon and see the tigers," the mother interpreted.

This was my last night living with the widow Jacobs and her children to observe, first-hand, their battle to live on the new, state-slashed relief funds. The mother had dropped the formal "Miss Marmaduke" and was calling me "Virginia." The children were taking turns sitting next to me during meals. I was one of them. And they were not afraid to dream in front of me.

"I read every horoscope and fortune-telling game I can find," the 35-year-old mother confided. "When I find one that tells me things are going to be better for us, I try to believe it."

Our confidences deepened. "I might even remarry if some nice man would want us," she said. "I could make a good home for him in return for his taking the children."

MANY SHARE PLIGHT

There are 52,000 Chicago relief recipients sharing Anna Jacobs' struggle to make ends meet on relief funds. When the state recently slashed its public fund, it took $14.35 from Anna's February allotment. All others suffered similarly.

"I'll keep on trying," Anna concluded. "But I don't see how we can make it." It was nearing bedtime. The coal had burned out. I was going to watch Anna put the little ones to bed and then say my good-by. Four days before, when I walked into the Jacobs home, I had found tears because there wasn't an extra nickel for a new hair-ribbon for Anna Marie. There were tears in my own eyes when I heard the little ones say their prayers. Always the ending was one they had adopted during the war. It was: "And please, God, bless America."

POLICE ALERT HOSPITAL TO AID BLAST VICTIMS

By Virginia Marmaduke

5/26/50

St. Bernard's Hospital was just settling down for the evening when a police ambulance, its siren screaming shrilly, skidded to a halt at the emergency door. Tonsillectomy patients who could be moved were asked to go home so their beds might be used for the injured. All cots that had been stored were brought out.

HYSTERIA SUBSIDES

The staff moved swiftly but with a quiet efficiency as the injured poured in. Even the most critically burned seemed affected by the calm handling and their hysteria subsided as they were brought into the hospital.

Within 30 minutes, the foyer of the hospital was filled with more than 100 persons anxiously seeking information about relatives or friends they feared were caught in the explosion. They kept their voices low in almost a reverent tone. From one end of the foyer a statue of Christ looked down and several in the room crossed themselves as they looked up.

SWITCHBOARD SWAMPED

The girls at the information desk answered their questions quickly and politely, and the crowd began to thin out within an hour. But phone calls continued to come in and several hours later the switchboard still was swamped as relatives inquired about loved ones who were feared injured.

St. Bernard's took care of the largest group of the injured. Similar scenes on a lesser scale were enacted at other hospitals in the area. Two persons, moaning from the pain of severe burns, were brought in on stretchers and a policeman said: "There must be another 100 up the street. A streetcar just hit a gasoline truck." [...]

PRIVATE EYE'S SPICY STORY
By Virginia Marmaduke
10/28/50

Champagne parties, swimming pool debauches, stolen embraces in the back seat of an auto and eventual hotel room trysts. These were the high points of a courtroom narrative by a private investigator employed by J. Leslie Younghusband to shadow his wife whom he suspected of infidelity.

Robert Parsells, personable young detective of the M.F. Smith National Detective Agency of Miami, Fla., told the spicy incidents before Circuit Court Judge Daniel A. Roberts Friday. It was the second day of the 54-year-old cosmetic king's hearing to determine whether he has grounds upon which to charge adultery in his divorce suit against his fifth wife, Mary Louise, 34.

'SHOCKING PINK' SUIT

Also competing for star billing in the courtroom drama were the respective attorneys, Samuel Rinella for Mrs. Younghusband and Taylor Wilhelm for her husband. Mrs. Younghusband participated as a feature witness, chic in a dressmaker suit that would be called "shocking pink" in nail lacquer vernacular.

Natty in a solid blue suit and maroon tie, her spouse watched the proceedings from a front row seat in the spectators' section. When he twice jumped to his feet to interrupt the proceedings, Judge Roberts ordered him to sit down and threatened contempt action if he continued.

She told how she had dinner with Frank Marlin, another detective, and then coffee in his room at the Blackstone Hotel to try to obtain a "report" he was preparing for her husband. Then Mrs. Younghusband had to sit for two hours and listen to another private eye's story of how she cavorted around a Miami, Fla. hotel in a manner which he said was unbecoming a young matron. [...]

ONE BUILDING IS CROSSROADS FOR A NATION
By Virginia Marmaduke
11/12/50

Can you guess where you are sitting from the following description? You are in a two-block long auditorium. The ceiling is 110 ft. high. There are 20 massive stone columns, each five feet in diameter, towering around you. From the top of two of them, huge statues look down upon the more than 65,000 people who tread this floor daily. Their names are "Dawn" and "Dusk." In this massive setting travelers from the east meet travelers from the west daily.

Did you say it's Union Station?

LARGEST IN THE WORLD

If you did, you are right. This sprawling building of stone and marble is the largest railroad depot in the world, in [terms] of single floor space. It spreads from Jackson to Adams, north and south, and from Clinton to the river on the east and west.

More than 300 trains a day pull in and out of its sheds. They bring travelers from Canada and Florida. They connect for transcontinental passengers from coast to coast. To many weary travelers, Union Station is more than a depot. "It's a national landmark to me," said Mrs. Anna May Goodyear, 27, of Yakima, Wash. "I have crossed the continent eight times and to me, this is the nicest, friendliest depot." [...]

W.F. Carlson, master of Union Station, said management of the huge depot presented many problems since most of its guests were such short-time visitors.

MINIATURE CITY

"But we've tried to meet all the reasonable demands a traveler might have," he explained. "And we think we have a miniature city all under our one roof." He said it cost $1,000 per day for the housekeeping department alone, with more than 100 persons constantly "sweeping, scrubbing and shining." "Think what it means," he said, "if each of the 65,000 persons we serve daily should toss away just one cigarette or match or chewing gum wrapper."

PART IN GRAND OPERA—A SUPER EXPERIENCE

By Virginia Marmaduke

11/19/50

Want to get out of this world for a few hours? Want to soar into a fascinating realm of make believe and actually become a breathing part of it all? Here's how: Get a job as a supernumerary in one of the operas now being presented in the current season at the Chicago Opera House.

"Supers" is operatic slang for persons [who are] not regular actors, but employed to appear in mob scenes or spectacular settings. On Hollywood movie lots they call them extras. I became a super so that SUN-TIMES *readers could get a first hand report on how it feels to do a part in grand opera.*

<u>MORE THAN 100 APPLY</u>

I was one of more than 100 applying for the 26 super jobs in the production of "Carmen." But it was first come, first served and I was lucky enough to have been early. I was honest with the man in charge of supers. I told him it would be my first experience.

"I think you'll do," said Ralph Spears of the New York Metropolitan Co., producers of the opera series. "Your eyes are dark. You'll make a good gypsy." I was early at the 20 N. Wacker stage door entrance to the Civic Opera House. It gave me some time for a visit with William Wright, 60, the doorman. [...]

There are two other women supers and 21 men. We women were to be gypsy peasants. The men were to portray soldiers, pirates and picadors of the bullfighting arena. A notice on the bulletin board said we were to report to the wardrobe lady on the fourth floor. She was gray-haired Mrs. Christine Martin, in her sixth season as dispenser of costumes for the New York company.

Mrs. Martin gave us two skirts, white peasant-necked blouses and gay kerchiefs we were to tie around our waists. The shorter skirt was for early scenes when we were to be cigarette girls working in a factory alongside the sultry Carmen. The long skirts changed us into spectators at the bull fight in the final act.

<u>GETS MADE UP</u>

Then came a short session with Michael Aranshky, head make-up man for the company. He patted greasepaint onto my face and ordered me to relax as he drew more distinct eyebrows and lips. An internationally known pantomimist, he often joins the cast on the stage for special character roles.

Then came a call over the loud speaker systems: "Supers on stage." [...] The orchestra began the stirring movements of "Carmen." The house lights went low. The mammoth curtain was drawn up. The show was on. There I was, all decked up in greasepaint, wearing a gay gypsy costume. There were glorious voices all around me. I was part of the torrid, tempestuous love story of Carmen, the little gamin who made men's blood boil. I forgot there were a possible 6,000 eyes staring at me. We were in a world of our own on the huge stage.

I was part of grand opera. It was SUPER.

In late 1950, in an attempt to personalize (or in the case of the Duchess, further personalize) some of their reporters, the *Sun-Times* ran a series of stories in its pages each profiling different reporters on its staff. And first up was Virginia Marmaduke.

MEET THE WOMAN BEHIND THE BYLINE OF...VIRGINIA MARMADUKE

12/18/50

No girl graduate, new to newspapering, views her job with more enthusiasm than SUN-TIMES *Reporter Virginia Marmaduke still displays after years of covering the news.*

One of the reasons for that enthusiasm is her genuine interest in people and the things that happen to them—and each new assignment gives this vigorous, friendly woman a chance to observe another intriguing quirk of human nature—

Born in Carbondale, Ill., and reared in Chicago, Virginia Marmaduke attended Walter Scott grammar school and Hyde Park High School. The pleasure she found in going places and meeting people as a reporter for the high school weekly influenced her in favor of a newspaper career. After two years at the University of

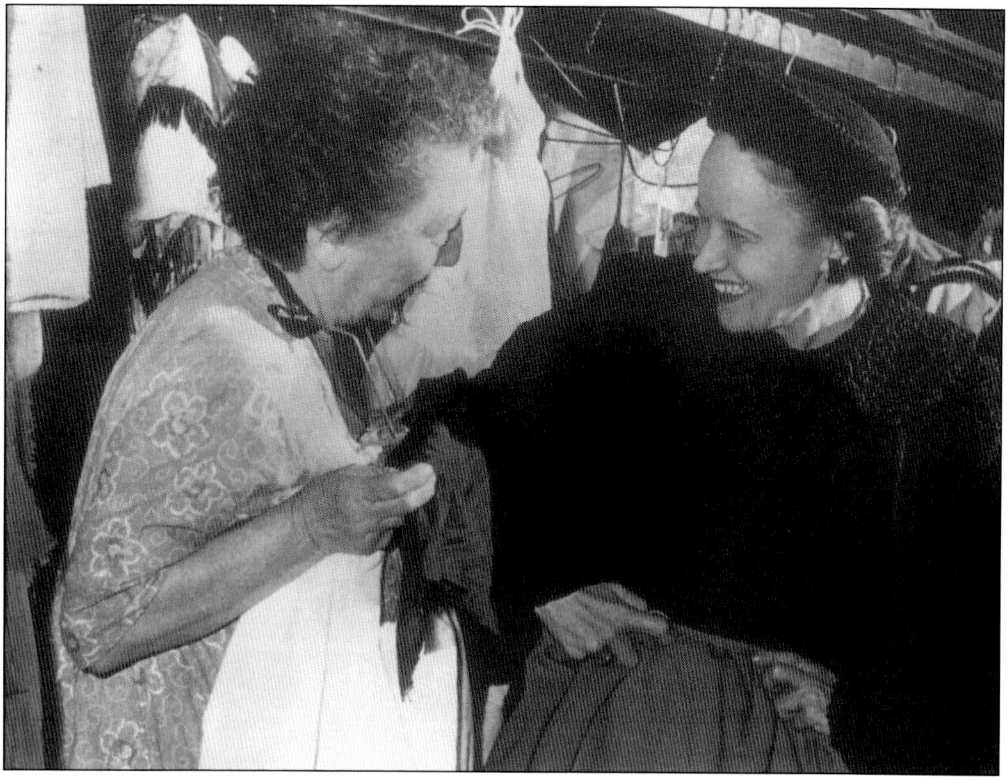

Meeting with the wardrobe mistress for her role as a "super" in a Chicago opera.

Chicago, she went on to major in journalism at the University of Iowa, Iowa City, where she served as a staffer on the school's Daily Iowan.

Her first postgraduate job was with the Daily Journal in the coal-mining town of Herrin, Ill. As time passed, she obtained extra work for two press services as a "stringer"—an occasional correspondent who periodically clips and pastes into one long column all the items that have been accepted and published, and is paid according to the length of the "string."

She also become a special correspondent for the St. Louis Star-Times. *Through constant practice, she sharpened her powers of observation. Over the years she has whetted them on assignments ranging from garden parties to electrocutions.*

Some of her stories in The SUN-TIMES *have had heart-warming sequels. In 1944, following her series of articles on the plight of children with cerebral palsy, the state legislature appropriated funds for the establishment of Illinois Children's Home Hospital—the state's first institution created specifically to meet the need of these unfortunate youngsters.*

As the result of an assignment at La Rabida Jackson Park Sanitarium she became deeply interested in the research program there to help child victims of rheumatic heart disease. She has since done much to further that work through her stories in The SUN-TIMES *as well as through her private efforts.*

A skilled horsewoman, Miss Marmaduke worked as a professional rider at horse shows during her high school and college years. She still rides for recreation. When she joined this newspaper in 1941 [sic], an editor learned of her equestrienne ability. From time to time since then she has been assigned to stories involving riding a varied assortment of animals—including a camel, a policeman's horse and an elephant.

Applying the reporter's principle of "see for yourself," she recently lived with a relief family to experience the pinching effects of a cut in relief checks. After publication of her articles in The SUN-TIMES, *the cuts were partially restored. Again, to get the true picture of the civic and social problems created by Chicago's wayward girls, she spent nine days as a policewoman assigned to the women's lockup, juvenile investigation and pickpocket details.*

Combining keen insight and close observation, Virginia Marmaduke's writing makes interesting, lively reading. Watch for stories under her byline in The Chicago SUN-TIMES. *You'll enjoy them.*

1951

From time to time, Virginia Marmaduke's career would intersect with aspects of her personal life. This was certainly true when she reported on the 100th birthday of the Illinois Central railroad, the company where her father was employed for over 53 years.

CHICAGO SUN-TIMES

I.C. CELEBRATION TO MARK FOUNDING 100 YEARS AGO

By Virginia Marmaduke

1/7/51

In the bells and whistles of a railroad that slices through the heartland of the Midwest there may be detected (with a little imagination) next month the strains of "Happy Birthday."

February will mark the beginning of a year-long celebration of the 100th anniversary of the founding of the Illinois Central R.R. The dramatic story of its growth is also the story of the rise of Chicago and the Midwest to greatness, and in the pages of the I.C.'s sage, are found the names of giants of Illinois and the nation.

BIG BANQUET PLANNED

Chicago is the headquarters of the system and one of the big events of the centennial year will be a banquet Feb. 16 at the Palmer House. Attending will be 1,000 representatives of business, industry, the arts and science and politics. They will pay tribute to the Illinois Central for its contribution to Mid-America. They will honor the men who laid the first rails, and those who now operate the streamlined speedsters. During the year, on-the-line birthday parties will be held in 150 communities in the 14 states served by the road. [...]

PUBLIC SEES COLOR TELEVISION; 1,000 JAM FIRST SHOWING

By Virginia Marmaduke

1/11/51

Crowds poured in Thursday for their first glimpse of color television after initial public showings brought a warm and friendly response from Chicagoans. "First-nighters" Wednesday night included housewives, businessmen and youngsters. Even a blind boy made a special trip to the preview because he wanted to be "in on the thrill of it." They jammed the lobby of the Wrigley Building an hour before the showings at the Columbia Broadcasting System's main floor studio.

SHOW TO CONTINUE

By the end of the two-hour free showing more than 1,000 persons had filed past the demonstration, spending a few minutes before five receivers. Each used the color TV system recently approved by the Federal Communications Commission as standard for color broadcasting. [...]

Mrs. Michael Waters, 3400 S. Union, housewife, liked the natural colors on the packages shown in the commercial advertisements. [...]

Lance Vaughter, 5, and his brother, Dick, 12, of 9943 Prairie, were there with their mother. "I don't know how it was done, sons," she told them, "but this is it and maybe we can some day have it like this in our own living room."

"I want to know the color of Howdy Doody's eyes," Lance said.

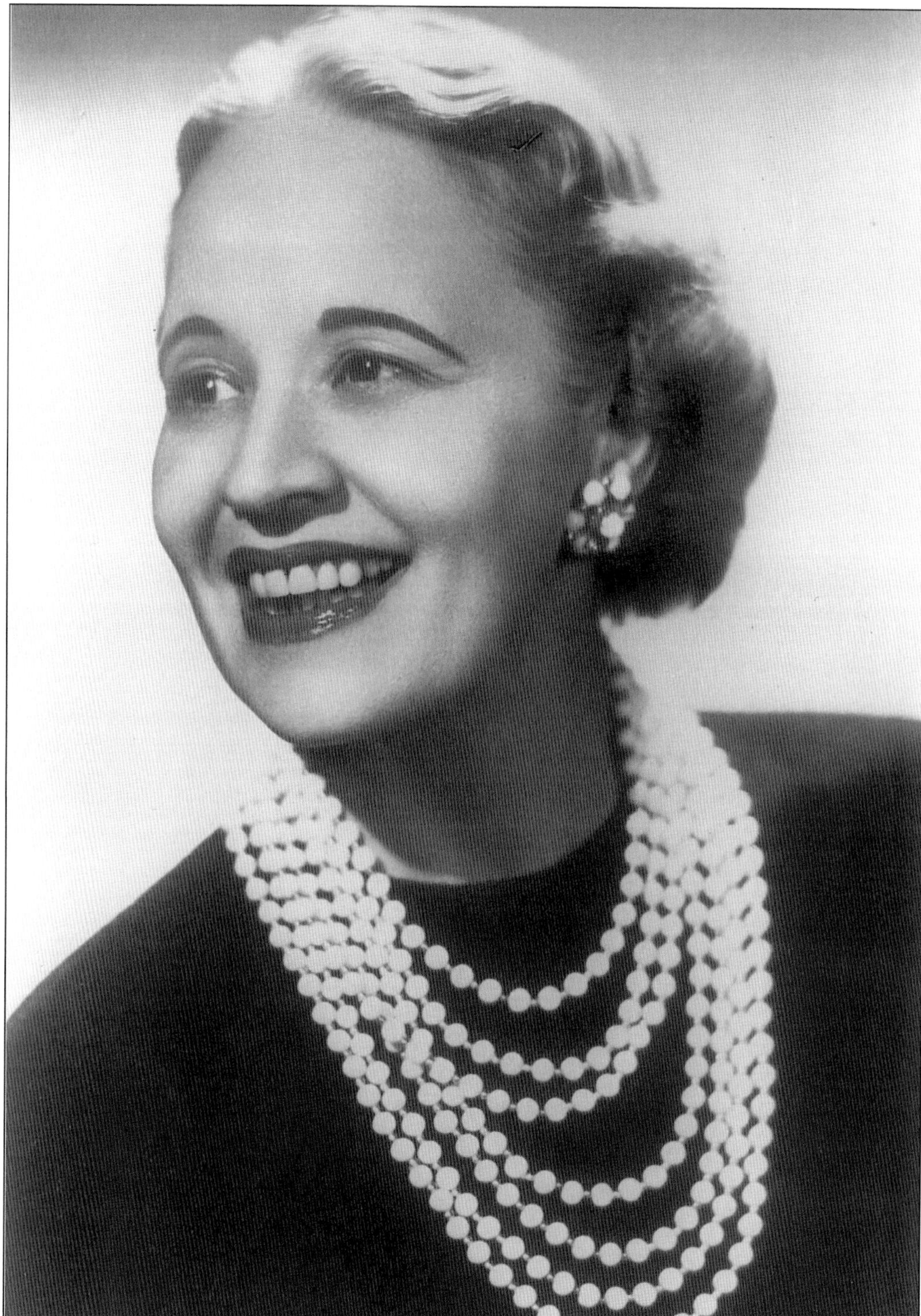

A mid-career portrait.

HONOR MISS MARMADUKE

2/5/51

Virginia Marmaduke, SUN-TIMES *reporter, will be among five Chicago newspaper women honored at Northwestern University Tuesday for "consistently fine performances in journalism." The awards will be presented during a dinner meeting of Theta Sigma Phi, women's journalism honorary society.*

TRUMAN LOAD GREATEST IN HISTORY—MRS. F.D.R.

By Virginia Marmaduke

2/17/51

A woman who should know said Friday that President Truman is carrying the "greatest load in history" and that when persons criticize him they also should remember the tremendous responsibility he must shoulder.

The speaker was Mrs. Franklin D. Roosevelt, in Chicago to address a "Salute to Roosevelt College" dinner at the Congress Hotel.

Her defense of President Truman's personal actions came when she was asked how she felt about his letter-writing and name-calling.

<u>'IT'S UNFORTUNATE'</u>

"It's unfortunate when anyone feels the strain so greatly that he loses the ability to think through the effects of what he says, but when you talk about the President of the United States, remember he is carrying the greatest load in history."

Asked if she thought Mr. Truman was faced with more problems than any other President, she replied:

"I do." [...]

SIX ROSIE THE RIVETERS OF WORLD WAR II GIVE KID SISTERS DEFENSE JOB HINTS

By Virginia Marmaduke

3/27/51

Settle back with that second cup of coffee, Mrs. Housewife. And you, Miss Career Girl, read on as you ride to work. This is the story of what may be a "new YOU" if the present national emergency continues. You may be asked to exchange your aprons and white collars for assembly line coveralls. Your next job might be in a war plant.

Joseph Borus, regional director at the U.S. Bureau of Employment Security, says an estimated 18,800 additional women workers will be needed in the Chicago area by May 15. With continued Selective Service withdrawals and further expansion of the defense program, more women may be needed later.

This means you may find yourselves in entirely new surroundings. Will you know how to act? What to wear? How to avoid the plant wolf?

* * *

To help you get off to the right start, six Chicago Rosies of yesterday have agreed on some straight-from-the-shoulder advice. Their first commandment: "Leave the sexy smiles and the tight sweaters at home and learn early in your job to squelch the factory wolf."

Florence Kramer, now 31, was one of the beauties behind a badge at Acme Steel's Archer Av. aircraft plant. The plant wolves, she now recalls, approached often and avidly. "My first answer to any romantic proposition was that I was married," she said. "When some of the would-be Romeos still persisted and tried to tell me that my husband was in the Navy far, far away I fixed them with a stern stare and said: 'Yes, and that's where you ought to be too!'" That, she found, usually shut them up. Mrs. Kramer now lives—and very happily, thank you—with her Navy veteran husband at 6405 S. Seeley.

MEET THE GENERAL'S LADY
By Virginia Marmaduke
4/26/51

A petite, dark-eyed woman with a flashing smile will reign as Chicago's No. 1 glamour guest Thursday when the city roars a Midwest welcome to her hero husband. She is Jean Marie MacArthur, 52, wife of the famous general. While eyes may first seek the general, the second glance will surely go to the gracious woman who has shared his life for 14 years.

MRS. WOOD AT SIDE

Riding with Mrs. MacArthur from the airport and during the parade will be Mrs. Robert E. Wood, wife of the chairman of the welcoming committee. The two women have much in common. Both married West Point graduates; both are Southern born. The former Jean Faircloth, Mrs. MacArthur is from Tennessee. The former Mary Butler Hardwick, Mrs. Wood was born in Georgia.

Gen. and Mrs. MacArthur spent their honeymoon in the Phillipines where he was serving. Wood, who retired from the Army as a brigadier general and is now board chairman of Sears, Roebuck & Co. and his bride spent their honeymoon in the Panama Canal Zone where he was in command.

SHUNS LIMELIGHT

Unless Jean MacArthur changes her pattern, she will wear a smile as she shares Chicago's welcome but she will shun the limelight in favor of her husband. In San Francisco, Washington and New York, she was constantly at the general's side but managed to evade quietly the illuminating spotlight. Thus far her public appearance wardrobe has been confined to two ensembles, a purple suit and dark fur scarf and a red wool suit. Weighing scarcely 100 pounds, she dresses simply but well.

The MacArthurs will occupy the Royal Skyway Suite on the 23rd floor of the Stevens Hotel.

GOLDEN JUBILEE
Touring Movie Stars Greeted by Stevenson
By Virginia Marmaduke
10/9/51

SPRINGFIELD—Movietime, U.S.A. came to Illinois Monday, beginning a week-long observance of the motion picture industry's golden jubilee.

Gov. Stevenson greeted a bevy of Hollywood stars and personalities at a breakfast in the Leland Hotel.

"Illinois is glad to congratulate the movie industry on its 50th birthday," he told them. "There is an importance and an urgency in this means of communication which can wield such a great power for good in the propaganda battle."

KAYE HEADS GROUP

Heading the Illinois Hollywood contingent is comedian Danny Kaye, spokesman for the visiting celebrities. Others include producer William Perlberg; writer-director George Seaton; actors Otto Krueger and Paul Harvey and actresses Nancy Davis [later Nancy Reagan], Susan Cabot, Sally Eilers, Alice Kelley, Barbara Hale and Bill Williams. [...]

$1,800 REWARD IS OFFERED FOR BABY'S RETURN
By Virginia Marmaduke
10/16/51

A belief that the kidnapper singled out Lawrence James Lyons because he was the "prettiest baby" in the nursery was advanced Monday by Michigan City (Ind.) police. Meanwhile, 2,000 residents began an intensive search of the city and surrounding area for the infant.

The baby was kidnapped from his crib in St. Anthony's Hospital last Saturday, when he was only 4 days old. A reward fund which quickly jumped to $1,800 was offered for the baby's "safe and immediate" return.

At the hospital, nurses and attendants who had been around the fourth floor nursery Saturday were given lie tests because of what police called "muddled stories." The tests are expected to take two days and the results will not be announced until they are over. [...]

MYSTERIOUS VISITOR

A nurse's aid, Miss Marlene Lubds, told police that about 4:15 p.m. Saturday someone had asked to be shown the Lyons infant, calling for him by crib number. She said she was too busy to notice if it was a man or a woman.

The mother, Frances, 37, also leaned toward the police theory that the kidnapping was done by someone wanting a baby, and not for ransom. In her 10-room, white shingle home at 616 Wabash, in Michigan City, Mrs. Lyons said: "The longer my baby is missing, the more I am sure that someone who loves babies has taken him."

She said she felt that whoever has the baby "must have just wanted such a pretty child."

'BRING HIM HOME'

"I feel sure that whoever has him wouldn't want to harm him. Please be good to him. Bring him home and I'll never hold any bitterness." She said the three doors to her house would be left open every night. She pleaded with the kidnapper to place the infant inside one and "leave without any questions asked." [...]

SUN-TIMES PHONES: TO ALL MANILA
'Pin Baby OK'
By Virginia Marmaduke
11/7/51

Elvira Difuntorum, the Filipino "pincushion" baby, was the star of another modern-age thriller Tuesday night when The SUN-TIMES *phoned her parents in Manila to tell them "all is well."*

The 11-month-old child was flown 8,000 miles to have two pins she had swallowed removed from her body.

One had lodged in her lung. A doctor at St. Luke's Hospital here removed it in a 59-second operation, with a bronchoscope Tuesday morning. The second pin, in her stomach, passed out naturally. By mid-afternoon Tuesday the brown-eyed child was sitting up in bed, delighted with the snow falling outside her window. It was the first she had ever seen. These were the heart-warming things her parents were told over the transoceanic radio telephone with the help of everybody along the way.

Standing by at the North Central Hospital in Manila, the father, Petra, talked for himself and his wife, both of whom speak English. [...]From Chicago the call moved to Oakland, Calif. There it was sent over to Manila.

'OAKLAND CALLING'

"Hello, Manilla...Oakland calling the residence of Petra Difuntorum, please." There was a pause.

"We have no listing for the name of Difuntorum, operator, but could this call possibly have to do with our pin baby?" The Oakland operator had been filled in on the background of the call.

"Yes, Manilla, we want to talk to the baby's parents." Manilla's Filipino operator had anxiety in her voice.

"Please, Oakland, I must know...the pin in the baby's lung—is she out?"

"Oakland" answered with a smile with her voice. "Yes, Manila, the baby is all right now." [...]

Within a few minutes, the Manila operator had located Elvira's parents. They had been waiting at a Manila hospital for further word on their daughter. Taking up where the father left off, a hospital spokesman asked to add his thanks to the people of Chicago. "Manila thanks you," he said. "Our citizens financed the baby's fight through public contribution. Everybody has had an interest in Elvira's case." [...]

LOVE AND KISSES TO 23

Lift From Korea Helps Little Girl Fight Illness

By Virginia Marmaduke

11/11/51

The 23 boys of Navy Fighter Squadron 874 can't look in on the joy they have brought to a sick little girl at 6833 Calumet. They are too busy in Korea, flying combat missions from the aircraft carrier USS Bon Homme Richard.

But they weren't too busy to take a 9-year-old girl to their hearts when they read in The SUN-TIMES *Chicago Briefs column about her lonely, sad grey eyes and her battle with rheumatic fever. Nor was* The SUN-TIMES *too busy to act as go-between, as requested by the boys in a letter to this newspaper. "Please deliver this package to Sharon," they asked. "Then tell us all about how she acted when she opened it."*

<u>SITTING UP IN BED</u>

Well, here it is boys: Sharon was sitting up in bed, three pillows at her back. She had pale-blue ribbon bows on her braids and looked as pretty as a picture although her heart is still very weak. We read her your letter to [the SUN-TIMES*] first so she would know where we come in.*

Then we read the letter you wrote to her. She hugged your squadron picture to her cheek and kissed it as she heard that you had named one of your fighting Corsairs after her and have inscribed her name on its nose.

Then came the opening of the packages. She opened the dainty, white satin box first. When she saw the two pairs of luxurious Oriental pajamas with robe to match, her gray eyes sparkled like diamonds. [...] Then came the big, wooden box—the one you had instructed us so carefully how to open. She pulled back the sliding top and cautiously removed the paper packing. Out came the big, gorgeous geisha girl doll.

"She's beautiful and I love her already," Sharon said. Then she asked again the kind of plane you fellows had named after her.

<u>NAMES HER DOLL</u>

"That's it," she decided. "I will name my doll Corsair."

We let Sharon's mother, Helen, read your note attached to the money order for $18.75. The mother cried a bit as she told Sharon that you sent it for a defense bond. But soon all was gay again. Sharon's happiness was infectious. Only one thing bothers her, boys. She isn't able to write her thanks to you. Even that is too strenuous for her present condition.

Once again you'll have to let The SUN-TIMES *carry a message for you. "Tell them I love them each and every one," Sharon said. "Tell them when I get well I will bake some cookies and send to them." And then, shyly, "I wish I could give them each a big kiss and hug."*

1952

<u>CHICAGO SUN-TIMES</u>

COUNSEL FOR PARENTS

Petting, Going Steady Are Teen-Age Dating Problems

By Virginia Marmaduke

1/28/52

Into the life of every boy and girl comes a time when they must learn to get along with the other sex. Usually the first time in this teen-age transition is dating. Before the mysterious transformation, boys think of girls as creatures to be pursued only for the purpose of teasing. Girls whisper and giggle about boys but admit no interest in them—even to each other.

THEN COMES A CHANGE. The boys still chase the girls. The girls still run away. But their hearts aren't in their work. The girls run while looking backwards, hoping they'll be caught. Soon the youngsters are purposely sitting next to each other at the Saturday movie matinee. The ice is broken. Boy-girl friendships begin.

After that problems come swiftly—both for the adolescent and the parent. The two biggest questions are: What about "going steady"? What about petting?

WRITING IN A NEW BOOKLET, issued by Science Research Associates [...] Edith G. Neisser counsels on these problems. [...] "Parents often object to the going-steady situation," she begins. "Some warn their offspring it's like putting all their eggs in one basket." But to the high school boy and girl, going steady spells no more than social security, no last-minute scrambling for dates, she believes. Furthermore, going steady means one at a time, she adds—not one forever.

Thus, trying to break up a devoted friendship between two young people—solely on the grounds that they must have wider associations—is not always wise, Mrs. Neisser cautions.

MUCH MORE DISTURBING, Mrs. Neisser warns, are the current customs about petting. How can we give our children the guidance that they need—and how can we help them to understand and control their sexual feelings? First, Mrs. Neisser states, we might as well admit that kissing and caressing are "natural" and "unavoidable" expressions of sincere affection for someone of the opposite sex. "The difficulty, as young people need to understand [it]," she writes, "is in keeping these expressions at a manageable level." [...]

FETED AT LUNCHEON
Mother Award Goes To Busy Homemaker
By Virginia Marmaduke
5/2/52

A busy homemaker who scraped 890 hours from her family responsibilities and offered them in volunteer service to the Logan Square Chicago Boys Club is Chicago's 1952 Mother of the Year.

Named Thursday at the State Street Council's sixth annual Volunteer Awards luncheon at the Palmer House was Mrs. Marie Liermann, 48 [...]. Mrs. Liermann was chosen from five finalists, narrowed from more than 100 candidates representing Chicago's 141,000 registered volunteer workers. [...]

<u>HEADS MOTHERS' CLUB</u>

The award to Mrs. Liermann was based on her "consistent, dependable service" to the Logan Square Boys Club. She is now in her second year as president of its Mother's club. She supervises the cooking and sells meals at the club, directs fund drives and conducts a boys' cooking class.

When she isn't holding sway in the club's kitchen, she is busy at home taking care of the needs of three sons and a husband. Louis Liermann, retail meat dealer and two of her sons, Jim, 17, and Tom, 14, were present to see their "Mom" receive her award, a hand-tooled gold pin set with a diamond. [...]

Having attended Hyde Park High for her freshman and sophomore years of high school, the story below was something of a homecoming for Virginia.

A BALMY DAY ON THE CAMPUS
Hyde Park Students Muse, Elect A 'Brainy' Beauty
By Virginia Marmaduke
5/19/52

Letting their fancies turn to spring, Hyde Park High School youths have lifted a pretty, dark-haired senior girl student to an unofficial pedestal. At the same time they defied other Chicago area high schools to try to match their "brainy beauty" in senior classes.

The fanciful "election" was a part of a dreamy noon-hour in Jackson Park, a handy campus to the big, South Side school [...]. The boys were taking about "queens," the movie star and the Atlantic City type and the kind selected to reign over conventions. Soon their talk drew closer to home. They decided there were a lot of girls in their school that could outshine "those synthetic" beauty queens.

Mulling over possible candidates, they decided: "We all ought to agree on one out-standing girl. We could call her queen of the Hyde Park 1952 graduating class and then invite other schools to see if they can match her."

CHOICE NARROWS

They picked a field of six girls, all of whom had been some kind of a queen during the school year at Hyde Park. Finally the boys agreed on a pert, dark-haired girl whose school activities have made her widely known throughout the 3,000 student body.

She is Francine Hokin, 17, president of the Senior Girls Club and as smart as she is pretty. She has been a member of the school's scholastic honor society all four years and has served as president during her senior year.

Ralph Rehbock, 17,[...] was one of Francine's loudest praise agents. "I've been Francine's classmate since we began at Kenwood grade school," he explained. "She's easily been the prettiest girl in class. But what I like best about her is the way she never shirked a job." He was the one who suggested her title to be "Hyde Park's brainy beauty." [...]

BOOM FOR LADY VEEP SOUNDS GOOD TO CONVENTION PETTICOAT POLITICIANS
By Virginia Marmaduke
7/21/52

Two women candidates for the Democratic vice presidential nomination were being talked up along convention corridors and hotel lobbies Sunday. Mrs. India Edwards, one of the possibilities, said it was good gossip—the kind women everywhere ought to be glad to hear. Mrs. Edwards is a petticoat power in Democratic political circles. She is a vice chairman of the Democratic National Committee and director of the Women's Division.

BOOM TAKES JUDGES

Also being boomed as a distaff candidate for the second highest job in the U.S. is District Judge Sarah T. Hughes of Dallas, Tex., a past national president of the Federation of Business and Professional Women's Clubs.

A headquarters for India Edwards-for-vice-president has been opened at the Conrad Hilton, but without her official sanction. Judge Hughes' candidacy has gone no further than a telegraphed recommendation to Texas delegates by Mrs. Vera Norman of Des Moines, president of the Iowa B.& R.W. state organization.

THINKS TALK IS FINE

Mrs. Edwards said she is not campaigning for herself nor any other candidate since it would be "unethical" in view of her position with the party. But as an individual woman in politics she thinks talk of a lady Veep is fine. "This is groundwork for the future," she prophesied. "It may be mostly talk now but when it comes up at future conventions—and it will—the thought of a woman vice president won't be such as shock."

Judge Hughes also feels she is lending her name primarily as spadework for her sex. "I'm not so naive as to believe we will have a woman vice president this year," she said. "But we do have to get into the political arena—and fight." [...]

81ST ANNIVERSARY
Great 1871 Fire Memories Still Burning Here
By Virginia Marmaduke
10/8/52

This is the day when the wail of a fire engine siren may bring back frightening memories to pioneer Chicagoans. It is the 81st anniversary of the Great Chicago Fire, the flaming destroyer that killed 300 persons and left more than one-fourth of the city's population homeless.

Some native Chicago octogenarians may remember their parents herding them from their homes as the spreading conflagration came nearer on that dreaded October night. Others may recall a flame-filled sky which they watched from the safety of an out-of-range rooftop. To many descendants of early Chicagoans, the anniversary of the fire will revive memories of "the stories grandma and grandpa used to tell."

ORIGIN OF MYSTERY

More than 17,000 buildings were leveled. Some which survived still carry the scars of the intense heat which scorched and seared as the fire burned itself out. More than 90,000 of the city's 335,000 population were without homes. Many lived in makeshift hideouts for days, unable to return to the site of their former homes because of hot embers. The origins of the Great Fire is now considered a mystery although many cling to the original story of the cow that kicked over Mrs. O'Leary's lantern. It is agreed that the first flames broke out in the cowshed behind Patrick O'Leary's frame cottage at what is now 538 De Koven, but historical detectives have not been able to pin the actual cause on the cow.

OFFERS THEORY

Through the years, until her death in 1893, Mrs. O'Leary protested she hadn't even been in the barn that night, and that she and her family were all in bed at 9:30 p.m., that Sunday evening, Oct. 8, when Dennis (Peglet) Sullivan from next door, pounded on the O'Leary's door and shouted that the shed was afire.

James O'Leary, a son, always claimed that a ton of green hay, in the barn loft, caused the fire through spontaneous combustion. There were other versions. Some whispered that a group of roustabouts had furtively used the O'Leary barn for a beer party and the fire started from a cigar butt or pipe spark. Another rumor had it that a neighbor, needing some fresh milk for a Sunday night oyster stew, sought to swipe some from one of the O'Leary cows and her lantern was kicked over during the attempted theft. [...]

As the presidential election of 1952 heated up, the Duchess became one of only a handful of female reporters assigned permanently to the Eisenhower campaign train. For the next few months, she would file her stories "from the road."

IKE MARKS HIS 62ND BIRTHDAY
By Virginia Marmaduke
10/15/52

ABOARD EISENHOWER SPECIAL—This is the biggest, longest birthday in all of Dwight D. Eisenhower's 62 years. He is celebrating it Tuesday in his native state of Texas where there is lots of everything—including big birthday cakes. The celebration began Monday in Wyoming and carried through Oklahoma to New Orleans, where he was given a pre-birthday present of what was called "the largest political rally ever held in Louisiana." New Orleans also gave him the birthday card of his life. It carried 1,000 signatures.

GETS TWO CARDS

Mamie Eisenhower gave her husband two birthday cards and a big kiss for his birthday present. She confided to newsmen she wouldn't have known what else to get him anyway, he's got so many things. [...]

Virginia always spoke admiringly of the Eisenhowers, especially Mamie Eisenhower and Virginia often liked to relate the story of how she put to rest a festering rumor about the future First Lady. During the long, traveling days of the campaign, Mrs. Eisenhower would often strangely disappear from the speaking halls and voter meetings in the early afternoons.

Stories began to float that Mrs. Eisenhower was suffering from a new, undisclosed illness or that she might even have been turning to drink to deal with the stress of the campaign and her afternoon vanishings were her "sleeping it off." Anxious to get the truth, the Duchess spoke to Mrs. Dowd, Mamie's mother. Marmaduke learned that Mamie had been a "blue baby," born with a congenital heart defect, and required sleep every midday to sustain her energy.

Armed with that information, Marmaduke disseminated the news and put the rumors to rest.

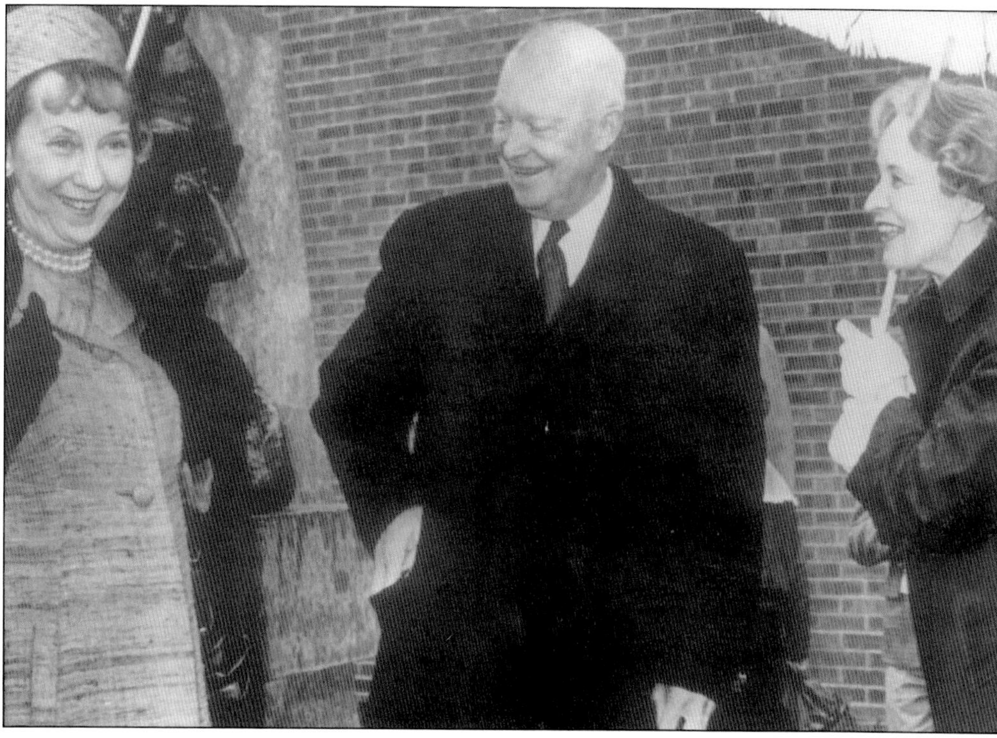

The Duchess with President and Mrs. Eisenhower.

CHICAGO SUN-TIMES

CANCER VICTIM'S WIFE—'I PRAY FOR A MIRACLE'

By Virginia Marmaduke

2/15/53

There is a hush in the home at 5643 S. Kilbourn. The mother does her housework as quietly as possible. The five children have learned to talk—and play—in whispers.

The father, Mark Keslin, 43, lies desperately ill. He knows, and so do the others, that these may be his last 30 days with them. He is a terminal cancer case. "My first prayer is that somehow, some way, God will make me well so I can stay and take care of my family," the father explained. "My second is that somehow, some way, my wife and children can be taken care of if I have to leave them." Tears welled in his deep, blue eyes as he spoke of the baby that is expected in July.

FAITH PRESERVED

"How will Sara ever manage?" he asked. "She will be all alone." But the faith that has made their 20 years together an inspiring family group is still very much with the couple. "I pray first for a miracle," said Sara Keslin. "Then, like Mark, I pray secondly for the spiritual strength I will need when he is gone." The Keslins were married in 1922. Since then the father has worked steadily toward providing a good life for his family. First came James, now 18, followed by Jean, 16; Grace 14; Thomas, 2 1/2; and Johnny, 17 months. [...]

THE SOUTHERN ILLINOISAN

VIRGINIA MARMADUKE LIFE STORY: FORMER AREA WOMAN ON TV PROGRAM

4/9/53

The career of Virginia Marmaduke former Carbondale and Herrin woman now a feature writer for the Chicago Sun-Times, *will be shown on Ralph Edwards'* This Is Your Life *television show from 1:30 to 2 p.m. Saturday over KSD-TV Channel 5, in St. Louis.*

Virginia's participation on the show will come as a surprise to her. She flew to California Monday at the request of the program producers. They had told her that she was to assist in helping honor some other person—not that she was to be the central figure in the 30-minute telecast.

Many of the details of Virginia's life were supplied to the TV producers by Mrs. Ruth Marlow, Herrin, a close friend. Virginia wrote for the former Herrin Daily Journal *and her column "Virginia's Reel" was one of its most popular features.*

She joined the Sun-Times *as a reporter early in 1943.*

Virginia is also well-known in the area through her activities at the DuQuoin State Fair where she [has] announced the society horse show for 10 years. Harvey Marmaduke, representative of the executive department of the Illinois Central Railroad in Chicago, flew to California Tuesday. Mrs. Blanche Marmaduke, Miss Marmaduke's mother, flew out Monday. Both will be on the set but Virginia will not know it. The Marmadukes lived in Carbondale for years until [Mr.] Marmaduke was transferred to Chicago with the I.C. [...]

In 1953, Virginia Marmaduke was utterly astonished when she was ambushed and honored on television's *This Is Your Life* show as the "typical American newspaper woman." About being caught off guard, she said afterward, "I kept thinking, 'How awful to get scooped in front of the nation.'"

The following two stories relate the broadcast and its behind the scenes preparations.

CHICAGO SUN-TIMES

OUR DUCHESS GETS SURPRISE OF HER LIFE

By Jack McPhaul

4/9/53

A SUN-TIMES *reporter went to Hollywood to cover a story. To her astonishment, she found herself the heroine of the story. A coast-to-coast TV audience Wednesday night witnessed the unfolding of Virginia Marmaduke's biography. The* SUN-TIMES *newswoman was the central figure in the Ralph Edwards' program "This Is Your Life." The program, which has an estimated audience of 5,560,000 viewers, presents each week highlights in the life of some person. It is seen in Chicago over WNBQ, Channel 5.*

OTHER IDEA

Miss Marmaduke, called "Duchess" by her colleagues, went to the coast in the belief that the program was to be based on the life of another Chicago woman. She had planned to write the story for The SUN-TIMES*' new Sunday TV Prevue magazine.*

Virginia was seated in the audience and Edwards asked her to read from a manuscript [actually, a mock newspaper, folded in quarters] the name of the woman who was to be the night's heroine. The camera caught the reporter's amazement as she saw her own name. [Virginia's, not the other woman's name, appeared in the "paper's" headline.]

On stage her first surprise was to hear the voice of her father, Harvey C. Marmaduke, a railroad Chicago executive, recalling his nervousness the day Virginia was born. He came into view and embraced his daughter. Virginia expressed regret that her mother was in Miami and could not be present. Then her mother's voice came from the audience and she too went on stage to greet her daughter. The surprise journey from Florida to California was Mrs. Marmaduke's first airplane trip.

The program recalled Virginia's days as an 18-year-old schoolteacher at Pinckneyville, Ill. A man came on stage and Virginia immediately recognized Dean Bartrel, now a Pinckneyville merchant, with whom she had attended dances nearly 20 years ago. There was still another surprise in the person of Mrs. Frank Turner of Bloomington, who had been Virginia's roommate at the University of Iowa. It had been 23 years since last they had met.

DEBUT IN CHICAGO

Her career was brought up to 1941 [sic] when she came from the Herrin Daily Journal *to be a reporter on* The Chicago Sun. *At this juncture, Irv Kupcinet,* SUN-TIMES *columnist, appeared and related some of Virginia's journalistic exploits. Photographs were shown of some of her activities, including the time she worked for a day as a cab driver for a news story, and again when she rode a motorcycle to learn something about how a traffic policeman works. Kup cited her series of articles on cerebral palsy—stories which resulted in legislative action providing for the establishment of a children's hospital.*

Proudly Mrs. Marmaduke related her daughter's work in behalf of La Rabida Jackson Park Sanitarium for children suffering from heart disease. A poignant moment came when Mrs. Anna Jacobs of Chicago appeared on stage accompanied—by her three small children. Edwards had flown the four to the coast. Mrs. Jacobs explained that she was appearing as a representative of 52,000 Chicago families whom Virginia had aided in a critical moment through her SUN-TIMES *stories. This concerned a 1950 episode. Action was underway to cut the amount of state funds to be given persons on relief.*

SHARED THEIR LOT

The Jacobs family was on relief. Virginia spent a week at their home, sharing their lot. Her stories showed just what relief families had to go through, and as a consequence, the severe reduction program was abandoned.

In closing the program, Edwards said that Virginia's life "has been a crusade with words...a continuing fight against injustice." Virginia, who was deeply moved throughout the program and several times had to fight back tears, said she was accepting the program as a tribute to all newspaperwomen.

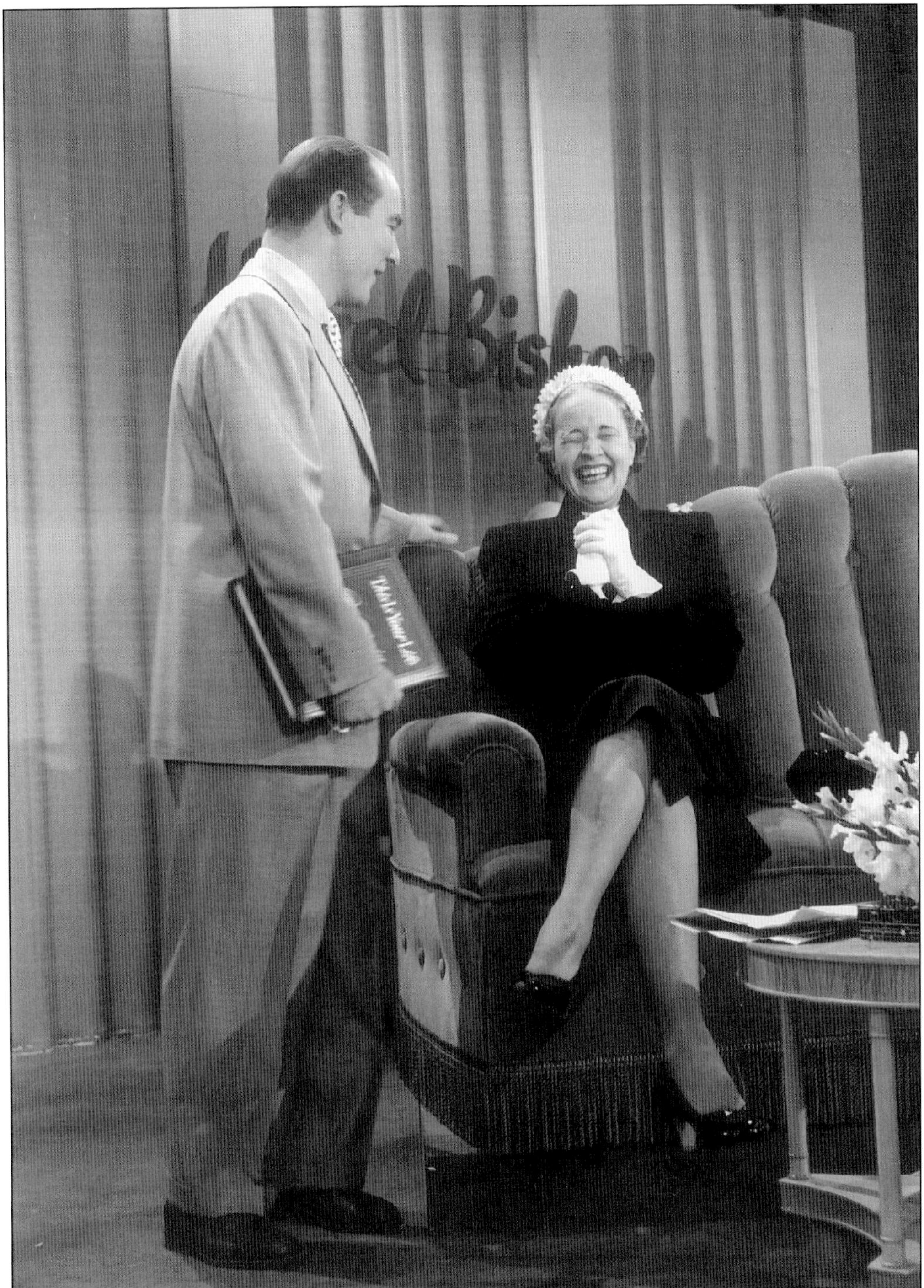

This Is Your Life. (Ralph Edwards Productions.)

KUP'S COLUMN
By Irv Kupcinet
4/10/53

WITH THESE words, "This is YOUR life, Virginia Marmaduke," Ralph Edwards pulled as neat a switch as it ever has been our pleasure to sit in on. For the "Duchess," as the ace SUN-TIMES *reporter and humanitarian is known to intimates and newspaper pals, had gone to Hollywood radiant in the expectation of playing a minor role in unfolding the story of another Chicago woman on Edwards' Wednesday night TV tear-jerker,* This Is Your Life. *Your television screen spoke far more eloquently than these words how completely taken by surprise was our "Duchess."*

THE ONE FACTOR that gives Edwards' shows tremendous pull among TV viewers is the surprise element—the surprise of the "victim" on learning his life story is to be unfolded; the surprise and often tearful reaction when relatives and old friends, flown to Hollywood from any part of the globe, are brought on stage to help paint the picture. Edwards has been consistently fortunate, through skilled efforts, in capturing this surprise element.

HOW EDWARDS AND HIS production manager, Al Paschall, pulled the wool over Miss Marmaduke's lovely brown eyes is indicative of the painstaking efforts poured into this program every week. Only Wednesday night's show provided an extra challenge because the "Duchess," with a superb nose for news, might easily have suspected a story—her own story—if the slightest clues had been dropped by the handful of persons in on the know. And any suspicion by the "victim," however faint, would detract from the surprise element.

IN THE CASE OF MISS MARMADUKE, Edwards reached all the way back to the story of Florence Hubbard, the "other Chicago woman" whose life story the "Duchess" thought she was going to help unfold. Miss Hubbard is the former Carson Pirie Scott & Co. clerk who gained nationwide fame a few years ago when she guessed the identity of the "The Walking Man" on Edwards' radio show, Truth or Consequences. *[…] Because this was a yarn filled with drama, the "Duchess" was assigned to accompany Miss Hubbard to Hollywood and back. The two became fast friends.*

EDWARDS CALLED ON THE ABOVE INCIDENT in Miss Marmaduke's life to spring the trap. By long-distance telephone, he and Paschall explained they thought it was time to revive the thrilling story of Miss Hubbard and they planned to do it by featuring her on This Is Your Life. *And would Virginia kindly come out and tell of her experiences in accompanying Miss Hubbard to Hollywood? Meanwhile, researchers had been put to work to dig up all the important and interesting chapters in Miss Marmaduke's life.*

IF ONLY EDWARDS AND HIS STAFF and the "victim" were involved, maintaining secrecy would be simple. But the researchers have to talk to friends, who conceivably and inadvertently might drop a hint to the "victim." And relatives and friends have to be brought to Hollywood to help tell the story. […]

EVERY PERSON SO INVOLVED is warned that if the "victim" learns the plot, the whole shebang will be called off, as happened in the case of Ann Sheridan a few weeks ago. But even when Edwards obtains a pledge to secrecy, he still isn't home safe. There's always the danger of having the "victim" accidentally run into the other members of the show in Hollywood. If the "Duchess," for example, had stumbled into her parents, the jig would have been up.

IN THIS EMERGENCY, EDWARDS AND PASCHALL summoned their finest ingenuity. They warned the "Duchess" that SHE had to take every precaution not to wander around Hollywood, lest she run into Miss Hubbard. They suggested she lock herself in her hotel room and go out only for meals. And Ralph arranged luncheon and dinner dates for Miss Marmaduke with members of his staff, who steered her to outlying restaurants. On such occasions as she left her hotel room, the "Duchess" wore sun glasses, a bandanna to cover most of her face and she peered around corners before making the turn. Little did she know that Miss Hubbard was in Florida, where she has gone into retirement. The "Duchess" actually was hiding from herself!

STILL ANOTHER PRECAUTION was taken by Edwards. He handed Miss Marmaduke a phony script upon her arrival in Hollywood and told her, "Here are your lines. You have to know them letter-perfect by Wednesday." This was the script in which "Duchess" was to introduce Miss Hubbard and tell of their experiences together. And to make sure Miss Marmaduke's time was well occupied with learning dialog instead of sight-seeing, Edwards' writers padded her part. The Duchess now knows an awful lot of dialog she'll never use.

AND TO COMPLETE THE PICTURE, Edwards went through a regular rehearsal with Miss Marmaduke—using, of course, the make-believe script. The rest of the cast rehearsed all Wednesday afternoon, finishing by 5:30 and then hiding in our dressing rooms so that the coast would be clear for "Duchess" to rehearse with Edwards at 6 p.m.—one hour before show time.

With all these precautions, is there any wonder that [an] exceptional expression of surprise came over "Duchess'" face when Edwards took her by the hand as he opened the show and said, "This is YOUR life, Virginia Marmaduke"?

1954

CHICAGO SUN-TIMES

CHICAGO FOUNDLING HOME PLACE OF WARMTH, UNDERSTANDING

By Virginia Marmaduke

1/31/54

The stanch old building at 15 S. Wood could be a house of sorrow. It houses unwed mothers-to-be and unwanted babies. It could echo with grief, with shame, and even anger. But the Chicago Foundlings Home is none of these things. It is a place of warmth and tenderness for its infants, a sanctuary of understanding protectiveness for its guests-in-waiting.

THREE SERVICES

Unique in modern social welfare practices, it houses three services under its one rambling roof. It is a "home" for expectant mothers, a nursery for foundlings and an adoption and placement agency, all in one package.

This follows the tradition as set up by Dr. George E. Shipman when he founded the institution 83 years ago. Alarmed at the 1871 report that more than 1,000 unwanted Chicago babies had been left in alleys, on park benches and other places to die unattended, Dr. Shipman rented a four-room bungalow at 54 S. Green and tacked a sign on its front door.

It read: "Those having children of which they wish to dispose, whether they are children of sin or of poverty, have but to leave them in the basket at the Home and they will be cared for. No questions will be asked or answered." The first child was taken into the home on Jan. 30, 1871. By May, 32 babies were being cared for. Dr. Shipman obtained larger quarters. Three years later he built the present four-story structure on Wood and [it has] served as many as 150 mothers at one time. [...]

PROBLEMS THE SAME

"We still have some of the old-fashioned rackers used during Dr. Shipman's first days of service," Mrs. Emilie Crenshaw, executive director, explained. "And a few pieces of the original furniture."

The problems they seek to meet remain much the same. "We have served 14,000 babies and 11,600 mothers during our 83 years," Mrs. Crenshaw stated. "And we are particularly proud of the more than 3,000 babies we have placed in adoption." Mothers-in-residence contribute services to the maintenance of the institution, exactly as they would in their own homes. They share cooking, washing, ironing and cleaning chores as they wait out their time.

SOME KEEP BABIES

Some are able to keep their babies. Some make advance arrangements to surrender their infants before leaving for one of the maternity hospitals which co-operate with the home. These babies are returned to the home—and kept until legal adoptions can be arranged. More than 5,000 friends and supporters have been invited to the home for its anniversary tea Sunday. Although a Red Feather agency since 1950, the home exists mainly on voluntary contributions.

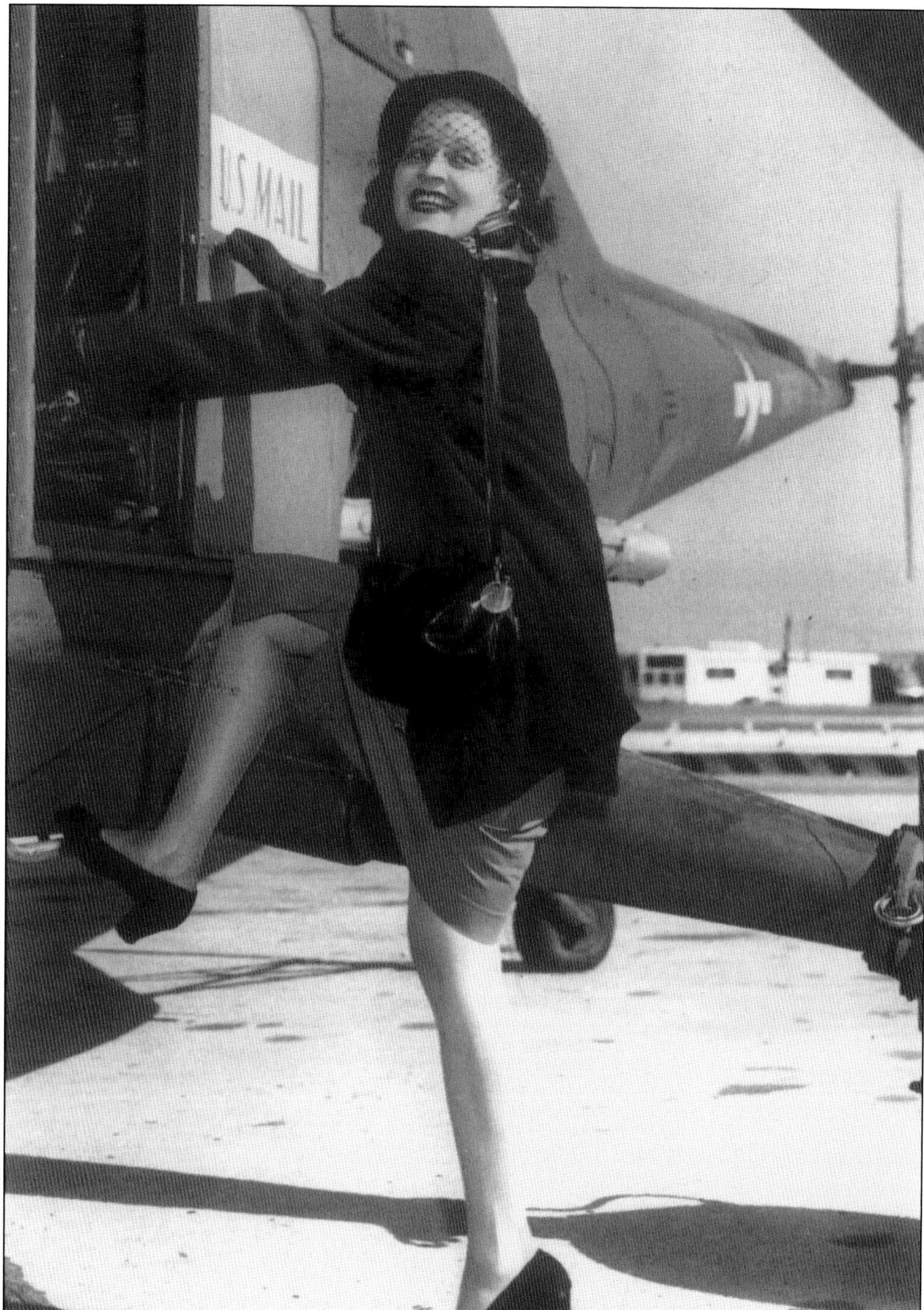

Wherever she had to go to get a story.

Always concerned about the welfare of children, the Duchess became so enamored with the work and mission of the Chicago Foundlings Home that she adopted it as one of her favorite causes and charities. Later she would edit its newsletter and join its board of directors, a seat she would hold for thirteen years. Years after that, in 1962, after retiring from reporting, Virginia was made executive director of the home.

CHICAGO SUN-TIMES

TAPERS OFF
Look—No Candles, But Liberace's Here
By Virginia Marmaduke
4/28/54

To the strains of the tune called "Chicago," the Liberace television show backed into North Western Station. Only thing missing aboard the City of Los Angeles streamliner were the candelabras.

Here for a series of concerts at the Opera House, the dimpled darling of the middle-aged bobby soxers detrained Tuesday in style. He sat at a spinet piano in his drawing room and played a "Chicago" serenade to the more than 600 fans who had jammed the Chicago & North Western Ry. train shed for his arrival.

MOTHER OFF FIRST

First off the private car (reserved entirely for Liberace and his 'party') was the pianist's mother, Frances, chic in a white fleece coat trimmed in ermine tails and a mink stole over her arm. Next came the great man's slightly lesser brother, George, a grayer, older version of the same face and features. Posing for a family portrait at the train steps the three Liberaces look like peas in a pod—the same deep dimples, clear and perfect complexions and even, pearly white teeth.

Making his way behind a police escort through the beseeching autograph seekers, Liberace explained the absence of the identifying candelabra, usually atop the piano he plays. "It's in the luggage," he said, pointing to a mountain of bags and cases. "If I had known it would be so missed I'd have had it [taken] out." [...]

DAD DEMANDS BAN ON DEFECTIVE CAR
Boy, 11, Dies—Wild Auto Victim
By Virginia Marmaduke
9/28/54

A grief-stricken and angry father is asking why his 11-year-old son lies dead—one of six children struck down by a hit-and-run driver. He is asking why cars with defective brakes are allowed on the streets. The child is Robert Sledzianowski of 2619 Iowa, who died at 6:58 a.m. in St. Elizabeth Hospital of a cerebral concussion. The father is Joseph Sledzianowski, 42, a railroad clerk for the Pacific Fruit Express Co., 11 S. LaSalle.

ON WAY TO SCHOOL

The six children were on their way to St. Helen's Roman Catholic School, 2319 Augusta, and were crossing Western at Augusta when a car, driven by James Hoover, 25, of 1137 S. Mozart, rammed into the little group. Thomas Shimanski, 11, of 6610 Schreiber, suffered a leg fracture and possible concussion. The other children were treated and released from the hospital.

Police arrested Hoover with a companion, Willie J. Peeler, 25, of 29-14 W. Madison, five blocks from the accident scene when their careening car rammed a building. [...]

BIG STORY WILL HONOR 2 ON SUN-TIMES STAFF
10/29/54

The Big Story of Sun-Times *reporter Virginia Marmaduke and photographer Joe Kordick will be televised at 8 p.m. Friday, Channel 5. It previously was dramatized on the radio version of Big Story, heard on WMAQ.*

Viewers Friday will see how Miss Marmaduke and Kordick made possible a life-saving operation for a little girl and how they told the story to Sun-Times *readers. Kordick is the first photographer ever to be honored on the Big Story series.*

1955

The horizons and celebrity of Virginia Marmaduke increased considerably in 1955. Along with her continuing high-profile work as the *Sun-Times's* number one "girl reporter," the Duchess moved into the electronic media, first with a 15-minute "Features in the News" insert for Chicago's NBC-radio affiliate, WMAQ and its daily newscast.

Through radio, and later TV, offered financial "greener pastures," the Duchess said, "My first love is the pen and it always will be." So, of course, she kept her day job at the *Sun-Times.*

CHICAGO SUN-TIMES

ELECTION EFFECT?

Mrs. Daley Busier: Outcome Won't Change Home Life, She Asserts

By Virginia Marmaduke

3/30/55

Whether the mayor's car ends up parked in front of 3536 Lowe will make no difference in the routine of the Richard J. Daley household. The pretty and efficient chatelaine of the four-bedroom brick bungalow is determined that the same warm, interfamily life shall continue no matter what is the outcome of the April 5 election.

And the seven children and husband of Eleanor Daley know that when Mom sets her sights, things are going to work out the way they are planned. A charming figure of precision, the petite Mrs. Dailey is nicely managing her large family with one hand and joining her husband in his campaign as Democratic mayoral candidate with the other. "I learned long ago how to adjust our family life to the demands of Dick's public life," she explained. "I'm just a little busier now than before."

A typical day last week included: Breakfast for eight; getting six children off to school; household chores till 11:30 a.m.; lunch for five; whipping up a big salmon loaf and setting the oven clock so it would be just right for [a] 6 p.m. dinner.

TEA IN AFTERNOON

Then a hasty change into a chic knit dress for an afternoon tea given by a neighborhood Democratic women's group; a press interview at 4 p.m.; dinner, and then a ward meeting with her husband at 8:30 p.m.

A slim brunette, Eleanor Daley is a youthful 47 years old. She is 5 feet 3 inches tall and weighs 115 pounds. She has laughing brown eyes and hair to match. [T]he seventh of 10 children, Mrs. Daley was a secretary for a paint company until her marriage in 1936. Close friends (and her husband) call her "Sis." Her four sons and three daughters have grown up in the same neighborhood where their Dad grew to manhood. They include Mary Carol, 16; Eleanor, 14; Richard, 12; Michael, 11; John, 8; and William, 6. Patricia (who was 18 last St. Patrick's day) is a postulant at Sisters of Mercy mother house in Des Plaines. [...]

There are "Daley For Mayor" posters in every window of the 3500 block of S. Lowe. "I think the demonstration of affection from our own neighbors is one of the nicest things that has happened to us," Mrs. Daley concluded. "Many of them have watched Dick grow from rompers to long pants, since he was born within two blocks of where we now live. They know him best and they are for him. It is the highest of compliments."

Richard J. Daley would win that mayoral election and become Chicago's most famous, influential mayor; a legend in his own time. The Duchess's mid-campaign meeting with "Sis" Daley would open up yet another avenue for the Duchess. After the election, Virginia became Mrs. Daley's "unofficial" head speech writer and press secretary.

Along with that change in her life, Virginia Marmaduke also initiated another big transition. In mid-1955, Virginia changed jobs, switching newspapers, moving her byline to the *Sun-Times's* chief competition, *The Chicago Tribune*. Asked later what her motivation was, the Duchess was characteristically practical and to the point, "They paid more money!"

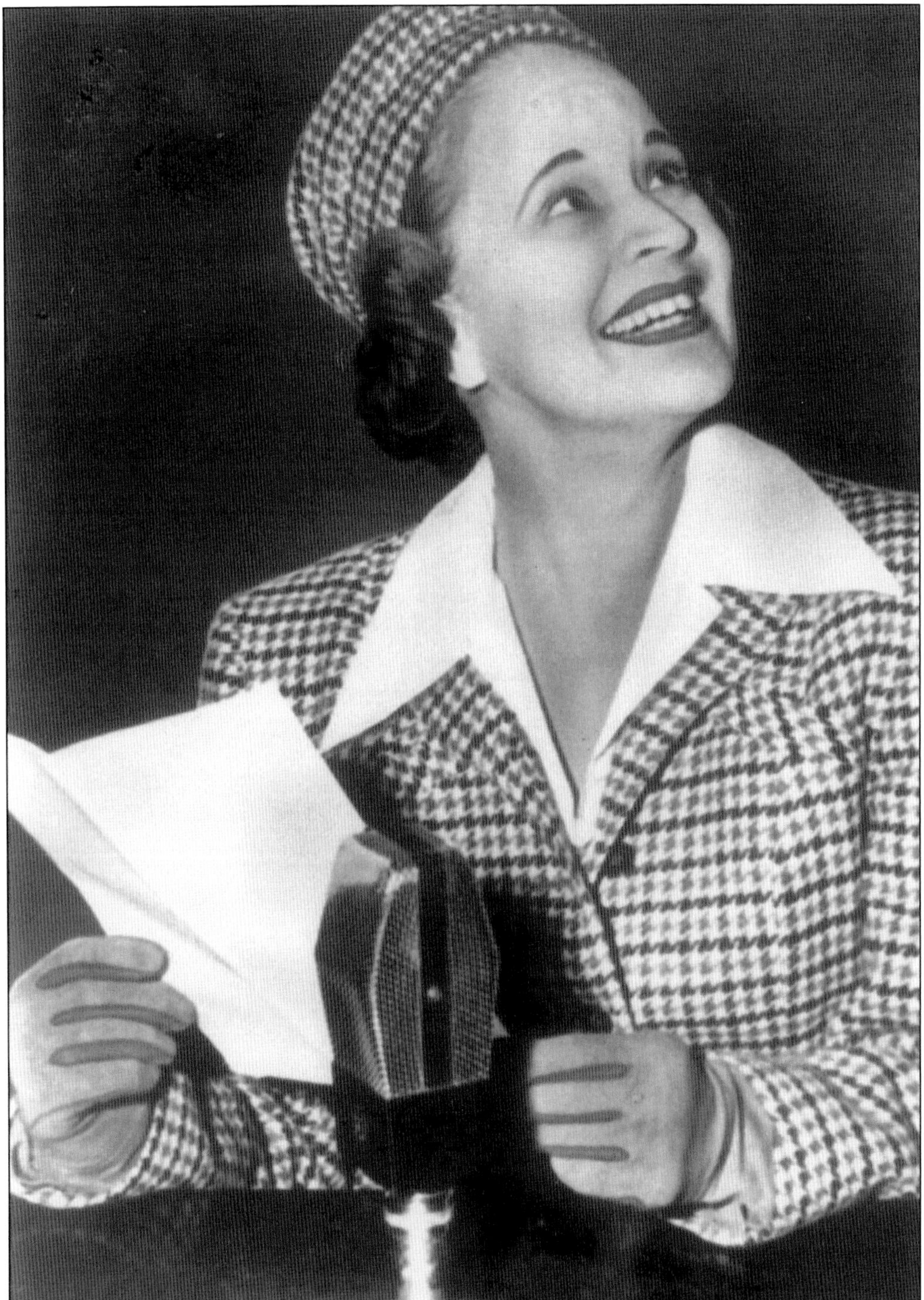

Around 1955, Virginia Marmaduke expanded her fame by moving her talents into Chicago radio, and then television. (V. Marmaduke.)

<u>CHICAGO TRIBUNE MAGAZINE</u>

THEY FIND MISSING PERSONS

There Are Stories of Heartbreak and Happiness in the Card Files at Police Headquarters, and Sheldon Cissna Knows Most of Them

By Virginia Marmaduke

7/10/55

A DESPERATE FATHER of five is begging help in locating his wife. A tear-stained mother is pleading for hope that her son, mysteriously missing for seven years, may some day be found. Another sad-eyed mother is collecting the clothes belonging to her teen-age daughter. She has just identified the girl's body, fished from the Chicago River.

This is the grim work of the bureau of missing persons of the Chicago police department, tracing the more than 6,000 pleas and complaints that move thru its files in a single year. One of the veterans of the bureau, Sheldon R. Cissna, retired this month after 24 years of looking into the eyes—and hearts—of people with troubles like these.

In some he has seen vindictiveness and shame. In most he has seen genuine grief and human need. One way or another, Cissna and his fellow workers have touched the lives of 100,000 persons, some of them intimately, during the last quarter century. "Most of the cases are cleared up quickly," Cissna explains. "They are the ones resulting from family mixups or squabbles." In 1954, 6,243 persons were reported missing. By the year's end, 6,002 cases had been stamped "canceled."

Chicago missing persons reports originate in the neighborhood police station, where relatives or friends make the initial complaint. The downtown bureau, at 11th and State, takes over when the station has exhausted its resources. [...]

A native of Bedford, Ind., Cissna joined the Chicago police force July 6, 1926, at the age of 26, after a brief career as a switch man for the Belt railway and World War I service in the navy. "I took the police examination on a dare that I couldn't pass it," he remembers. "If I could find that fellow today, I'd thank him."

A crinkly-eyed, graying grandfather of 55, Cissna has two sons, a daughter and five grandchildren. Sheldon, Jr., 34, is pastor of the Assembly of God church in Jacksonville, Fla. Aside from being a grandfather, Cissna's hobbies include wood and leather carving and a deep interest in the work of the Illinois Epilepsy league, in which he is joined by his wife, Ella. [...]

Probably the case that was most Cissna's own was [the] "Little Miss Bobby Socks" mystery that aroused the entire nation. The body of a girl was taken from the Chicago river Jan. 28, 1953. There were no marks of violence, no identifications. Her skirt had snagged on a wood abutment of the wharf at the foot of Dearborn and Wacker. She had been in the water for about a week.

Police teletypes spread the word: Female, between 17 and 19 years old; 5 feet 4 inches tall; about 110 pounds; wearing [a] gray sweater, green skirt, gray cloth coat, floral print scarf, probably worn babushka style, black bobby socks and saddle-type oxfords. [...]

The next day Mrs. Cecile Coulter, widow of a former Roundhead postmaster, and her son, Derwin Coulter, Jr., identified Little Miss Bobby Socks [as her daughter Shirley]. "I bought those black wool ankle socks for her," the mother sobbed. "She was wearing them Dec. 3 when she [went] out to start her Christmas shopping."

The mother had brought with her the hood to the gray coat Shirley had been wearing. All doubt was removed when it matched Little Miss Bobby Socks' in fabric, fiber and lining. The mother could not explain how or why her daughter came to be in Chicago. Since there were no marks of violence, police believe she either fell or jumped into the river. If Little Miss Bobby Socks had to choose a big city to lose her life, Sheldon Cissna said he was glad it was Chicago. "Some other city might not have joined so wholeheartedly to establish her identity," he concluded.

As the Duchess would often say, one of the benefits of being in journalism in the same city for as long as she was, was the chance to witness the final outcome of a story that was close to her heart. Icing on the cake of course was when that story had a happy ending, as in this article for the *Tribune*, a coda to the heart-tugging saga of little Pam Lamphere.

PAM'S ALMOST OUT OF THE WOODS!
Child Born with Exposed Bladder, Who Was a Center of Controversy in 1948, Now Is a Healthy, Happy Nine; She Soon Will Undergo Her Final Operation, a Minor One
By Virginia Marmaduke
11/13/55

WHEN Irene and Fred Lamphere cross glances over the head of their 9-year-old daughter, their eyes soften. They know this is the year that may see the end of her tribulation. They know, too, that it can mean the close of a chapter that upturned their lives. Pamela Lamphere is the beautiful, brown-eyed child whose plight stirred the nation's heart the summer of 1948.

Born with a rare abdominal deformity, she needed immediate surgery if she was to reach maturity. Her mother rebelled at the long-shot chance it might mean. The father was equally determined the risk should be taken. It brought about such bickering between the youthful parents that Irene went home to her mother and took baby Pamela with her.

How America took sides on the question of the wisdom of the proposed operation; how the dilemma was solved; how the parents were reunited, and how Pamela today is a happy, healthy fourth grader with a little brother and little sister, is a modern American love story. The conclusion will be written sometime this year during Pamela's tenth year of life, when plastic surgery will erase the last trace of her body malformation.

The story of Pamela Lamphere began on a hot, sticky day in August, 1948, in the court of Superior Judge Walter R. O'Malley. The screenless windows of the stuffy courtroom were opened wide. Flies buzzed over the empty benches. Judge O'Malley was hearing divorce cases. There were the usual complaints: desertion, nonsupport, and cruelty. When the clerk called the case of Irene Lamphere versus Fred Lamphere, Attorney Charles C. Cooley stepped up.

"My client wishes to reveal some additional reasons for her request for a divorce," he told the judge. "She did not tell them when we filed suit a month ago.

"My client's husband is demanding that she agree to some very dangerous surgery for their daughter, Pamela, 22 months old. This mother has been told that chances for survival in this type of operation are not good. She knows that little Pam may live only a few years the way she is, but she prefers to have her that long rather than take a chance on losing her now."

Judge O'Malley questioned Cooley: "Have you determined the medical facts in this case?"

"As well as we could," the attorney declared. "Mrs. Lamphere has been told the child's chances for recovery are about 1 in 1,000." [...]

[After the case became public,] thousands of letters poured in to Mrs. Lamphere. Some urged her to permit the surgery. Others said she was right to keep her daughter—as long as she could. These were only words, and mostly from strangers. The young mother was not influenced.

Then came a personal visit by Mrs. Helen Ulrich, 38, and her daughter, Christine, 19 months old. "I've been reading about you and little Pamela," Mrs. Ulrich began. "I had to come and talk with you." The two mothers, one young and distraught and the other graying and calm, sat on a divan. The little girls played with dolls on the floor. They became friends at once, almost as if they knew the thing they shared.

Mrs. Ulrich continued diffidently: "I know what you are going thru...my little Christy was born with the same thing as your Pamela. Four months ago I faced an identical decision. My religion helped me make up my mind. I trusted in the Lord, and He brought my daughter thru."

She said that she had brought the child—so that Mrs. Lamphere could have living proof. The younger mother's eyes welled with tears. "But you have other children," she began. "Pam is all I have. And I am the only one fighting for her..."

Mrs. Ulrich nodded sympathy and understanding. "Come into the bedroom with Christy and me," she urged. "We want to show you something." Clutching Pamela in her arms, Irene Lamphere followed.

There, on the bed, Mrs. Ulrich revealed her daughter's wholesome little body, free of the ugly deformity with which she had been born. Only a dainty scar remained. Mrs. Lamphere lifted Pamela's dress and removed the surgical dressing on her abdomen.

"Was Christy like this?" she demanded.

"Exactly," Mrs. Ulrich answered.

Irene Lamphere gathered up her child. "Then Pamela shall have the same chance," she said. "I have seen with my own eyes."

A sympathetic mother and her toddling daughter had won for Pamela Lamphere what judges, doctors, lawyers, and a pleading father had failed to get—her mother's permission for a chance for a full and normal life.

Two days later, Judge O'Malley received the recommendation of a "medical jury." It strengthened Irene Lamphere's new resolve. The doctors advised, unanimously, that surgery for Pamela was needed and that, from their examinations, chances for her recovery were "excellent." Irene sent word to Fred that she would like to "talk things over" with him. Within minutes after their reunion they were in each other's arms—reconciled.

On Sept. 22, 1948, little Pamela spent one hour and 55 minutes in the operating room at Cook county hospital. She came thru it fine. After two other minor operations, doctors sent her home—a normal child.

They said a final "clean-up," when her body was more mature, would be all she would ever need again. They told the parents to bring her back sometime during her tenth year for minor plastic surgery. This, then, is it. Pamela was 9 years old Oct. 11, meaning this is the beginning of the fateful year. Gathering with her around her birthday cake in their modest home at 3217 Hamlin av. were her sister, Susie, 6, and her brother, Michael, 5.

Says her mother: "I'm not worrying about this final operation, but we will all be glad when it is all over."

For whatever reason, after contributing only five stories, the above feature was the last the Duchess wrote for the *Chicago Tribune*.

With its publication, Virginia Marmaduke's full-time employment as a newspaper reporter concluded.

III.
Duchess Emerita (1956–2001)

At this point the written record of the life of Virginia Marmaduke shifts (by and large) from articles *by* her to stories *about* her, from daily diary to scrapbook. With her late 1955 resignation from the *Chicago Tribune*, Virginia Marmaduke signaled that she was—at least for the time—through with printed journalism. But if the Duchess was done with newspapers, newspapers were not done with her.

Thanks to her radio and, soon, television work, and to a couple of high-profile political appointments, the name and face of "Virginia Marmaduke, former newspaperwoman," remained in the public eye and in the news, carefully detailed in the *Sun-Times*, the *Tribune*, and other newspapers. But even a career as deeply documented—and celebrated—as Virginia Marmaduke's nevertheless ends up yielding a few gray areas.

One of the least recorded and most confusing aspects of Virginia's life is her work in radio and television. Articles uniformly disagree with each other about the sequence and dates of her broadcast career. The records of her TV and radio employers and the local performer's union, AFTRA, are either nonexistent or totally contradictory. And finding tapes of these program (audio or film) is impossible—churned out five days a week, if these programs were recorded at all (and most programs at that time weren't) the transcriptions of them have long since been lost.

Many sources peg 1955 or 1956 as the year radio and TV became a regular part of Virginia's work day. These dates make a sort of logical sense. The Duchess once said that her 1953 appearance on *This Is Your Life*, not surprisingly, increased her local fame greatly. Thereafter she was soon heavily sought after as a guest (or a fill-in host) on Chicago-area radio and television news and talk shows, especially radio's *Monitor* program and TV's *The Ernie Simon Show,* where the Duchess was a frequent co-host.

TV director, and Duchess friend, Richy Victor said of Virginia's on-air talents, "In those days when they said you were on, you were ON,...and it was tough and in those days Virginia handled herself well. Virginia gave you a strong half-hour, hour, and maybe if you'd listen, she'd give you a whole week. . . ."

Virginia was definitely working in radio in 1955, the year she was writing for the *Chicago Tribune,* as their biographical blurb after her articles state she can be heard three-times weekly in segments over WMAQ. And she was still there as late as 1958 as other clippings attest.

Many accounts suggest that not long after her start in radio in 1955, Virginia got her very own show over WMAQ radio, *Coffee with the Duchess*. It was a program that was, in the Duchess's words, "typical chit-chat and phone-ins; easy money—and fun." *Coffee* was sponsored by Maxwell House (hence the title) and, allegedly, aired every weekday morning.

(If some sources are to be believed, *Coffee with the Duchess* would later move to morning television, airing daily over WMAQ, Chicago's NBC affiliate, perhaps with both the radio and television versions airing concurrently.)

Eventually, Virginia would audition for and get her own late-night talk show—a "Johnny Carson-type show"—over WBKB (now WLS), the local ABC station. This program, *A Date with the Duchess*, aired nightly from 10:30 to 11:30 p.m., with Virginia welcoming celebrities—local and non—and chatting about area happenings. This show was on the air probably around 1957.

Whichever, whatever is truly the case, no one disputes that these programs, radio and television, existed for the Duchess; they just aren't sure of exactly the sequence of them or for how long they lasted. No matter how brief, or lengthy, the Duchess's tenure in broadcasting was, she always remained firmly committed to the mediums of radio and television. Later, when she devoted ample time and money to Southern Illinois University at Carbondale, she distributed her largess equally between the school of journalism and the department of radio-TV.

Unquestionably Virginia starred in one of her many programs—and perhaps one of TV's most interesting programs ever—in mid-1957 on WBKB-TV. On it she was given the task of

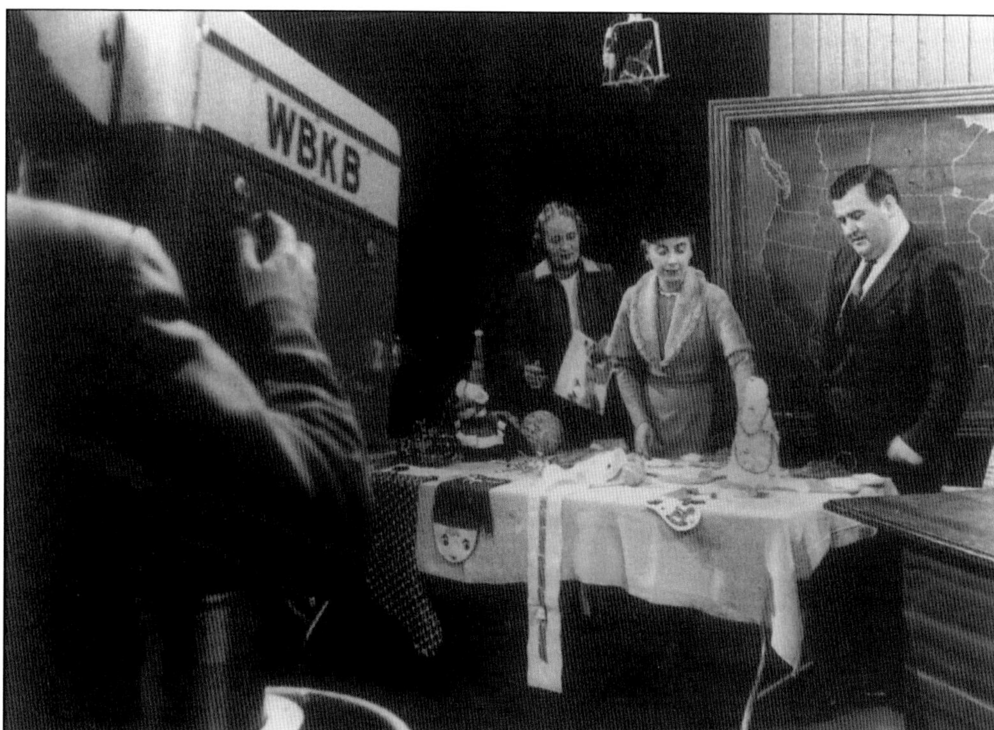

Discussing Christmas crafts with guests on one of Virginia's television shows.

offering advice to the lovelorn. (This was not the Duchess's first encounter with dispensing advice. In early 1955, while still at the *Sun-Times*, she sat on the committee which dreamed up the original *Ann Landers* column, helping to choose the name "Landers" because it did not indicate any particular ethnic background.)

The Duchess's name and face though was considered too well-known in the Windy City and, just as Eppie Lederer became Ann Landers for her famous advice giving, so would Virginia Marmaduke's identity be largely concealed. For the program, the Duchess would be seen only from the side, in silhouette, though her distinctive profile and voice might have given her away to a few sharp-eyed viewers. The program, titled *Ruth Jamison* (a name also chosen for its ethnic generalness), was favorably reviewed, in '57, by the show biz bible *Variety*.

VARIETY
TELE REVIEWS
RUTH JAMISON With Virginia Marmaduke, Fred Kasper
Director: Richy Victor
Writer: Virginia Donahue
15 min., Mon.-Fri, 3:30 p.m.
PARTICIPATING
WBKB, Chicago
7/24/57

Of five new daytimers which WBKB is unwrapping this summer, this lonelyhearts entry is perhaps the surest to remain when the fall blueprints are drawn. The show is tastefully produced, the advice intelligent, and there's plenty of drama in the mailbag for the hausfrau to bend her imagination to.

Veteran reporter for the local gazettes, Virginia Marmaduke, undertakes her first [sic] tv chore as an adviser on personal problems, under "pen" name Ruth Jamison. Not only to cover her identity but to give her a supra-human quality, she's shown only in magnified silhouette, armed with an authoritarian pencil. Miss Marmaduke, if she works as well full face before the cameras as she does in shadow, could well be the local television find of the season. She's articulate, smooth and clinical but kindly, hitting that rare middle ground of the personal-impersonal in her advisory role.

Letters—seven of them on segment caught—are fed to her by announcer Fred Kasper, who reads them with earnest sobriety against barely audible organ tones. Problems ranged from the simple boy-girl intrigue to the desperate situation of an unwed mother-to-be, and Miss Marmaduke's counsel, never hackneyed, was sincere and appeared spontaneous. What keeps this show well above the soaper level is its unfailing good taste, the drama soft-pedaled and the emoting always thinner than schmaltz.[...]

In time, other activities of Virginia Marmaduke's, both personal and professional, would also find their way into print.

BATAVIA HERALD (Batavia, IL)
VIRGINIA MARMADUKE TO M.C. HORSE SHOW
8/1/57

Miss Virginia Marmaduke, known in her professional circles as "The Duchess," will be announcer-commentator for the Kane County Horse Show Aug. 4, according to an announcement this week by Howard Huntoon, Horse Show Superintendent.

A veteran member of the horse show fraternity, Miss Marmaduke has served at such major shows as the Audubon Horse Show in New Orleans, the DuQuoin Society Horse Show in Southern Illinois and the Illinois State Fair Horse Show in Springfield.

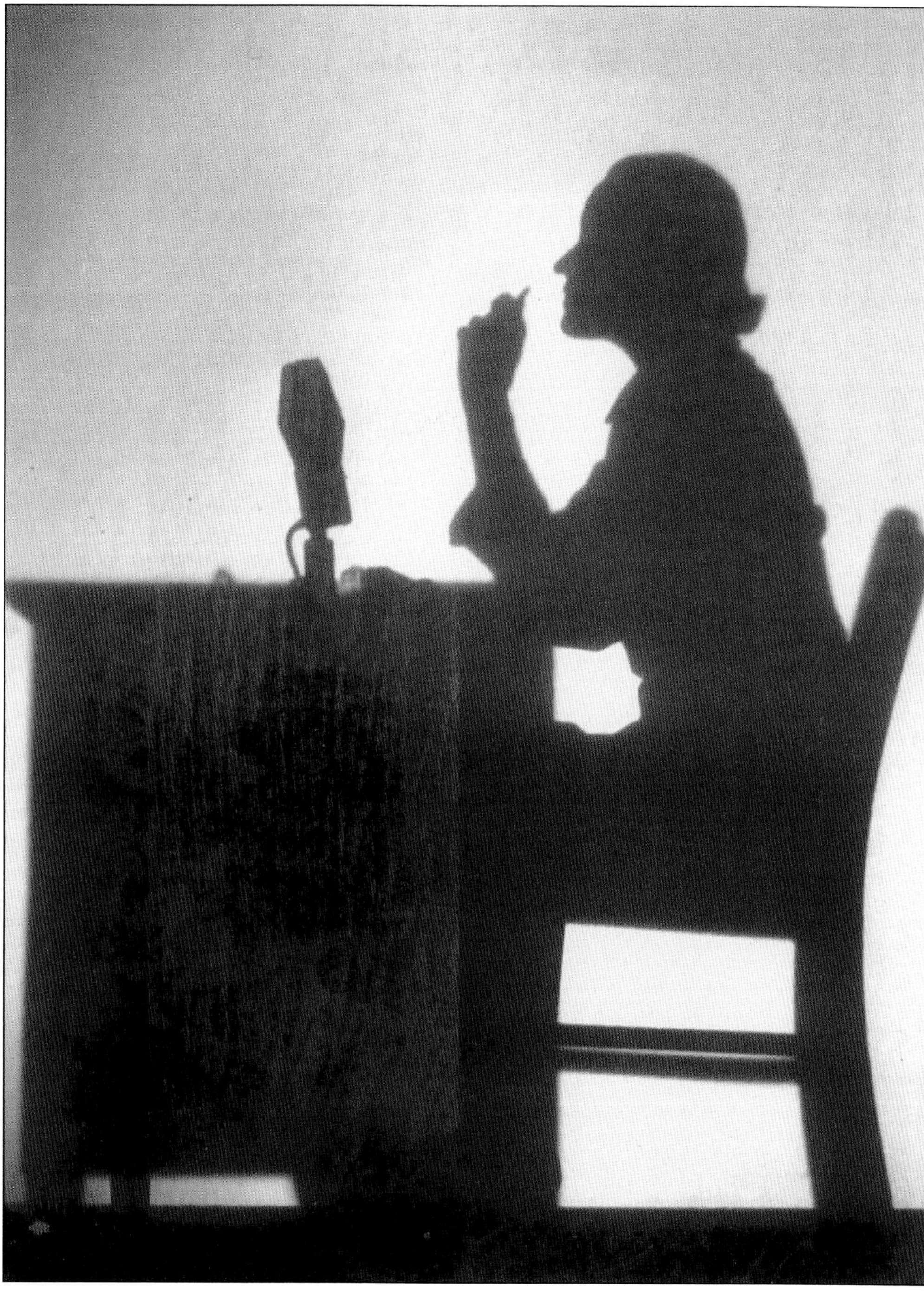

In Silhouette and On TV: Virginia as she appeared on television's Ruth Jamieson *program. (WLS-TV Chicago.)*

Herself a former rider and exhibitor, Miss Marmaduke is an authority on show ring etiquette and rules and has covered the major shows of the nation for the metropolitan newspapers of Chicago. [...]

She is one of the few women horse show commentators in the nation and is believed to be the first ever to receive assignment at a major show. [...]

CHICAGO SUN-TIMES

KUP'S COLUMN

By Irv Kupcinet

10/10/57

*...Newsgal **Virginia Marmaduke** will be cited as "Woman of the Year" by the Old Town Chicago Boys Club on Thursday. The award will be presented by garage tycoon **David (Dixie) Meyer**, whose next presentation to her may be a ring!...*

Renowned columnist (and friend of the Duchess's) Irv "Kup" Kupcinet has seldom been off target in his news scoops in his daily "Kup's Column," so, if Mr. Meyer did pop the question at some point to Virginia, she must have declined, for neither an engagement nor a marriage ever took place. Which is not to say that she and Meyer weren't an "item." The two were longtime companions but marriage just wasn't in the cards—the Duchess always said, "We were both just too set in our ways."

DALEY NAMES FIRST WOMAN TO CHICAGO BOARD OF HEALTH

By Charles Pierce

11/27/57

A woman has been appointed to the Chicago Board of Health for the first time in its history.

Mayor Daley named Virginia Marmaduke, a radio commentator, Tuesday to fill one of the two vacancies on the board. Selected by the mayor for the other vacancy was Stephen M. Bailey, business manager of the Chicago Journeymen Plumbers Union. [...]

The appointments, referred to the Council's Health Committee, are subject to Council approval. Five members of the nine-man board are doctors. All appointees serve without salary. [...]

Daley said [...] Miss Marmaduke's background as a reporter in covering affairs of youth and schools should make [her a] valuable member of the Board of Health.

In early December 1957, Virginia Marmaduke was sworn in as the first female member of the Chicago Board of Health.

H.C. MARMADUKE, RETIRED IC AID, DIES

2/26/58

Harvey Creigh Marmaduke, retired executive assistant to the president of the Illinois Central R.R., died Monday night of a heart attack at Edgewater Park, Miss. He was 73 and lived at 7020 S. Jeffrey with his wife Blanche and his daughter Virginia, member of the Chicago Board of Health, TV and radio commentator and former Sun-Times *reporter.*

For the last four months, Mr. and Mrs. Marmaduke had been wintering at the southern resort. Their daughter returned to Chicago Sunday night after a three-week visit with them. [...]

OFFICE MAINTAINED

Since his retirement he had been a consultant in employee relations for a number of oil companies and railroads, including the New York, New Haven & Hartford. The IC, however, paid him a unique tribute. It kept his office open for him, and although he was on the pension rolls, his desk was waiting whenever he wanted to drop in. [...]

KUP'S COLUMN
By Irv Kupcinet
3/12/58

...Radio will be shocked to learn Mary Merryfield *is parting company with WMAC on March 28. Her noontime Radio Journal has been a listening delight for seven years. The split came over differences with her bosses on programming. The Phil Bowman show will be expanded (with* Virginia Marmaduke, Johnny Erp, Art Van Damme *quintet and signer* Mike Douglas*) to take over Mary's time...*

KUP'S COLUMN
By Irv Kupcinet
5/28/58

*...*Virginia Marmaduke *packs her tape recorder and hikes herself to London for a 10-day stay. She'll record a series on "Springtime in England" for her WMAQ show...*

Along with going to England in June of 1958 for her radio show, the Duchess also put on her press badge one more time during that trip and sent back to Chicago a special series of reports, "Five Letters to London," for her old paper the *Sun-Times*. Wielding letters of introduction from Chicago officials, and acting as both reporter and good will ambassador, Virginia voyaged across the Atlantic to see how British institutions compared to those of the Windy City.

FIVE LETTERS TO LONDON
Virginia Visits Famed Scotland Yard
By Virginia Marmaduke
6/24/58

Most tourists go to London to see the Changing of the Guard at Buckingham Palace, or to tour the Houses of Parliament across the River Thames. When Virginia Marmaduke, NBC Commentator and former Sun-Times staff writer, visited London, she had tea with the London Fire Brigade chief; she visited the London zoo director, [and had] lunch with the head of England's socialized medicine system. She also talked crime with Scotland Yard officials. And she almost met Sir Denis Truscott, lord mayor of London.

How'd she do it? Letters of introduction. Hers happened to be from Mayor Daley of Chicago, Fire Comr. Robert Quinn, Brookfield Zoo Director Robert Bean, Dr. Herman N. Bundesen of the Board of Health and Police Comr. Timothy O'Connor. Maybe you couldn't assemble such an impressive collection. But you can read what Virginia was able—or wasn't able—to do with hers. (Virginia Marmaduke is heard daily on WMAQ-NBC at 11:35 a.m.)

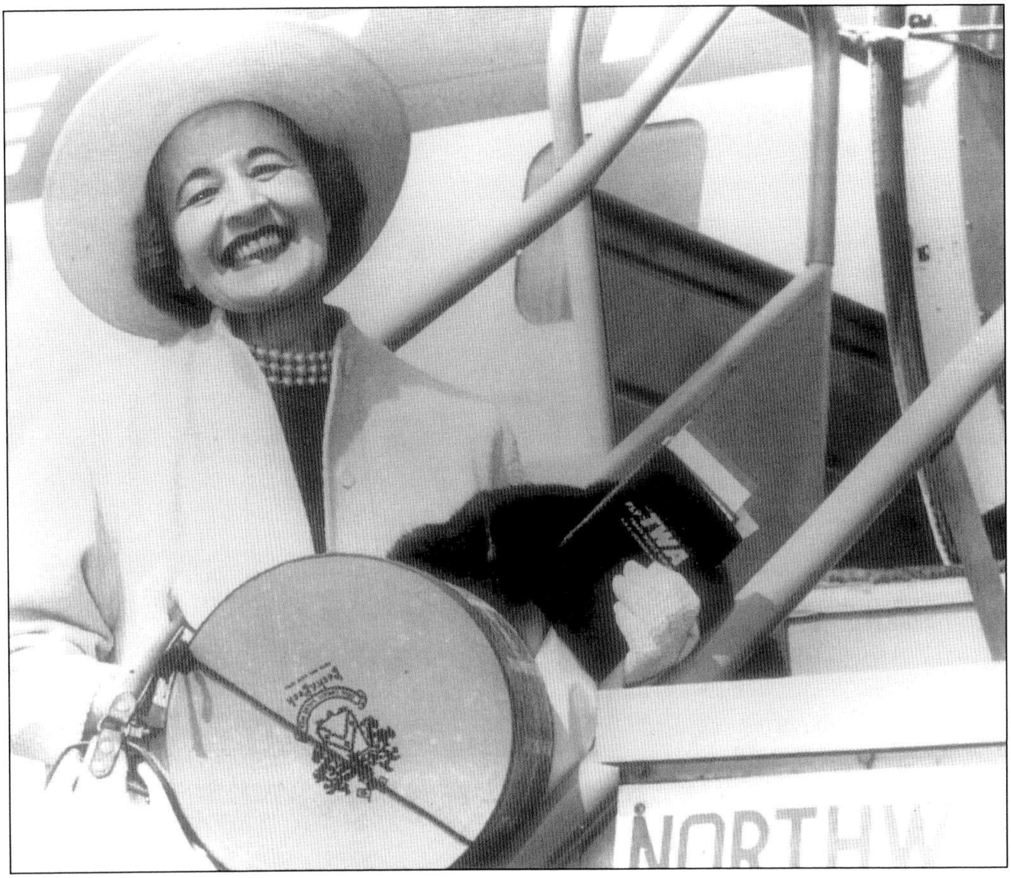

Off to England, and back for a time, to the newspaper world with her "Letters to London" series. (V. Marmaduke.)

The letter I carried from Chicago Police Comr. Timothy O'Connor to "All Peace Officers of London" proclaimed me a "highly respected citizen" of Chicago. But this proved no qualification for entry into Scotland Yard's Chamber of Horrors. Said Gilbert Wiles, chief press officer: "No woman has ever viewed our collection. It is only open to visiting police officers to use as a research and study museum."

Capt. Thomas (Rosie) McLaughlin, Chicago's North Side supervising captain had told me of the gory but fascinating place. A friend of his had seen it and had described in detail the torture instruments and eerie wax models of criminal faces that line its cavernous shelves.

While waiting for my interview at Scotland Yard, I had stopped by the press room and told the bevy of police reporters of my objective. Graham Laxton of the London Star said: "Go ahead and try...but none of us has ever been able to worm through the iron gates of the Horror Chamber."

I couldn't squeeze through either but I learned some other, probably more important, things about London crime. Londoners don't have much, according to our standards! Their police officers carry no guns. They are permitted to draw their billy club (they call it a truncheon) only in self-defense and have to file a written report each time it is used.

The London police establishment includes about 20,000 men. The Scotland Yard detail is an exclusive, highly trained segment that works in plainclothes and goes in when local police have bogged down on a case. There are 180 police stations, each marked with blue lamplights at the sides of the entrance as are our Chicago stations.

But their police blotters tell a far different story. Armed robberies and assaults are few and far between. The penalty for carrying arms is rough and the punishment is swift. Murders are few and mostly are poison cases. Death sentences are the rule, rather than the exception, and are carried out within a few days after the sentencing.

Officer Wiles said the four most important fields of crime in London are (in order): Stolen autos, of which 98 per cent are recovered; housebreaking with forced entry; walk-in larceny, where doors are left unlocked; and pickpocketing and purse snatching. He said London has no narcotics detail, no special homicide and no juvenile delinquency bureau.

London's crime problems may be different than Chicago's but police reporters are the same—everywhere. When I offered to buy the next round of lager—they LET me. [...]

FIVE LETTERS TO LONDON
Virginia Finds Fire Fighting Ideas For Chicago
By Virginia Marmaduke
6/26/58

Virginia Marmaduke, who carried five letters of introduction from Chicago officials to London leaders, is telling about her visit to London. In this article—the fourth of five—she describes her call on London's famed Fire Brigade.

I've always liked—and admired—firemen. They usually also take to me. They did in England when I called at the headquarters of the London Fire Brigade to deliver a "hello letter" from Chicago's Fire Comr. Robert Quinn to London's chief, Frederick W. Delve.

The British fire fighters invited me into their lounge that sits on Albert Embankment alongside the Thames River. We had tea with hot milk and biscuits. And, as at every firehouse, lots of conversation. But if London's firemen brag a bit, they're entitled to it.

During the war, the lives of about 11,000,000 people (including the boroughs) were in their care. From the time Adolf Hitler's first bomb dropped (on Saturday, Sept. 7, 1940) they fought almost continuous enemy-made fire. They fought destruction, caused by enemy action, 50,155 times in five years and of these, 2,380 were flying bomb explosions.

That they fought with the international firemen's code of bravery is shown by the number of gallantry awards they received. These come no easier in London than they do in Chicago; 185 medals and 94 commendations were awarded by the close of the war.

One of these went to an auxiliary firewoman. She was Ann Tanner who drove a petrol lorry all over London during a mighty intensive bombardment so that vital fire-fighting service could be maintained. [...]

Two of London's applied ideas might serve equally well in Chicago. Chief Delve is engaging in a city wide campaign to get London business houses to prepare—and display prominently—maps of their building basements at all entries. He said such advance knowledge can save firemen's lives as well as help cut down on property damage when a conflagration starts in the basement.

Their other innovation is a mobile headquarters that enables over-all direction at the scene of the fire. It is a renovated old London bus, turned into a central control unit and has every possible type of two-way electronic equipment including walkie-talkie hookup with firemen inside burning buildings. [...]

Probably their most unusual call came recently when firemen responded to a call about a horse stuck in the mud in the middle of the city. The delivery animal had strayed to a nearby park, softened by the spring rains, and sunk to its hocks. The firemen fashioned a stomach sling and then gently lifted the horse with the [...] tackle. [...]

The daily sojourns of the "Letters to London" series would not be Virginia's only encounter with venerable British institutions. As has been widely reported, the Duchess, at least once, met and interviewed royalty, chatting up Queen Elizabeth II and Prince Phillip. Where and when though is open to question. Some written accounts state that Virginia interviewed the royal couple on their widely-covered visit to Chicago in the 1950s. But the royal couple didn't journey to the Windy City until 1959, well after Virginia had retired from print journalism. Could she have come back to newspapering—as in the "Letters" series—for a very brief time as a guest writer? If so, it wasn't for any Chicago-area paper; a thorough review of all Chicago papers published during the royal visit yielded no Duchess bylines.

Perhaps she didn't interview the royal couple at all *in Chicago*, but in Britain, combining that great news coup with this June 1958 trip to England. And perhaps Virginia didn't interview the royals for print but for one of her radio or television endeavors—with the recorded transcriptions now, sadly, long since gone.

Whichever, the Duchess was at least able to acquire and keep one memorable souvenir from her trip to the UK. While in England, she illegally stole from the garden of the Archbishop of Canterbury a sampling of spearmint. One day, while standing in the garden, sipping her afternoon tea with dainty lady-like aplomb, Virginia, all the time, was determinedly digging into the dirt with the heel of her shoe in order to extract some leaves and roots of bona fide English mint.

After obtaining her purloined plant, Virginia clandestinely wrapped it in Kleenex and slipped it into her handbag. She smuggled it back to the US and replanted it in her own garden. For years after, even after her move back to Southern Illinois, the Duchess nurtured her little sprig and passed seedlings from it—a touch of the British Isles—onto many of her American friends.

FUNDS FOR FOUNDLING HOME
7/28/59

Virginia Marmaduke of the Chicago Board of Health and Chicago surgeon-philanthropist Dr. Karl A. Meyer add to a wishing-well fund for [the] Chicago Foundlings Home. Money will be used to defray cost of home's new building, rising at 1780 W. Polk. The two attended a meeting at 847 Asmand, River Forest, to discuss plans for a fund raising dinner Wednesday at the Chateau Royale, 5743 W. Chicago.

THE SOUTHERN ILLINOISAN
EX-REPORTER ASSUMES POST
8/9/59

Miss Virginia Marmaduke, former reporter for the Herrin Daily Journal, *has volunteered to serve on the editorial staff of the new publication of the Illinois Council for Mentally Retarded Children, it was announced Monday.*

Miss Marmaduke, 7020 Jeffrey Ave., Chicago, was [...] on the staff of the Chicago Sun-Times *for 16 [sic] years. She is now featured on NBC's* Coffee With the Duchess *program. She was featured on* This Is Your Life *in 1952 [sic]. The newsletter will appear in mid-August for distribution to 5,000 family members, state legislators, newspapers and state agencies.*

CHICAGO DAILY NEWS
PERSONALITIES—-PLUS
12/8/59

***Virginia L. Marmaduke** has been named vice-president in charge of public relations for Consolidated American Life Insurance Co. of Illinois.*

CHICAGO DAILY NEWS
1/5/60

[...]Virginia Marmaduke declines a WMAQ invitation to take over permanently the Jack Eigen radio interview show. Too busy with her new career with an insurance company.

THE SOUTHERN ILLINOISAN

EX-HERRIN REPORTER: MISS MARMADUKE TO VISIT

5/6/60

Virginia Marmaduke, veteran newspaper woman and former broadcaster, now a vice president of Consolidated American Life Insurance Co. of Illinois, will revisit Southern Illinois this weekend.

Miss Marmaduke was born in Jackson County and started her career as a reporter on the old Herrin Journal *from 1933 [sic] to 1942. She will be honored guest of Union County Tourists and Recreation Assn. for a Southern Illinois tour and featured speaker Saturday night for a countrywide meeting at Jonesboro. [...]*

Miss Marmaduke will speak at the dinner at 6:30 p.m. Saturday at Kelley's Motel and Cafe west of Jonesboro, and at the county meeting at 8 p.m. at the American Legion Community Center in Anna. On Sunday, Miss Marmaduke and her companions will visit other scenic spots in the area before starting back to Chicago. [...]

CHICAGO SUN-TIMES

HEALTH BOARD OKS NEW DIETARY MILK

1/19/61

Chicago dairies got official approval Wednesday to market a dietary milk preparation for customers who want to take off weight. The Board of Health adopted a resolution that permits milk producers to market skimmed milk flavored and fortified with vitamins that will have a 900-calorie count.

That will be the recommended intake for persons wishing to lose weight without cutting down on food. Ordinary skimmed milk provides around 500 calories per quart, but the added flavoring will boost it to 900. [...]

Virginia Marmaduke, only woman member of the health board, was elected permanent secretary to succeed the late Dr. Francis Dulak. While she offered to serve without salary, the board directed she should be paid $100 monthly for her added work. Dr. Dulak had received a little more than $12,000 annually in the post.

THE SOUTHERN ILLINOISAN

At Banquet: Miss Marmaduke To Speak

5/18/61

Miss Virginia L. Marmaduke, native Southern Illinois newswoman, now vice-president of a Chicago insurance firm, will be the guest speaker at the third anniversary dinner meeting of the Carbondale Altrusa Club Tuesday, according to the president, Mrs. Araminta Bigelow.

The dinner, to be served at 7:30 p.m. at the Gardens, will be open to any of Miss Marmaduke's friends who would like to attend. Members of the Herrin Altrusa Club plan to attend, as Miss Marmaduke is a former resident of Herrin.

Miss Marmaduke will use the title "Interesting Persons" for her address. Recounting high-lights of her 26-year career as a reporter and interviewer through the media of newspaper, radio and TV, covering news events which included tea parties, murders and political conventions, she will have on display glossy photographs of some of her most interesting interviewees and tell behind-the-scenes stories regarding them. [...]

CHICAGO-SUN TIMES

KUP'S COLUMN

By Irv Kupcinet

3/23/62

OUR BEST WISHES *go to* Virginia (Duchess) Marmaduke, *who has resigned as vice president (in charge of press) of an insurance firm to become executive director of the Chicago Foundlings Home,* ***Dr. Karl Meyer's*** *pet charity.*

CHICAGO TRIBUNE

20 APPOINTED TO WOMEN'S SERVICE GROUP

4/18/62

WASHINGTON, April 17—The Pentagon today announced appointment of 20 women, including the wife of the comedian Milton Berle, to three-year terms on the defense advisory committee on women in the service.

The 20 will be new members of the 50-woman committee which advises the defense department and helps interpret women's role to the public. The committee, whose members serve without pay, will hold its semiannual meeting here April 29. New members of the committee from Chicago are Miss Virginia L. Marmaduke, vice president, Consolidated American Life Insurance company, and Mrs. Jules Lederer.

CHICAGO DAILY NEWS

2 ON BOARD OF RETARDED CHILD GROUP: ACCOUNT EXEC, WRITER CHOSEN

10/6/62

Account executive Donald Erickson and Virginia Marmaduke, secretary of the Chicago Board of Health, were appointed directors of the Illinois Council for Mentally Retarded Children Saturday at a board meeting in the Morrison Hotel. [...] Miss Marmaduke, a free-lance writer, is the first woman member of the Board of Health.[...]

WOMEN PLAN TALKS ON DEFENSE: 2 CHICAGOANS REPRESENT STATE

10/20/62

Two Chicago women will represent Illinois next week at the semi-annual meeting of the Defense Advisory Committee on Women in the Services. They are Mrs. Jules Lederer, who writes a syndicated column under the name of Ann Landers for Field Enterprises Inc., and Virginia Marmaduke, secretary of the Chicago Board of Health.

The three-day meeting will open Sunday in Washington, D.C. Members will develop programs for increasing public awareness of women's role in the armed forces.

In 1964, at the request of then Illinois Governor Otto Kerner, Virginia Marmaduke took on a new job—public relations director for the Land of Lincoln Pavilion at the New York World's Fair.

With the help of a robotized Abe Lincoln, courtesy of the Walt Disney company, the Illinois pavilion had the second heaviest attendance of the fair, second only to the building devoted to the Vatican. During her time at the fair, along with teams of tourists, the Duchess would also welcome to "her" pavilion, Lucille Ball, Gina Lollobridgida, and Carol Channing, among other notables.

In addition, the Duchess sent back to Chicago a daily radio program, *Post Card From The Fair*, which aired every morning at 10:55 a.m. over WGN Radio 720. The Duchess's fair duties would last for two years. At its end, the Duchess would call it "one of the highlights of the closing of my public career."

CHICAGO SUN-TIMES

IT'S THE MOLLOY: THE DUCHESS LOVES HER FAIR KINGDOM

By Paul Molloy

6/12/64

NEW YORK—To anyone who has ever dreamed of running off with the circus, Chicago's Virginia Marmaduke is a source of nagging envy. She has one of the sweetest jobs in the world.

A handsome, effervescent lady, Miss Marmaduke is director of special events for the Illinois Commission at the World's Fair. The commission operates the Illinois Pavilion at the fair, and it's Miss Marmaduke's task to see that special events, particularly those involving VIP visitors to the pavilion, are smoothly coordinated.

She is also the "voice of the fair" for both WGN-Radio and Ch. 9, the only Chicago stations to play a regular role at the Flushing Meadows spectacle. She sends in five weekly taped-reports (Post Card from the Fair) *which are played on WGN Monday through Friday at 11:55 a.m. Besides that she does a five-minute videotape* (World's Fair Prevue) *which rolls on Ch. 9 each Saturday at 5:55 p.m.*

IT'S 'HER' PAVILION

SHE LIKES her varied assignments so much that she works at them seven days a week, turning up her pretty nose at a vacation. As she sees it, the fair itself is a vacation—and who wants to take a vacation from a vacation?

No visit to the fair is complete without a stop at the Illinois Pavilion, and no stop at the Illinois Pavilion is complete without at least a glance at Miss Marmaduke scurrying about with note pad and pencil, portable tape recorder over her shoulder. She interviews famous personages who visit "her" pavilion, looks in on the hundreds of exhibits and projects for her radio and television reports and, all in all, is one of the busiest individuals on the fairgrounds.

Her enthusiasm, to put it simply, has no bounds. She's in love with the Illinois Pavilion and she wants the world to know it. But then zeal for her work and an intense curiosity about life have always been Marmaduke trademarks, especially during her years as a newspaperwoman in Chicago. [...]

FIRST-RATE SALESMAN

AN ANECDOTE she told me is typical of Miss Marmaduke's "salesmanship." On the 15-cent subway ride to work one Sunday morning, she thought the "nice-looking gentleman" who shared her seat seemed familiar. It was Casey Stengel who also was riding to work (Shea Stadium, house of the New York Mets, adjoins the fairgrounds). Miss Marmaduke, after telling Stengel that the White Sox would take the pennant, insisted he be a VIP visitor at the Illinois Stadium. Stengel said he'd try and make it. "If you don't," snapped Miss Marmaduke, "I'll phone your Edna (his wife) and tell her you flirted with me on the subway."

Two days later, Mrs. Stengel visited the pavilion. "Casey told me we'd enjoy knowing each other," she said. "He'll make it later."

VIRGINIA MARMADUKE QUITTING HEALTH BOARD

By Robert S. Kleckner

8/8/64

Mayor Daley has received a letter of resignation from Virginia Marmaduke, only woman member of the Chicago Board of Health. Miss Marmaduke, former newswoman and television-radio commentator, has been in New York since last March where she is acting as director of social events for the commission which operates the Illinois exhibit at the World's Fair. [...]

Though he had earlier stated "we would hate to lose her," Mayor Daley reluctantly accepted Virginia's resignation from the Board of Health in late October of 1964.

Though the Illinois Pavilion had been a successful endeavor and a personal joy, in 1965, at the end of the World's Fair, Virginia was out of the job. And though she was by this time a woman of independent means, she still wanted to work. She said, "At the end of the fair, I stood in front of the mirror and said, 'Do I want to go back to reporting, back to that rat race?' I said, 'no.'

"I said to myself, 'You're too old to chase fire engines anymore. You're too opinionated—you'll be trying to tell the bosses how to run it.'"

So, since returning to reporting wasn't a allure, and neither were other jobs in journalism (the Duchess once said, "Being a reporter is fun. Being an editor is work!"), Virginia was very fortunate when her friend, Governor Otto Kerner, once again lead the way with an offer of another high-profile appointment.

NAME 10 FOR SESQUICENTENNIAL
10/15/65

SPRINGFIELD, Ill.—Gov. Kerner appointed a blue-ribbon group of 10 Thursday to help plan an Illinois sesquicentennial observance in 1968. The governor's appointees, plus 14 previously named by Illinois Senate and House leaders, were given $500,000 by the General Assembly to plan for the 150th anniversary of Illinois' admission to the union in 1818.

Kerner's appointees named to two-year terms, were John D. de Butts, of Winnetka, president of the Illinois Bell Telephone Co.; Lenox Lohr, director of the Chicago Museum of Science and Industry; Virginia Marmaduke, former Chicago newspaper woman, and John H. Sengstacke, publisher of the Chicago Defender. [...]

In 1966, at the age of 57, Virginia Marmaduke said goodbye to the Windy City and returned to Southern Illinois. This time for good. Nine miles south of Pinckneyville, on a 350-acre plot of land, which had originally been given to the Marmaduke Family in a grant from President James Monroe in 1831, Virginia had built a modern-day, two-story white cedar log cabin.

Virginia christened her new home with the name Four Cedars and her mother and her widowed aunt, Mrs. Leah McCants, moved in with her. In her "retirement," among other things, Virginia began work on writing three books: an autobiography, a novel and another she coyly told a reporter, "I won't tell you about."

Sadly, none of these works were ever published, if they were even finished. Perhaps writing without a daily deadline was just not well-suited to the Duchess. So, it was back to writing on assignment in the late 1960s when Virginia was pegged by the Illinois Division of Tourism to pen a state-wide syndicated column titled *Enjoy Illinois*. These articles eventually entailed writing two articles on Illinois for the *Chicago Sun-Times*, where once again the byline of Virginia Marmaduke looked up at the reader from the printed page.

IT'S THE YEAR TO DISCOVERY OUR OWN STATE
By Virginia Marmaduke
4/7/68

This is the first of two articles by Virginia Marmaduke on her favorite subject, the glories of Illinois. The second will appear in next Sunday's *Sun-Times* travel pages. Miss Marmaduke, former *Sun-Times* reporter, is now retired to her old family farm near Pinckneyville in far southern Illinois and doing free-lance writing. Named in 1965 by Gov. Kerner as the only woman member of the Illinois Sesquicentennial Commission, Miss Marmaduke is now busy up and down the state participating in historical celebrations and other Sesqui events.

This is the year for you to discover your home state—its beauty and geography and places of recreational and historic interest. Illinois is observing the 150th anniversary of its 1818 entry into the Union and a year long, statewide birthday party is in progress. Every one of its 102 counties will be having some kind of celebration this summer. The red carpet of hospitality is stretched up and down its 385 miles. [...]

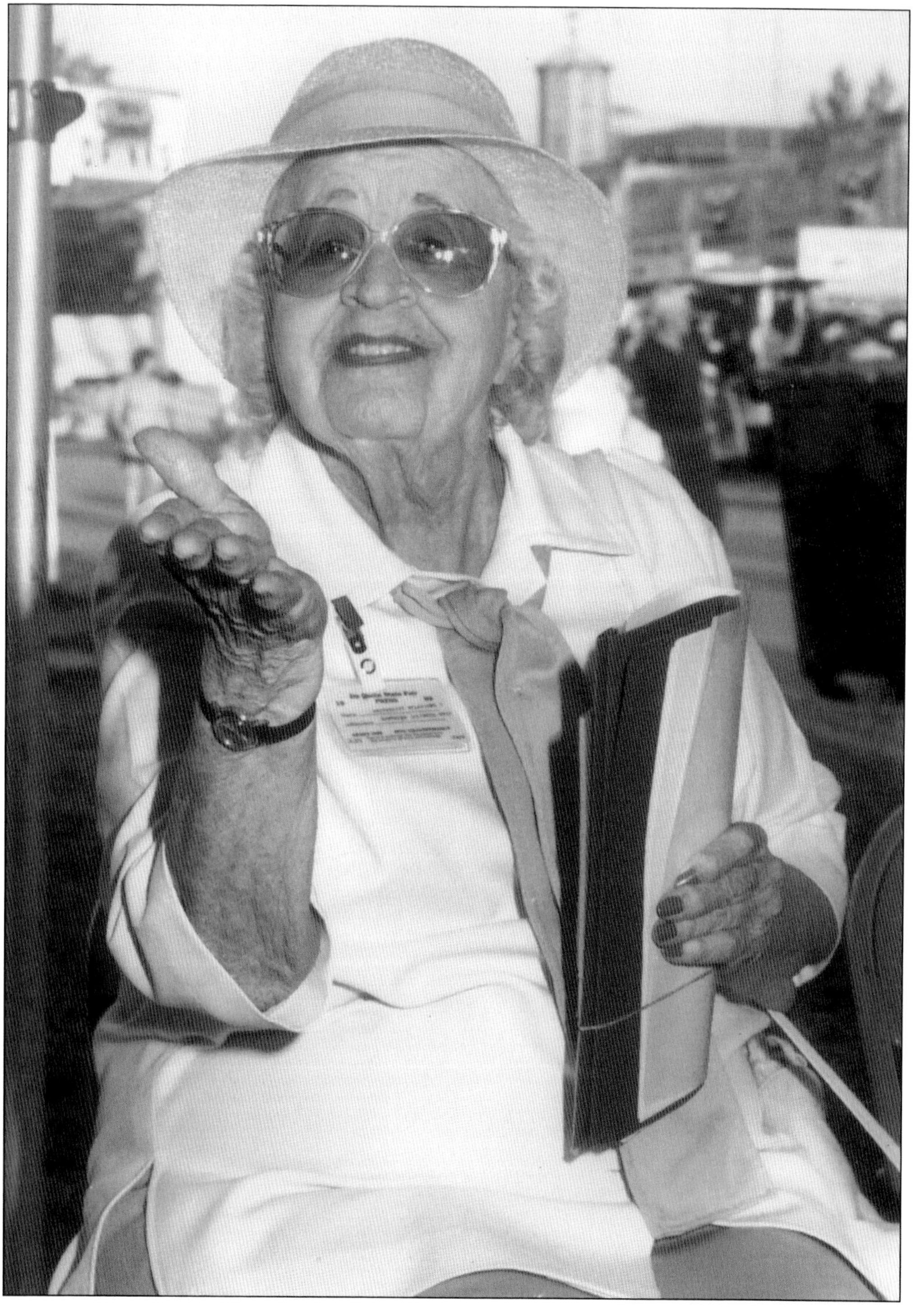

The Duchess, enthusiastic as ever, at the DuQuoin State Fair. (WSIU-TV.)

THE SOUTHERN ILLINOISAN

MATRIX SPEAKER

11/5/68

Virginia Marmaduke of Pinckneyville will address the Beta Tau Chapter of Theta Sigmi Phi Nov. 16 in Carbondale. Miss Marmaduke will speak on "What Women Can Do in Public Relations." She will speak at a 12:30 p.m. Matrix Table luncheon in the Regatta Room of Carbondale's Holiday Inn.

CHICAGO TRIBUNE

TOWER TICKER

By Robert Wiedrich

2/28/69

...DOWNSTATE NEWS: Our dear pal, ***Virginia (The Duchess) Marmaduke****, not only collected a blue ribbon for her pickles at the Du Quoin State Fair, but took first-place awards with her apple butter and corn relish. Then she announced her retirement from culinary competition. What a shame. That corn relish is great!...*

Along with her other culinary delights, the Duchess was also well-renowned for her home-made "Newspaperman's Beer Bread." It was a rich and hearty loaf made from a can of brew—"I find Olympia beer works best with this recipe." Beer bread was said to be part of the perfect breakfast for the hard-drinking newspaperman.

Though earlier in 1960, Virginia began to work on behalf of Southern Illinois University when she was named to the board of their SIU Galleries, it wasn't until 1970 that the Duchess more or less formalized her long association with SIU, her adopted alma mater. Besides endowing scholarships and being one of its biggest boosters, Virginia took on the job of being an (unpaid) consultant to the college's University Relations. For her new job, Virginia had SIU business cards made up; printed on them, the words "No pay, but lots of power."

Along with her consulting, the Duchess also found herself frequently called upon for other college-related endeavors: speaking on campus and off-campus; to students and to area civic leaders. She said about her new role as ambassador and cheerleader, "I'm very much in demand—because I'm free."

But the Duchess reserved most of her energies for the young people of the Department of Radio and Television and the Department of Journalism, giving them the benefit of her experiences. Virginia Marmaduke always said the relationship between her and "her" students were reciprocal, "[They're] the ones who make me feel WANTED and NEEDED here on campus and at this time in my life, it's mighty wonderful to be wanted and needed...for anything...." Of course, along with her University efforts, Virginia also did just about anything she could to promote her beloved home state, especially its southern portion.

THE SOUTHERN ILLINOISAN

WOMEN'S ACTIVITIES: REPORTER WILL SPEAK

8/13/71

Virginia Marmaduke, semi-retired newspaper writer and newscaster living on a farm near Pinckneyville, will headline the women's activities luncheon of the American Agricultural Economics Association annual meeting at Southern Illinois University in Carbondale Monday. [...]

Miss Marmaduke's luncheon talk will be on "The Last of the Sob Sisters," recounting her experiences as a reporter in Chicago for a dozen years and later in radio and television. A native of Carbondale, she began her newspaper career in Herrin. She lives in a modern log house she had constructed on the family farm south of Pinckneyville, writing, speaking, gardening, promoting tourism in Southern Illinois, and taking part in civic and charitable affairs. [...]

MARMADUKE, VAUGHN, SWEENEY

Three honored for area service

By Karen Rothe Of The Southern Illinoisan

2/22/73

Southern Illinois Incorporated (SII) honored three area residents for years of service to the area with special awards at the promotional groups' annual dinner Wednesday. Recipients of the Certificate of Appreciation for service to Southern Illinois were the Rev. Jettie Vaughn, Cambria; Morgan Sweeney, Herrin; and Virginia Marmaduke, Pinckneyville.

About 200 attended the event at the Southern Illinois University Student Center, where high-lights included a slide show produced at SIU by University Exhibits, and a concert by an SIU student group. [...]

"As knowledgeable about the area as any who ever cared, she (Miss Marmaduke) stands big in the eyes of all who have had the privilege of meeting—and then afterward loving her," James L. Seed, Marion, said during the presentation. [...]

HAMBLETONIAN: OFFICIALS DISCUSS HOW TO KEEP RACE

By DeMaris Berry

5/16/73

"The only criticism that can justly be made against keeping the Hambletonian in Du Quoin is that the grandstand has never been sold out for the race," said Virginia Marmaduke of Pinckneyville. The Hambletonian is a race for light harness horses.

She spoke Tuesday to a group gathered to learn how to keep the Hambletonian, the richest race for three-year old trotters, in Du Quoin. [...]

Miss Marmaduke said, "The Hambletonian not only helps Southern Illinois economically and public relations-wise, it serves as a binding influence. The Eastern establishment wants the trotting classic, not for the sport of it, but for the betting of it. The establishment is conducting smear campaigns against Southern Illinois."

BLANCHE MARMADUKE DIES

7/27/78

Blanche Crain Marmaduke, 92, of rural Pinckneyville, died Wednesday, July 26, 1978, at the Pinckneyville Community Hospital, after a brief illness. She was born July 30, 1885, in Perry County, to Worth and Estelle Tessier Crain. She was married in 1906 to Harvey Creigh Marmaduke, who preceded her in death.

Survivors include a daughter, Virginia L. Marmaduke of Pinckneyville; and a sister, Leah Crain McCants of Pinckneyville. Until returning to her native Southern Illinois 12 years ago, for 40 years she had made her home in Chicago, where her husband was assistant to the president of the Illinois Central Railroad.

Following cremation in St. Louis, private graveside memorial services will be at 4 p.m. Friday at the Oakland Cemetery in Carbondale. There will be no visitation. [...]

After her mother's death, and due to the declining health of her aunt, Virginia Marmaduke left the countryside of Pinckneyville in 1978 and rented out her log home. Her aunt, Leah McCants, moved into a nursing home and Virginia took an apartment in Pinckneyville, just down the street from the town square.

In her apartment at 410 West Mulberry, in a spare bedroom which doubled as an office, the Duchess put up photos, plaques, and mementos of her long career. She said, "You know when you get old, people think you get flaky. And when I'd say things like 'I knew Frank Sinatra' or 'Ike was the sexist man I ever met,' people would look at me funny. So, I went through what must be 300 pictures I have and came up with 88 that proves it."

With her tongue in her cheek, and to prove that this stroll down memory lane wasn't meant to be an ego trip, Virginia commissioned a wooden sign to be made and then hung it right above the pictures and certificates. It read: "Marmaduke's Brag Wall."

The Wall proved to be a highly sought-after destination for all visitors to Virginia's home.

ANNUAL DINNER APRIL 17

Friends of Morris Library to give awards to four veteran journalists

3/8/79

Four veterans of the writer-journalism world will be honored at the annual dinner meeting of the Friends of Morris Library[...]

A volunteer area group dedicated to special support of Morris Library, the "Friends" will present their unique Delta Awards to three retired Southern Illinoisans and one active columnist-editor. They include: [...] Virginia Marmaduke, whose career in journalism began in Herrin and later included reporting for the large city dailies in Chicago [...] The Delta Awards were initiated some years ago to honor writers, historians, researchers, and others of the literary world. [...]

VIRGINIA MARMADUKE of Pinckneyville, better known as "The Duchess," will be honored shortly by Chicago newsmen

9/16/79

She will be the first woman journalist ever named Chicago Press Vet of the Year by the Chicago Press Veterans Association. The award will be made at a dinner-dance Oct. 31 at Chicago's Club Martinique.

The citation refers to Miss Marmaduke's role as a "pacesetter for women." She worked for the Chicago Sun-Times, *the* Chicago Tribune *and NBC in Chicago. [...]*

CHICAGO SUN-TIMES

THE MAYOR AND 'THE DUCHESS'

10/22/79

Virginia Marmaduke, 71, longtime Sun-Times *reporter, now retired, gets a friendly chuck under the chin from Mayor [Jane] Byrne Sunday at a dinner of the Chicago Press Veterans Assn. in the Martinique restaurant [...] Marmaduke, known to her colleagues as "the Duchess," was honored at the dinner as Press Veteran of the Year.*

THE SOUTHERN ILLINOISAN

SIU-C ALUMNI TO HONOR MISS MARMADUKE

3/26/80

Former newspaper woman Virginia L. Marmaduke of Pinckneyville has been named the 1980 recipient of the Service to Southern Illinois award presented annually by the Jackson County Southern Illinois University-Carbondale Alumni Club.

The award, given by the alumni club to persons who contribute outstanding service to Southern Illinois, will be presented May 4, at the SIU-C Student Center. [...]

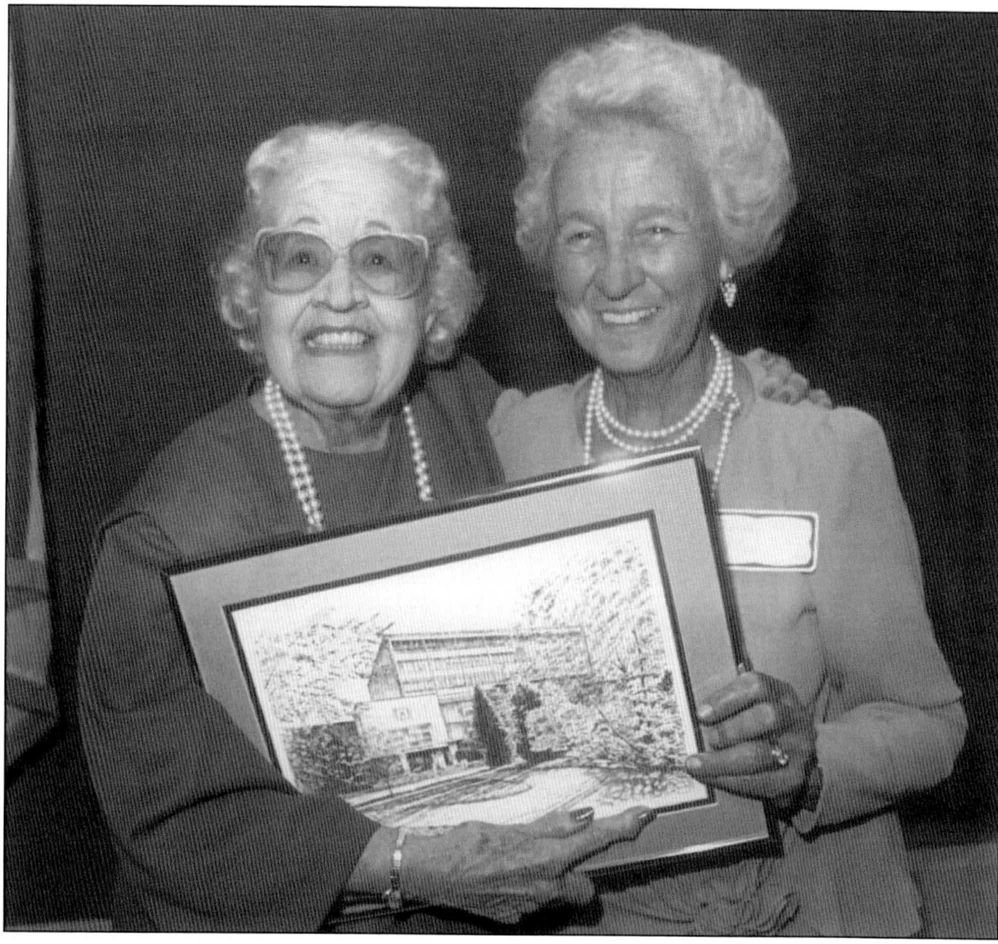

Honored for her work on behalf of SIUC's Morris Library, the Duchess poses with Dorothy Morris, widow of former SIU President Delyte Morris. (SIUC.)

MARMADUKE IS HOSPITALIZED
5/6/80

The ceremonies went on without the guest of honor Sunday night when the Jackson County Southern Illinois University-Carbondale Alumni Club presented its annual Service to Southern Illinois Award to Virginia Marmaduke.

Miss Marmaduke, 74, a veteran Chicago newswoman and Pinckneyville resident, became ill while en route from Chicago to Carbondale to attend the event. She has been in Chicago to attend the Lincoln Academy convocation and ball. George Mace, vice president for university relations at SIU-C, was on the university airplane with Miss Marmaduke and helped transfer her to Memorial Hospital of Carbondale.

George Maroney, Memorial Hospital administrator, said today Miss Marmaduke was treated for "possible cardiac problems." She was transferred Monday evening to St. John's Hospital in Springfield for "further evaluation and possible cardiac surgery," Maroney said.

At St. John's, where Miss Marmaduke is in the intensive care unit, a spokesman said today her condition is satisfactory and that no diagnosis has been made yet. She is expected to remain at the hospital for several days, the spokesman said. Ralph Dunn, a relative of Miss Marmaduke's, accepted the award on her behalf.

The Duchess fully recovered from this brief health scare. But one of her doctors gave her the following (unsolicited) advice, "You better start acting your age."

The Duchess retorted, "That's boring as hell." Despite some failings in health, the Duchess did not let her body undermine her enthusiasm for her causes (especially SIUC) and she kept up her busy schedule of committee meetings and public speaking engagements. She said, "I can't walk very well and I can't see very well, but I can still talk like hell!"

Two years after her own health problems, the Duchess had to come to the aid of someone else due to a physical concern. John Sheley, editor of the local Pinckneyville newspaper, fell sick for a short time and Virginia came in to help run the paper during his illness. At least one article was printed specifically credited to her.

(NOTE: Proof that the world, or at least Southern Illinois, is a very small place, John Sheley is the son of newspaperman L.B. Sheley, who in 1930 wrote the *Herrin Daily Journal's* front page story on the wedding of Virginia Marmaduke to Harold Grear.)

PINCKNEYVILLE DEMOCRAT (Pinckneyville, IL)
EDITOR JOHN SHELEY GETS SCOOPED ON HIS OWN GOOD FEATURE STORY
As told to Virginia Marmaduke
2/17/82

Editor John Sheley is back in his own hometown, gratifyingly recovering from bypass surgery in St. Louis and having to take some smiling ribbing from some of his pals. He got scooped—even though he was at the very center of a heartwarming story evolving all around him.

He knows all about it today. Maybe this recap of the story will give him some chuckles. The story began when it was decided he needed surgery to help get blood flowing more freely into his lower extremities. He was transported to Missouri Baptist Hospital in St. Louis with surgery set for the following Monday morning.

Mrs. Sheley came back home to pack a suitcase, tie up some loose ends around the house and get neighborly and heartwarming offers to feed the birds and watch the cat during her upcoming absence. She had planned to return to St. Louis the following Sunday and be right there for John's big moment and to be handy after it was over.

But that Sunday was the first day of the big snow of '82. Jerry Kuhnert, a Sheley pal, had offered to chauffeur Pat in his 4-wheeler but highways were all reported closed. Next morning the word was still "roads impassable." Pat says it was like trying to "use your head instead of your heart," to stay off the roads.

Came Tuesday. Information was that I-64 was mostly one-lane-traffic and advancing only about 30 miles an hour. Pat's heart won over her head so she started to St. Louis determined to get as far as she could.

She got as far as the Albers Exit on I-64, about 40 miles from her goal. It happened all at once, she now remembers. Her car hit an ice patch, spun completely around and then slid sideways into a four-foot snow bank on the side of the road.

While she was still testing to see if she was unhurt, a smiling, well-dressed man pulled open her door asking, "Are you all right?" She answered she thought she was and he said, "Come with me, you can send back for your car." Today Pat says she never thought of robbery or fowl play but followed the man's orders with no questions. "We drove along slowly," she remembers, "and I told him my whole story of how my husband was in intensive care at Missouri Baptist Hospital and how much I needed to be right there with him."

Without hesitation the man replied, "I live in St. Louis and I know the way direct to the hospital. If we can get through, I'll take you." Pat said when he helped her out at the Hospital door, she offered to pay for his wonderful help and he told her not to even mention money.

"He gave me his name and address but asked me not to use it in a public way," she concluded.

So, even as he was the center of the story, newspaperman Sheley got scooped. His own wife was the star in a heartwarming feature story and she never told him a word about it, fearful it might make him nervous and hinder his recovery. [...]

Besides helping out in the area's print media, the Duchess was lured back to the television airwaves in 1983 when she and WSIU's Erv Coppi began narrating the annual parade of the Murphysboro (Illinois) Apple Festival.

It would be an on-air task and partnership that would continue for many years with Marmaduke and Coppi also helming the station's annual on-air fund drive, "WSIU Festival." Later she would team with WSIU's Jak Tichenor and others for programs originating from the Du Quoin State Fair.

THE SOUTHERN ILLINOISAN

VIRGINIA MARMADUKE TO LEAD WORLD TROTTING DERBY DIVISION

By Paula J. Finlay

9/2/83

To some people, horse racing and the Du Quoin State Fair and nearly synonymous, and Virginia Marmaduke is no stranger to either one. The retired newspaperwoman was at the first Du Quoin State Fair 60 years ago. On Friday, she will be grand marshal of the filly division of the fair's World's Trotting Derby. [...]

With her gray hair and glasses, Marmaduke could be pictured as a grandmother baking cookies and her warmth and easy laugh help strengthen that image. But at age 75, she is sharp and on the move and when she sits behind her typewriter, her role as an experienced reporter comes through. Marmaduke excitedly told of her love of horses and of Friday's honor when, in her words, she'll be a "75-year-old filly for a day." [...]

Marmaduke reminisced about an occasion in her long career as a newspaperwoman when her knowledge of horses proved useful. She spent 36 years [sic] working for Chicago newspapers and when horse racing began in the mid-1940s at Chicago's Maywood Park, she was the one sent to cover it. "I was really the only reporter who knew the difference between a trot and a gait," she said.[...]

Also in 1983, the Duchess, ever tireless, launched a new program at Pinckneyville Junior High, where every Friday she would meet with students to help them understand and interpret the news.

Co-sponsored by the *Southern Illinoisan* newspaper, the initiative took place every Friday with the Duchess interacting with 28 Pinckneyville students. Said the Duchess about her efforts, "God didn't give me any youngsters, but look what I've got today."

MURPHYSBORO AMERICAN (Murphysboro, IL)

MARMADUKE TO RECEIVE THE ORDER OF LINCOLN

5/9/84

On May 19 the Lincoln Academy of Illinois will confer the Order of Lincoln on Virginia L. Marmaduke, a well-known newspaper woman who was born in Carbondale and has traced her career from a small town weekly newspaper to the big papers of Chicago. [...]

NEWS FROM SIU-C

5/11/84

Long-time Morris Library supporter and retired newspaper personality Virginia Marmaduke received the second annual Friends of Morris Library Golden Friends Award, presented Sunday (May 6) at Southern Illinois University-Carbondale. [...]

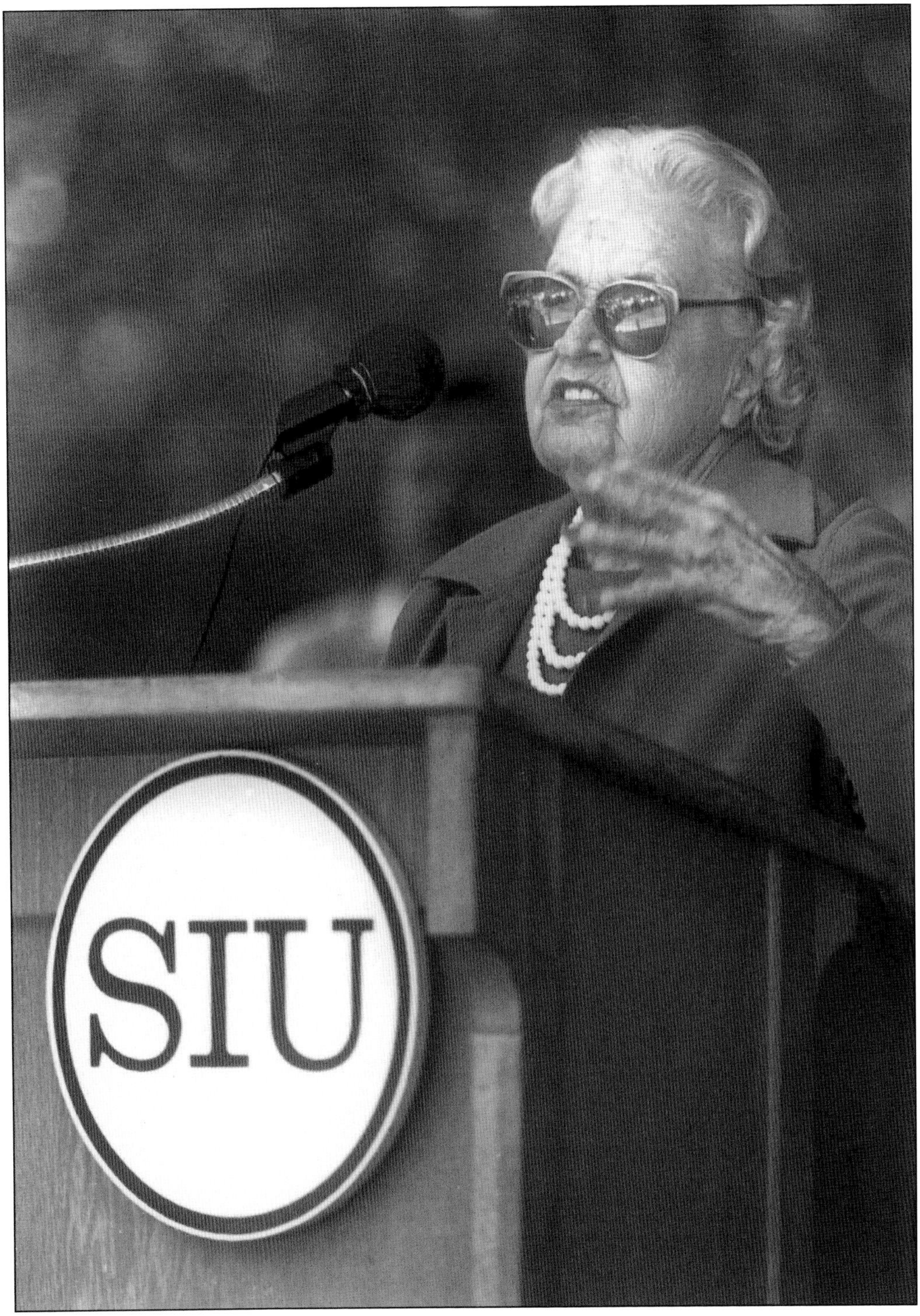

Always Working for SIU: The Duchess speaking on campus. (SIUC.)

ST. LOUIS POST-DISPATCH

VETERAN WOMAN REPORTER NAMED TO LINCOLN ACADEMY

By H.B. Koplowitz

5/14/84

[...] Virginia Marmaduke covered a lot of big stories in the 20 years she worked for various Chicago media. She interviewed celebrities and presidents, wrote feature stories and advice-to-the-lovelorn columns, and starred in a TV program called "Date With the Duchess." She covered every presidential nominating convention between Franklin D. Roosevelt and John F. Kennedy; appeared on the network TV show This is Your Life *as "a typical American newspaperwoman"; and was in charge of publicity for the Land of Lincoln Pavilion at the 1964 World's Fair in New York.*

[...] But on Saturday, she will receive her greatest honor yet, when she is inducted into the Lincoln Academy of Illinois. "It's like the icing on my cake," Miss Marmaduke said. "My biggest thrill was becoming the first woman Chicago press vet of the year, but that award was for what I was being paid to do. The Lincoln award also recognizes my volunteer work."

Each year the Lincoln Academy honors Illinoisans "whose contributions to the betterment of mankind have been accomplished in or on behalf of the State of Illinois." [...]

The Duchess's many letters to the editors of various southern Illinois papers were legendary. Written on her 30-year-old typewriter and mailed out from the Pinckneyville post office, they were missives at once opinionated, pointed (especially when taking to task some of the commentary of former colleague Mike Royko), and enchanting. Compiled by the News Service of Southern Illinois University, they were published in booklet form by the university in 1984. The collection, titled *Marmaduke at Large: Running the World From a Typewriter*, culled letters mostly from the early 1980s and had a forward by *Southern Illinoisan* columnist and Marmaduke friend and admirer Ben Gelman. Virginia used the proceeds of the book to set up another University scholarship.

THE SOUTHERN ILLINOISAN

THE DUCHESS: VIRGINIA MARMADUKE AWARD INITIATED AT SPECIAL BANQUET

3/6/85

It was an evening of love and respect for Virginia Marmaduke of Pinckneyville as some 90 Southern Illinoisans turned out for a dinner in honor of the woman known affectionately as "The Duchess." Specifically, the event was designed to recognize Miss Marmaduke's recent gift through the Southern Illinois University Foundation to provide an annual scholarship to a deserving SIU-Carbondale journalism student.

The first two scholarship recipients, Paula Finlay of Mendon and Mary Henry of Lewistown, received their awards from Miss Marmaduke at the dinner. But the principal speaker, Ralph Otwell, former editor of the Chicago Sun-Times, *also paid tribute to Miss Marmaduke's distinguished career as a journalist and a radio-TV personality in Chicago and to her service to SIU and to the Southern Illinois area.*

Otwell referred to her "irresistible, irrepressible, irrefutable" personality and to her "inquiring mind and involved heart" that brought "compassion and concern" to her reporting.

For her activities promoting the area and the university, including participation in the WSIU-WUSI Telethon that helped bring in nearly $250,000 for SIU's television stations over the past two years, Otwell praised Miss Marmaduke as "an exceedingly remarkable lady." He called her an "effective, unselfish advocate of Southern Illinois and Southern Illinois University." [...]

NEWS FROM SIUC

4/11/85

CARBONDALE, Ill.—Two people with longtime tries to Southern Illinois University at Carbondale will receive the University's Distinguished Service Award at spring commencement exercises May 12. Receiving citations will be retired SIU educator and administrator Willis E. Malone and Virginia L. Marmaduke of Pinckneyville, retired newspaper reporter.

[…] Now living in Pinckneyville, she serves as the University's "unofficial consultant for public relations."

[…] In addition to lending emotional support to dozens of aspiring journalists, Marmaduke has endowed a scholarship through the SIU Foundation for SIU journalism students.

The Distinguished Service Award citation describes her as an "active, effective and unselfish advocate of Southern Illinois and the University for many years" and lauds her "unswerving dedication to the institution and its students, the region and for her encouragement to others to join in this support."

DAILY EGYPTIAN (Carbondale, Illinois)

CBS director to speak at lecture

4/11/88

Lane Venardos, director of the CBS special events unit, will be the guest speaker for this year's Virginia Marmaduke Lecture, which will be at 7:30 p.m., April 11 in Lawson 221. Venardos, a 1966 graduate of SIU-E, started work in Chicago at WBBM news radio. In 1974, he joined The CBS Evening News *and held three different titles before becoming the show's executive producer. […]*

THE SOUTHERN ILLINOISAN

Virginia Marmaduke to greet America

7/8/91

Southern Illinoisans will recognize a familiar face—and voice—on ABC television's "Good Morning America" Tuesday. Virginia Marmaduke, the brassy newspaperwoman who spent 35 years working as a journalist in Chicago and Herrin, will greet viewers with a hearty "Good morning, America" during one of the program's station breaks.

"I'm probably the only 83-year-old babe who ever did it," Marmaduke said. "The Duchess," as she has been known […], taped the segment in front of the historic bell on the Pinckneyville Square. […]

DAILY EGYPTIAN (Carbondale, Illinois)

'DUCHESS' HONORED FOR LIFE-LONG WRITING TALENTS

Pioneer journalist wins induction into Chicago Journalism Hall of Fame

By Christine Leninger

1/29/92

Strike up the band once again for the Duchess. Southern Illinois native Virginia Marmaduke will be inducted Feb. 7 into the Chicago Journalism Hall of Fame.

"I feel like a kid again with all this recognition and I hope it will go on for as long as possible," Marmaduke said. […] "In all my 83 years of my life, today is my day and I really feel important," Marmaduke said.

"I can't retire now because it seems I'm needed more now than ever to help young journalists achieve their goals and go out into the world of newswriting that I love so well," she said. SIUC grants three scholarships in Marmaduke's name and Marmaduke says she is considering a fourth. […]

SIUC NEWS

LOCAL SHOW TRACES STEPS OF GUTSY NEWSWOMAN IN 1930S

2/13/96

CARBONDALE, Ill.—Mobsters, murders and the race track. Newswoman Virginia Marmaduke covered them all in a ground-breaking career that took her from "Bloody Williamson" to the Big Windy some 50 years ago.

Nicknamed "Duchess" by an editor, Marmaduke—now 87 and living in Pinckneyville—is the first woman to have covered a newsbeat at the Chicago Sun. *She retraces the steps of her action-laced career in a new hour-long television program created at Southern Illinois University's Carbondale campus.*

A Date with the Duchess *premiers at 7:05 pm. Monday, Feb. 26, on WSIU-TV (Ch. 8) in Carbondale and WUSI-TV (Ch. 16) in Olney. [...] "It's filled with anecdotes and nostalgia," promises Jak Tichenor, who produced the program for the University's Broadcasting Service. [...]*

SPRING DISCOVER DAYS BEGIN AT SIUC MUSEUM
By Tracy Taylor
4/24/96

The University Museum, with the help of a renowned SIU alumna [sic], kicked off a spring program Tuesday that a museum official says will help children and other community members see positive aspects of the University.

Virginia "The Duchess" Marmaduke, an award-winning retired newspaper and television reporter from Southern Illinois, welcomed museum visitors Tuesday as they came to view the Spring Discovery Days exhibits.

[...] Marmaduke said it is pleasing that SIUC can show the things that all of Southern Illinois should be bragging about at a time when many people and their children, who would not otherwise be able to see the exhibits, can visit. [...]

In the winter of 1997, the Duchess slipped and fell on some ice on the front porch of her apartment in Pinckneyville. She was hospitalized with an injured leg. Prior to her fall, Virginia had begun to show symptoms of Alzheimer's Disease; the symptoms became more pronounced after her hospitalization. Friends and Virginia's personal attorney soon realized that even after her leg healed, she would no longer be able to live independently.

In Chicago, her long-time friend and colleague Irv Kupcinet reported the sad news of Virginia's condition.

<u>CHICAGO SUN-TIMES</u>
KUP'S COLUMN
By Irv Kupcinet
5/1/98

ANOTHER ALZHEIMER'S VICTIM: former Sun-Times *reporter Virginia Marmaduke, one of the first and best of the famous female newspeople. After her reporting days, she became a publicist for Southern Illinois U. She now is in the skilled-care unit of Downstate Pinckneyville Community Hospital. We're saddened to report the fate of such a once-dynamic personality...*

From late 1997 on, Virginia "The Duchess" Marmaduke resided in the long-term assisted care wing of the Pinckneyville hospital.

There, she was visited often by friends and colleagues. With time, she gradually forgot their names but, to the end of her life, those who went to see her found the Duchess to be talkative, enthusiastic and vivacious company.

On November 8, 2001, at 2:45pm, Virginia Marmaduke passed away from pneumonia. She was 93 years-old. The following day, extended obituaries and tributes were published in *The Chicago Sun-Times, The Chicago Tribune, The Southern Illinoisan, The Daily Egyptian, The St. Louis Post-Dispatch,* and other newspapers.

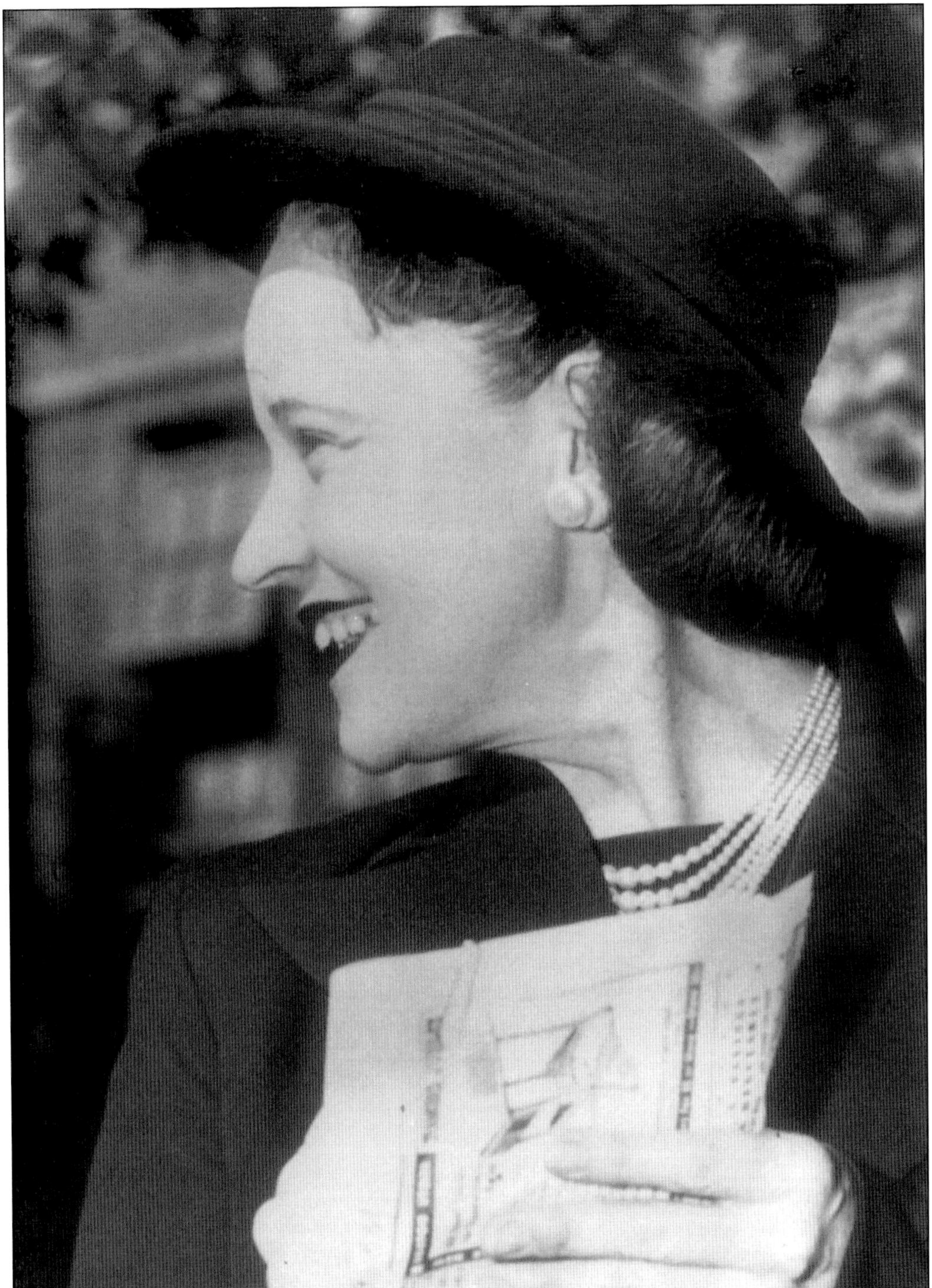

The Duchess in an undated shot—hat on head, pencil in hand.

Epilogue

Several years before her decline in health, on May 11, 1985, a very active and still spirited Virginia Marmaduke added yet another "first" to her long list of personal and career firsts. SIU, after years of having just one mass graduation ceremony for all its students, in 1985 splintered off each of its departments and colleges, allowing each to have smaller, more intimate and individualized ceremonies for their students.

For its inaugural ceremony, the College of Communications and Fine Arts selected Virginia Marmaduke to be their keynote speaker.

In her short talk, the Duchess was characteristically to the point and customarily optimistic, exhibiting the same gusto for life which saw her through early horse-and-buggy accidents, a failed marriage, grisly Chicago crime scenes, stories on five-alarm fires and post-war poverty, and even through her own battle with Alzheimer's Disease. Her zest for life was quelled only by death.

Though Virginia's remarks that day were tailored to an audience of future journalists, broadcasters, performers, and public speakers, in some ways she could very well have been talking about, or to, her younger self. The Duchess's speech was recorded and later transcribed by the college for use in various SIUC-related initiatives.

First, let me thank you for inviting me here today! You're helping me add another "first" to my long and gratifying career. You're enjoying your first SIU "personalized" graduation where you of Communications are the STARS and all in your own right and this also makes me the first female to address this group—so come on, let's shake hands on it...I'm a first for your school—and YOU are a first for me...

I think many of you know that I worked a WORLD BEAT for more than 40 years as a newspaperwoman and broadcaster and I saw and covered many changes in our nation and in our world. BUT TODAY, I see new, exciting and important things looming in the future and you know what? YOU... YES, YOU...are going to be an important part of every bit of it...

For instance: somebody is gonna open up the universe just like our ancestors opened up the WEST...and you are going to be a part of it. Somebody is going to travel to Saturn, to Jupiter, to Mars and other galaxies—and again, these explorers might very well be you... [...]

[S]omebody's going to have to report, and write and talk and explain about all of this, AND MOST CERTAINLY, THIS IS GONNA BE SOME OF YOU!... You're gonna be IN on some mighty wonderful happenings, you guys and gals. And you'll be "selling" it all as advertising agency reps, promoting it all as PR, public-relations experts, writing about it as playwrights, singing about it on Broadway and spreading the news of it all on radio and television and in newspapers. [...]

YES, why not some of you? Why not some of YOU?